THE VEGETARIAN COMPASS

Also by Karen Hubert Allison

How I Gave My Heart to the Restaurant Business: A Novel

KAREN HUBERT ALLISON

THE VEGETARIAN COMPASS

NEW DIRECTIONS IN VEGETARIAN COOKING

little, brown and company

boston   new york   toronto   london

First Edition

Recipe for Pizza Crust from *The Book of Bread* by Judith Jones and Evan Jones. Copyright © 1982 by Judith and Evan Jones. Reprinted by permission of HarperCollins Publishers, Inc.

LIBRARY OF CONGRESS CATALOGING-IN-PUBLICATION DATA

Allison, Karen Hubert.
   The vegetarian compass : new directions in vegetarian cooking /
  Karen Hubert Allison. — 1st ed.
     p. cm.
  Includes index.
  ISBN 0-316-03843-1
  1. Vegetarian cookery. I. Title.
TX837.A38 1998   97-46897
641.5'636 — dc21

10 9 8 7 6 5 4 3 2 1

MV-NY

Book design by Julia Sedykh

Published simultaneously in Canada by Little, Brown & Company (Canada) Limited
Printed in the United States of America

To my children:

Matthew Mark, Halley-Cyd Marie, and Luke Edward, Allisons all.

And to the fine man who brought them into my life,

Dr. Len Allison.

Throughout the 1980s my wife, Karen Hubert Allison, and I operated four successive restaurants in New York City. The first started in our small mews home in Brooklyn, the second was in a neighborhood outside of Brooklyn Heights, the third in Manhattan in Grammercy Park, and the last was uptown in the high-fashion world of Park Avenue and Sixty-third Street. Although each successive incarnation was a bit more dressy and slightly more sophisticated than the one that came before, for Karen, they were all the same restaurant.

Detractors said we grew too fast. Every new restaurant was like a phoenix rising from the ashes of the old, and every new location brought with it a shift in culinary geography, a different region to explore, another cuisine. Customers were often disappointed that the menu had changed. But for Karen, cooking was *about* change; she wanted the food we served to express our growth. Food transported her to places, but she never dreamed of cooking a dish according to the traditional recipe of a specific locale. It was not in her nature to diligently duplicate one of the seven *mole* sauces of Oaxaca. Instead, she used her cooking skills and imagination to evoke the feeling and flavors of Oaxaca. Marianne Moore once said that poetry was "real toads in imaginary gardens." At best, Karen tried to realize this through cooking.

For her, food was the heart of the matter. "Bring it on!" she would say. "Let's have it. Party favors to the last cognac!" If her novel, *How I Gave My Heart to the Restaurant Business*, is about her fate colliding with the roller coaster of restaurant life, *The Vegetarian Compass* is more straightforwardly about her passion for food. She was one of the few people I've ever met with a magnificent palate. Like a musician with perfect pitch, she could recite an entire score, name each ingredient in the composition, specify relative amounts, discourse on the affinities of one seasoning to another, and then tell you precisely why tonight's calamari was more succulent than its predecessors.

At our restaurants she would taste most every dish. Her energy was boundless. She would boogie into the kitchen like some latter-day Ferdinand Point, eager to chat with everyone who cooked: Peter Hoffman, John Dudek, Jim Pender, Nina Fraas, Romy Doraton, Seiji Maeda, Katherine Alford, Tony Brush, Masami Kawata, and me. Her comments were like hot music on the radio. She was definitely for having a good time. "Hey, boss," she would smile after trying a recipe I was preparing, "if you want to keep folks dancing in the aisle, better add some more bounce to that rabbit sausage."

Of course, she had her quiet times. Our restaurants were inevitably staffed by cooks who loved to discourse on food. In one of Karen's more reflective moments she might ask us a question like "What gives this dish its meaty quality?" and leave us cooks to ponder whether she was pulling our leg or urging us toward a more acute consciousness of our work. We were always taken by the accuracy of her senses.

At any meal, she occupied the center of the table. It was a treat to dine out with her. She would quickly assimilate the menu, request different preparations, and end by ordering an array of dishes for everyone to taste. When it was over, she would laughingly throw back her head, delighted by the task. Her approach was equally encouraging with cooks, waiters, customers, and friends. Including us in her talent was the way she drew us closely to her and made us feel loved.

————————

The wonderful panorama of recipes that make up *The Vegetarian Compass* are a riot of scent, color, flavor, and taste. They realize Karen's movement in attaining a harmony of the seses. Though Karen loved fish and meat, she was foremost and always a vegetarian.

There was a period of seven years before we opened Huberts Restaurant when we prepared only vegetarian dishes, and within those seven years, a six-month stretch when we ate nothing but root vegetables. Karen was determined to learn the entire range of taste of a given vegetable and the effect that different cooking techniques might have on its flavor. Our kitchen was her laboratory, her moment in life to concentrate on essence and to entertain possibility.

The two decades at Huberts Restaurant were further elaborations of this quest. Whether or not customers were aware of Karen's particular interest, it was her sense of vegetarian preparations that helped shape the character of each dish. She believed that vegetables need to be presented according to their shapes and textures, that they need to be handled delicately and artistically so as to preserve their distinctive character. It was why a dish that we ate in China, Mountain Spring Noodles with Brown Sugar, so stood out in her senses.

It was her passion for vegetables that made them more prominent in our mind and helped us to expand a direct connection between what we ate and how we felt. Creatively, she influenced all of us who worked in the kitchen, and from her encouraging comments came an array of truly original dishes, such as Huberts Goat Cheese Lasagna, Wild Mushroom and Radish Pudding, Fried Grits with Wild Mushroom Sauce, Huberts Vegetable Strudel, Curried Yam and Apple Soup with Young Thai Coconut, to name a few.

When we first started in the restaurant business in our home, Karen taught me all of my appreciation for food. She was the cook, the creative force, the inspiration for what we did; I was the pupil who learned well. During the course of our restaurant years, our roles shifted many times and our collaboration grew stronger. This book, however, marks a synthesis, a plateau that she alone was capable of reaching. In the last months of her illness, she worked with all her remaining strength on the recipes for *The Vegetarian Compass*. I saw her energy pouring forth until late at night to finish each chapter. There is a prodigious outburst here. She wanted to leave us in our mind's eye with more respect for the splendor of the earth. Had she lived through the final editing, she would have written more extensive headnotes for each of the recipes and a more complete introduction, but it was most in her heart to finish these recipes and get them out of the kitchen, so to speak.

I remember in the early days of Boerum Hill Restaurant, I would occasionally see her struggling with the arrangement or presentation of a dish while a waiter stood by impatiently, wanting to take the food to a customer. Gently, I would try to remind her, "Let it go, Karen, it's already great." I could see how hard it was sometimes for her to separate from something that she felt was still in progress. However, during the last four years, when she worked on the recipes of *The Vegetarian Compass*, that person was already a shadow. Every aspect of each recipe bears her thinking. Her final letting go was without reservation, compulsion, or anxiety. She simply allowed herself to become an instrument for the ground we walk on and what it sends forth to nourish us all.

ACKNOWLEDGMENTS

I visited many kitchens while I wrote this book. I received support, encouragement, and help from many people, in many corners of the world.

Rick Kot, my editor at Little, Brown
Susan Lescher, my agent
In New York while I was at the Culinary Institute of America:
    President Ferdinand Metz, Tim Ryan, Mary Donovan, Gary Allen, and the librarians
On the big island:
    Debbie, Eva, Rona, Lani, and Meg
In Seattle:
    Cousin Robin, who supported me in every way while I researched and wrote the book
In California:
    Aunt Carrie and Uncle Art, who put me up while I researched some more
In Taiwan:
    Joyce Yang, now in Hong Kong, who helped me uncover so much about Chinese vegetarian cuisine
Daniel Cohen, for his amazing computer help
Kathy Beach, for her major help and for putting more work than anyone else into the book

THE VEGETARIAN COMPASS

Historically, vegetarian cookbooks have always felt the need to justify themselves, something no meat-centered cookbook ever considered doing. Before writing this book I read hundreds of vegetarian cookbooks written in the last century. Without exception each one posed the same question: *why become a vegetarian?* The rationale for vegetarianism remains the same today as it was a century ago. People become vegetarians for spiritual, nutritional, political, and ecological reasons.

Whether we are saving our bodies, our planet, or our place in heaven we are putting more vegetables on our plates than ever before. Times have changed. Self-justification is a thing of the past. The vegetarian cookbook has emerged and is finally its own genre without apologies, without manifestos. The new vegetarianism is health centered, taste centered, and now technique centered. The question is no longer *whether* to put vegetables on our plate, but *how* to put them there. The appearance of greens, beans, and grains in our diets may no longer be news, but the question remains: how to prepare them in appealing ways that allow us to eat somewhere between our best judgment and our greatest pleasure.

My love of food and my belief in it remain colored by the privilege of feeding strangers and friends on a daily basis for almost twenty years. A professional cook lives a life of food that is rarely experienced outside a restaurant kitchen. Restaurants are the very image of abundance, and though that is exhilarating, it can also be overwhelming. I have known great joy from cooking, but I have also experienced the numbing effect of the sheer volume of food that came and went each day in our restaurant. The dark side of restaurant life is that food can so easily become fabric.

Cooks burn out and need to cleanse and refresh their palates. We have such sympathy for the rest of our body, we exercise and relax our muscles, but we forget that tongues get tired, too. Simplicity is restorative. I knew one chef who took regular holidays for his palate, eating such simple things as zucchini or bread and spring water for days, sometimes weeks, until he felt the taste buds return. Gustatory burnout is one reason many cooks experiment with different systems of eating in order to cleanse and refresh their palates. The best cooks know that good food and good health are the same.

Whatever food adventures or misadventures I have had, I've never lost my pleasure in cooking. Food celebrates life, and cooking represents an intuitive creativity we wish we could bring to the rest of our lives. I believe that the most enduring inspirations are found in the simplest and healthiest food choices.

The complex nature of today's new vegetarian audience demands that a contemporary vegetarian cookbook be like a compass pointing out not just one culinary direction but several, different by degrees. A compass makes no value judgment about starting points or destinations; it helps travelers find their way. *The Vegetarian Compass* is based on my own culinary true north, and I hope it will help people looking for a more balanced approach to eating and cooking find theirs. While the recipes in this book emphasize health, nutritional balance, and flavor, they also emphasize cooking technique.

Good cooks enhance recipes by putting in or leaving out ingredients according to their own taste. Feel free to mix your ideas with mine, and then I am sure you will enjoy this book. Trust your own teaspoon and use mine as a guide. Use the ideas in this book but cook according to your own tastes and pleasures. If you are a vegetarian, or if you are considering eating a more vegetable-centered diet, then you have already formed opinions about what you need for your own body to be happy and satisfied. Your sense of taste will point your culinary compass in the right direction, and it will surely lead you the right way.

SALADS

SALADS

CONTENTS

Americans have always wondered whether salads were the beginnings, middles, or ends of a meal. A case in point was my aunt Cleo, a Swede who spent half her life on the plains of Nebraska before she defied her husband and brought her family east to live in New York City. Aunt Cleo was one of the best cooks in our family. Along with her Midwestern twang, she brought recipes for things our East Coast family had never tasted. Although she made Swedish dishes like romfromage that married her native love of butter and cream, she also learned to cook American, straight out of the ladies' monthly magazines, and produced a steady supply of tuna casseroles and aspic molds.

One constant in my aunt's repertoire, though, was her Ambrosia Salad, which she always served at holidays and family events. During an engagement party for a young niece and her fiancé, Aunt Cleo complained that the prospective groom had not touched his serving of her famous salad. The young man considered the plate to the left of him, bursting with cream and mayonnaise and Jell-O with marshmallows and cherries. He scratched his head and apologetically explained that he had mistaken it for dessert. Aunt Cleo, for whom the only thing more important than food was family, attended their wedding, but forever after referred to her niece's husband as "that young man who can't tell the difference between a salad and dessert."

These days salads come in all shapes and sizes, and we start meals in ways that years ago we might have finished them. How we choose to cheer the appetite along has become a matter of personal taste. My aunt Cleo has passed on, but I suspect she would approve of the way the world has changed, at least when it comes to salads.

AVOCADO AND ROASTED GARLIC BRUSCHETTA

2 whole heads of garlic

Canola oil

8 (1/2-inch-thick) slices sourdough or country bread

2 ripe avocados, or about 1 1/2 cups cubed or mashed avocado

Salt and ground black pepper to taste (optional)

This is serious heaven, and a great appetizer for company. You may want to serve this with lemon wedges, but I prefer the rich flavor without any piquant contrast.

Preheat the oven to 350 degrees. Gently remove the outer layers of papery skin from the garlic heads; with a sharp knife, slice off and discard the top third of each head. Oil a small ovenproof dish and rub the garlic heads with oil. Place in the dish in one layer without touching. Cover and bake for 30 to 40 minutes or until the garlic cloves are soft enough to be pierced by a sharp knife. Remove from the oven and allow to cool.

Meanwhile, turn the oven heat to broil and arrange the bread slices on a baking sheet. Toast the bread for 1 1/2 to 2 minutes on each side, until the edges are browned. Separate the cooled garlic cloves and push out the softened insides from the skins. You will need 12 large cloves for this dish; reserve the remainder for another use.

Put the garlic cloves in a small mixing bowl and mash them coarsely with a fork. Mash the avocado coarsely in another bowl. Mix the garlic into the avocado. Season with salt and pepper if desired. Spoon the filling onto the toasted bread and serve as a first course.

ARTICHOKE TAPENADE

The unique taste of fresh artichoke hearts makes the effort of preparing them a worthwhile endeavor for this tapenade. If you do have to use hearts packed in water or oil, be sure you dry them well first. Walnut oil adds a delicious accent to the dish, but it will also work with olive oil.

- 3/4 cup walnut meat
- 2 tablespoons good-quality pitted brine-packed green olives
- 1 1/2 cups cooked and coarsely chopped artichoke hearts (hearts and leaf scrapings from 3 large fresh artichokes)
- 1/4 cup walnut oil, or as needed
- 1 tablespoon minced fresh onion
- 2 teaspoons chopped fresh oregano
- 1/4 teaspoon chopped fresh jalapeño or good chile pepper
- 1 1/2 teaspoons whole capers, rinsed, dried, and chopped
- Juice of 1/2 lemon, or to taste

Place the walnuts and olives in a food processor fitted with a steel blade and pulse until chopped very fine. Add the artichoke hearts and pulse just long enough to chop fine and blend with the walnuts. With the processor running, slowly drizzle in walnut oil until the purée is smooth. Add more oil if necessary. Fold in the onion, oregano, jalapeño, and capers. Add lemon juice to taste. Store in a tightly covered container in the refrigerator for at least 24 hours before serving to allow flavors to blend.

Serve with crackers or toast. This spread is also good on sandwiches, vegetables, and pasta; or it can be used to enrich and thicken soups.

BEETS AND RASPBERRIES
IN RASPBERRY VINAIGRETTE

▶ **RASPBERRY VINAIGRETTE**

1/3 to 1/2 cup excellent-quality
raspberry vinegar

1 teaspoon sugar (optional)

1 clove garlic, minced

Salt and ground black pepper
to taste

1/4 cup olive oil

1/4 cup canola oil

3 or 4 medium beets, peeled and
sliced as thin as possible (about
3 cups)

1 1/2 tablespoons minced red or
sweet white onion

3 to 4 cups fresh ripe raspberries

Salad greens

Garnish: 2 tablespoons chopped
chives

The thinner you slice these beets, the better. Use a mandoline, if you own one, or slice by hand, slowly and evenly, enjoying the Zen of the process.

If you live close to a well-stocked market or a good country farm stand, you can vary this amusing dish by using yellow beets and yellow raspberries. Whichever you choose, this color-coordinated salad is a knockout.

Make the vinaigrette: Combine the vinegar, sugar, garlic, salt, and pepper in a large mixing bowl. Slowly whisk in the oils until the sauce is slightly thickened. Taste and adjust seasoning with salt and pepper. Set aside.

Put the sliced beets in a vegetable steamer basket over boiling water. Cover tightly and steam until tender when tested with a fork. Immediately place the beets in the vinaigrette; stir briefly and allow to cool.

Sprinkle the cooled beets with minced onion and toss to combine. Gently fold in the raspberries.

Cover and place in the refrigerator for an hour or until chilled. To serve, spoon the mixture onto chilled salad plates lined with greens; sprinkle with chives.

COLLARDS IN
SESAME-GINGER DRESSING

Serves 2 to 4

When I get a little bored with steamed or sautéed collards or kale, I like to toss them in this sesame-ginger dressing. Any favorite vinaigrette will also do; I like a lemon or cider vinaigrette with or without a touch of Dijon mustard.

▶ 1 pound collard greens or kale

SESAME-GINGER DRESSING

2 tablespoons rice vinegar or balsamic vinegar

2 tablespoons fresh lemon juice, or to taste

1 teaspoon sugar, or to taste (optional)

1 or 2 cloves garlic, minced

2 tablespoons peeled fresh ginger cut into fine matchsticks

1/4 cup toasted sesame oil

1/4 cup canola oil

2 tablespoons shoyu

Wash the greens well in cool water to remove sand and grit. Remove and discard the large stems and leaf midribs. Cut the greens into bite-size pieces and place in a large vegetable steamer basket. Cover tightly and cook over boiling water for 15 to 20 minutes or until tender. Transfer to a serving bowl and keep warm.

Meanwhile, make the dressing: In a medium bowl, combine the vinegar, lemon juice, sugar if desired, garlic, and ginger. Whisk together the sesame and canola oils and the shoyu in a small bowl. Gradually add to the vinegar mixture, whisking until well combined.

Pour the dressing over the hot greens. Toss and serve immediately.

COUSCOUS SALAD
WITH BARLEY, CORN, AND CHIVES

▶ 2 1/3 cups vegetable broth

2/3 cup medium pearl barley

2 cups quick-cooking couscous

4 ears raw sweet corn, kernels sliced off (see Note)

Olive oil

1 cup finely chopped onion

2 to 4 cloves garlic, minced

1/2 cup chopped chives

Apple Cider Vinaigrette (see page 13) (optional)

Grain and pasta salads are thought of as entrées, but they can also be a promising beginning to a meal. Here, couscous — which is not a grain, but a tiny pasta — is steamed after it has absorbed some liquid, making it lighter and fluffier. It is best to cook the barley first and about 20 minutes later, start the couscous. If you're using raw corn kernels, you can add them to the hot grains mixture and let them steam naturally. This can be served with or without a cider vinaigrette.

In a medium saucepan, bring 1 1/3 cups of the vegetable broth to a boil; add the barley, return to a boil, lower the heat, cover, and simmer for about 45 minutes. Remove from the heat and let stand for another 15 minutes. Transfer the barley to a mixing bowl.

Meanwhile, prepare the couscous: Bring the remaining 1 cup of broth to a boil and combine with the dry couscous in a bowl. Cover and let stand for 10 to 15 minutes, stirring frequently, until the liquid is absorbed.

Turn the couscous out onto a double thickness of cheesecloth. Place this in a steamer over boiling water and steam, tightly covered, for 5 to 10 minutes. When the couscous is no longer crunchy, empty it out into the mixing bowl. While the grains are still hot, add the kernels of corn to the mixture. Fluff the couscous, barley, and corn with a fork; do not use a spoon.

Heat 2 tablespoons of olive oil in a small skillet and add the onion. Cook, stirring, for 5 minutes or until tender. Add the garlic and cook 1 minute longer. Add to the couscous, mixing with a fork.

Sprinkle with chives and serve as is or toss with 1 cup of cider vinaigrette.

NOTE: Cooked corn cut off the cob may be used, along with previously cooked and cooled grains.

APPLE CIDER VINAIGRETTE

Mix ingredients in a blender or with a whisk. Adjust seasoning with salt, pepper, and sugar.

▶ 1/2 cup canola oil

1/2 cup olive oil

2/3 to 3/4 cup apple cider vinegar

3 cloves garlic, minced
(1 1/2 teaspoons)

1/4 teaspoon salt

Ground black pepper to taste

1/2 to 1 teaspoon sugar

FAVAS, FIGS, AND FENNEL
IN LEMON CREAM

▶ 1 cup fresh fava beans, shelled, cooked, and cooled (see page 143)

6 ripe but firm fresh figs, sliced into thick rounds or quartered

1 fennel bulb, trimmed of feathery tops, sliced in very thin rounds across the width

LEMON CREAM

1/2 cup cream

3 tablespoons fresh lemon juice

2 small cloves garlic, minced (1 teaspoon)

1/4 teaspoon sugar

1/4 teaspoon salt

Ground black pepper to taste

Your favorite vinaigrette will do for this dish, but the lemon cream is a special treat. It is a version of citronette, a simple, rich dressing in which cream takes the place of oil.

Arrange the fava beans, figs, and fennel in a shallow dish.

Make the lemon cream just before serving: Combine the cream, lemon juice, garlic, sugar, salt, and pepper in a bowl and beat with a whisk until well combined. Taste and adjust seasoning.

Pour the dressing over the salad and toss lightly, being careful not to bruise the figs.

GINGER COLESLAW
WITH GREEN PAPAYA AND FIGS

Serves 6 to 8

Green, or unripe, papaya is crisp, slightly sweet, and almost lemony in fragrance. A fine julienne of the fruit works well in this dish. The sprightly addition of figs or mango is a personal favorite.

▶ 1 medium head cabbage
(about 1 1/2 pounds)

1 green papaya, peeled, seeds removed, cut into slices and cut into thin matchstick strips

2 tablespoons fresh ginger cut into fine 1 1/2-inch-long matchsticks

1 to 1 1/2 cups low-fat mayonnaise, or half low-fat mayonnaise and half plain yogurt

2 cloves garlic, minced

1 1/2 to 2 tablespoons sugar, to taste

1/3 to 1/2 cup fresh-squeezed lemon or lemon and lime juice

8 ripe but firm figs, cut into chunks, or 1 1/2 cups sweet mango chunks

Salt and ground black pepper to taste

Remove the coarse outer leaves of the cabbage, cut the head in half, and remove the core. Slice the cabbage into fine shreds with a long sharp knife. You should have about 6 cups.

Combine the shredded cabbage, papaya, and ginger in a mixing bowl.

In a separate bowl combine the mayonnaise, garlic, sugar, and lemon juice. Pour over the cabbage and green papaya and mix with your fingers, as you would a salad. Add the figs at the end and mix again gently, careful not to tear figs.

Adjust seasoning with salt, pepper, sugar, and lemon to taste.

GRATED BEETS AND CARROTS
WITH AVOCADO

▶ 2 cups peeled and finely grated
carrots

2 cups peeled and finely grated
beets

1 ripe avocado, peeled, pitted, and
cut into chunks

1/4 cup canola and/or olive oil

1/4 cup freshly squeezed lemon
juice

1 or 2 cloves garlic, minced

Pinch sugar (optional)

Salt and ground black pepper to
taste (optional)

Fresh ricotta cheese

Sometimes you don't want to cook vegetables, but to savor their raw flavors and textures. I include this grated, beautiful salad as a delicious way to fulfill that desire.

Combine the carrots and beets in a serving bowl and toss lightly. Scatter the avocado chunks on top.

In a small bowl, whisk together the oil, lemon juice, garlic, optional sugar, and salt and pepper if desired. Pour the vinaigrette over the salad and serve with a dollop of fresh ricotta cheese.

DAIKON SALAD WITH PONZU

Daikon is a long white, crisp, juicy turnip often used in Japanese cooking. Combined with ponzu, a citrus-soy–flavored sauce, it is very refreshing. You can buy ponzu sauce in Japanese specialty stores, but homemade ponzu is best.

▶ **DASHI**

3-inch piece kombu (dried seaweed)

1/4 cup dried bonito flakes

PONZU SAUCE

1/2 cup shoyu

1/4 cup rice vinegar or red wine vinegar

1/4 cup fresh lime juice

1 tablespoon umeboshi (pickled Japanese plum paste)

2 to 3 tablespoons mirin, to taste

1 pound daikon

Garnish: Fresh coriander leaves

First make the dashi: Bring 1 cup of water to boil in a small saucepan. Add the kombu and remove from the heat. Add the bonito flakes. Let stand for 10 to 15 minutes, then strain the dashi into a mixing bowl, discarding the solids.

Make the ponzu: Add to this dashi the shoyu, rice vinegar, lime juice, pickled plum paste, and mirin to taste. Set the ponzu aside.

Peel and grate the daikon. Mix with the desired amount of ponzu, and serve garnished with fresh coriander leaves.

RUTABAGA AND CELERIAC
IN TOFU RÉMOULADE

Serves 4 to 6

▶ **TOFU RÉMOULADE**

1 (10-ounce) package firm silken tofu

3 tablespoons olive oil

3 tablespoons cider vinegar or lemon juice

1/4 teaspoon ground red pepper (cayenne)

Salt to taste

2 cloves garlic, minced

1 teaspoon sugar, or to taste (add more if lemon juice is used instead of vinegar)

1 tablespoon Dijon mustard

1 tablespoon fresh lemon juice, or to taste

1 tablespoon plain yogurt, or to taste (optional)

2 tablespoons chopped gherkins

Tofu is a great way to thicken a vinaigrette, and makes this dressing look richer and creamier than it really is. Use packaged silken tofu for the smoothest texture. A blender will work for this recipe, but a food processor will be easier, because the dressing is as thick as mayonnaise.

1 tablespoon capers, brine rinsed off

1 tablespoon chopped fresh tarragon, or 1 teaspoon dried

2 1/2 cups julienned raw celeriac (celery root, or knob celery), about 3/4 pound

2 1/2 cups julienned raw rutabaga (yellow turnip), about 1 pound

Garnish: 1/3 cup chopped fresh parsley

Make the rémoulade: Place the tofu, olive oil, vinegar, cayenne, salt, garlic, sugar, and Dijon mustard in a food processor fitted with a steel blade and pulse until the mixture is thick and smooth. Taste and adjust seasoning with salt, sugar, and lemon juice. If you want to thin the sauce, add a tablespoon or two of yogurt. Add gherkins, capers, and tarragon.

Pour the rémoulade sauce over the celeriac and rutabaga and toss to combine. Sprinkle parsley over the salad before serving.

ROASTED YELLOW AND RED PEPPERS
IN MANGO VINAIGRETTE

Serves 4

This salad is almost as beautiful as a sunrise, and the sweetness of the mango in the vinaigrette is a perfect complement to the peppers.

▶ MANGO VINAIGRETTE

1 ripe mango

1/4 cup canola oil

1/4 cup olive oil

1/3 cup fresh lime juice

1 teaspoon sugar, or to taste

1 1/2 cloves garlic, minced

Pinch of ground red pepper (cayenne)

Salt to taste (optional)

1 tablespoon cream (optional)

2 or 3 roasted yellow bell peppers, torn into strips

2 or 3 roasted red bell pepper strips

Make the vinaigrette: Peel the mango and cut it into chunks. Purée until smooth in a blender or food processor. You should have 1 scant cup of purée. Measure out 1/2 cup and reserve the rest for another use.

Combine the oils, the 1/2 cup of purée, lime juice, sugar, garlic, and cayenne, and salt and cream if desired. Whisk vigorously until well mixed.

Pour this thick dressing over the pepper strips and chill. Serve over Bibb lettuce as a salad or on toasted Italian bread as a bruschetta topping.

VEGETABLE SATAY
WITH SPICY PEANUT SAUCE

These vegetables are delicious grilled, but can also be prepared in a broiler. There are two ways you can marinate them for this dish: Either skewer them first, dip them quickly into boiling water, then drain and place the vegetables, already skewered, into the marinade; or dip the loose vegetables in boiling water, drain, place in the marinade, and skewer them after they have marinated. Heating the surface of the vegetables helps them absorb the marinade. I happen to like the vegetables listed below in a satay, but you can use any vegetables you prefer.

You will need 8 or 16 metal skewers for this dish, depending on their size. Allow 2 per person.

▶ **MARINADE**

1/4 cup toasted sesame oil

1/4 cup shoyu

1/4 cup fresh lime juice

1/2 cup Thin Coconut Milk (see page 376)

2 cloves garlic, minced

1 teaspoon grated fresh ginger

1/2 teaspoon ground cinnamon

1/2 teaspoon ground turmeric

1/2 teaspoon ground cumin

1/2 teaspoon ground coriander

1 to 2 tablespoons sugar, to taste

2 medium onions, cut into quarters, connected at the roots

2 red bell peppers, seeded and quartered

8 to 10 broccoli florets

8 to 10 cauliflower florets

Sweet potato chunks, peeled and cut 1 1/2 to 2 inches thick (2 medium sweet potatoes)

1 bulb fennel, cut into eighths, connected at the root

SPICY PEANUT SAUCE

1/2 cup smooth or crunchy peanut butter

1/4 cup boiling water

1 tablespoon honey or sugar

1 tablespoon dark rum

1 teaspoon shoyu

1 teaspoon grated fresh ginger, or 1 tablespoon ginger cut into thin matchstick strips

1 teaspoon minced garlic, or more to taste

1/4 to 1/2 teaspoon minced jalapeño or small red chile, or 1/2 teaspoon sambal oelek (optional)

1/2 cup Thin Coconut Milk (see page 376), water, or rice milk, or as needed

1/4 cup chopped cilantro leaves

Fresh lime juice to taste (optional)

1/2 teaspoon shrimp paste: trasi, bagoong, or petis (optional)

Bring a large pot of water to a boil.

Make the marinade: Combine the oil, shoyu, lime juice, and coconut milk in a blender. Add the garlic, ginger, cinnamon, turmeric, cumin, coriander, and sugar to taste. Blend until smooth.

Prepare the vegetables, skewering them or leaving them loose. Dip them into the boiling water for a few seconds, only long enough to heat their outer surface, not to cook them. Drain and pat dry on a kitchen towel. Place the vegetables in the marinade. Turn frequently so that marinade and spices coat the vegetables evenly. Marinate for at least an hour.

Prepare a grill or preheat a broiler.

Prepare spicy peanut sauce: Put the peanut butter in a bowl and slowly stir in boiling water until the peanut butter is smooth. Add the honey, rum, shoyu, ginger, garlic, and jalapeño, and stir over low heat until incorporated. Slowly add coconut milk until you reach the desired consistency. The sauce should be thick, but you should be able to pour it. Stir in the cilantro and, if you want piquancy, the lime juice. For a more authentic flavor, add the shrimp paste. Makes about 1 cup.

If you have not skewered the vegetables, do so now.

Place the skewered vegetables over a grill of hot coals or under a preheated broiler. Grill for about 30 minutes or until tender and done, turning them halfway through the cooking time. As they become soft, transfer them to a platter and cover with foil to keep warm until all the vegetables are cooked. Serve with spicy peanut sauce.

SOUPS

CONTENTS

SOUPS

STOCKS

The stock, or broth, you use for a dish often defines its characteristic flavor. Professional cooks are notoriously proud of their stocks and often argue about the ingredients they prefer in them. In fact, there are times in restaurant kitchens when stocks are more often discussed than sex or politics.

Although when making a vegetarian stock, you have to forgo the flavors of meat, chicken, or fish, you do have the rest of nature's substantial bounty to draw from. Any vegetable, when cooked in water, will produce a broth. The question is, what combination of vegetables should you use for a given purpose? A broth colored by red Swiss chard, for example, might give you the meaty, mineral flavor you desire, but not the neutral color. Knowing you can obtain the same flavor from a bunch of green Swiss chard stems becomes useful information if you are interested in cooking lighter, vegetable-centered meals.

You might also consider including grains and beans. Some grains and beans add flavor, density, and color. For example, buckwheat groats contribute a toasty nuttiness, pinto beans lend a hearty flavor without imparting much color, and mung bean stock, though cloudy, is as sweet and fragrant as chicken broth.

There is almost nothing you cannot add to a stock, provided you have considered the flavor it imparts and do not overuse it. You will rarely find a professional cook adding cabbage or any other member of the strongly flavored brassica family to a meat or poultry stock. You can break that rule in a vegetarian stock, though, as turnips, rutabagas, and even cauliflower can be great additions to stocks if chosen judiciously.

Here are recipes for four good basic stocks that are different enough in flavor to be suitable for a wide range of dishes. One is a light, all-purpose stock you can use in soups, rice, and braised vegetable preparations. The second is a darker stock to use in ragouts or casseroles with more vivid character. The third stock is the deepest and richest, and is an ideal base for robust stews à la bourguignonne or hearty daubes. The fourth is a sweet, or orange, stock a good choice when you want to add a little sweetness to a soup, gratin, or sauce. (I have noted certain vegetables or beans as optional, to suggest that the stock does not depend on this ingredient for its success. If you have time or curiosity, you may wish to try them.)

The recipes for these stocks are intended to be jumping-off places for your own creativity. Stocks are, by their nature, amalgams of flavors. It also helps to know ahead of time what ingredients you will be using in your main recipe. Add rosemary to a stock, for example, when it figures in the final dish. Vegetarian stocks have the same complexity as their meat-based counterparts. Consider a stock as you would a wine. If you want a light, fresh flavor in your stock, then use grassy, enlivening vegetables and herbs: celery, chervil, chives, and perhaps a little mung bean. If you are looking for a more robust and earthy flavor, use mushroom stems, carrots, onions, thyme. A sweet stock will send you toward parsnips, sweet winter squash, yams, carrots, marjoram.

A good rule of thumb is to use twice as many cups of vegetables as you use water. Stocks should be strained through a chinois or cheesecloth and reduced further if a stronger flavor is desired. Vegetable stocks freeze well, in any quantity.

I prefer not to use much salt in a stock, but to add it later to the dish in which the stock features. Because you may want to reduce the stock or use it for a sauce, too much salt will only ruin it. If you can't taste the progress of the stock as it is cooking without adding more salt, remove half a cup of the liquid and salt that, to taste. It's a good idea to reacquaint yourself with the taste of fresh flavors. In our culture palates are on overload, so tasting something as it really is should be a refreshing and interesting idea instead of a bland one.

If you don't have the time to make your own stocks, try to find a good, preservative-free vegetable bouillon powder or cube whose flavor you enjoy.

This stock balances several flavors and colors and makes for a good, strong base. The optional potato skins and lentils will produce a cloudy liquid.

▶ 2 tablespoons olive oil

3 cups chopped onion

1 1/2 tablespoons shoyu

1 whole head garlic, split horizontally

1 cup chopped dark green, tough outer leaves of leeks

2 1/2 cups chopped celery stalks

1/2 cup chopped celery leaves

3 cups peeled and chopped carrots

3/4 cup chopped parsnips

1 cup mushroom stems (about 1/4 pound)

2 cups scrubbed potato skins (optional) (see Note)

1 cup rinsed lentils or presoaked pinto beans (optional)

1 tablespoon fresh thyme leaves, or 1 teaspoon dried

1 tablespoon fresh marjoram leaves, or 1 teaspoon dried

1 tablespoon chopped fresh sage leaves, or 1 teaspoon dried

1 bunch fresh parsley, leaves and stems

2 bay leaves

Heat the oil in a large stockpot and add the onion and soy sauce. Cover and cook over medium-low heat until the onion is tender; do not let it brown.

Add all the other ingredients to 8 cups of water. Bring to a boil, lower the heat, and simmer, covered, for 30 minutes. Uncover and continue cooking for 30 minutes to 1 hour. Taste occasionally and remove from the heat when the stock is flavorful. Strain through a colander, then through several thicknesses of dampened cheesecloth. Discard the solids. If you want a stronger flavor, boil the stock rapidly, uncovered. Depending on how long you cook and reduce this, you will have 4 to 6 cups of stock.

NOTE: Scrub potatoes thoroughly and peel them rather thick. Store potatoes and skins in water to cover to keep them from turning brown. Use the peeled potatoes in another recipe.

BASIC STOCK: LIGHT

3 cups chopped onion

10 garlic cloves, peeled and left whole

1 cup chopped leeks, white part only

1 cup chopped celery stalks

1/2 cup chopped celery leaves

2 cups chopped celeriac (celery root, or knob celery), or substitute 2 additional cups chopped celery stalks

3 cups peeled and chopped carrots

2 cups sliced zucchini or summer squash, if available, or 2 cups soy bean sprouts (optional)

2 cups presoaked mung beans

1 bunch parsley leaves and stems

This stock is rich in taste but has a lighter flavor and color than the preceding recipe. Mung beans will add some cloudiness but also enrichment. Kombu is a wide green seaweed available in Japanese and health food markets.

1 ounce kombu, washed, or 2 cups chopped kale

2 tablespoons chopped fresh basil, or 2 teaspoons dried

1 tablespoon fresh chervil leaves, or 1 teaspoon dried

1 tablespoon fresh marjoram leaves, or 1 teaspoon dried

1 tablespoon chopped fresh sage leaves, or 1 teaspoon dried

1/2 teaspoon salt

Combine all the ingredients in 8 to 10 cups of water in a large stockpot. Bring to a boil, reduce the heat, and simmer, covered, for 30 minutes. Uncover and continue to cook for 30 minutes to 1 hour. Taste occasionally; when the stock is flavorful, remove from the heat. Strain through a colander, then through several thicknesses of dampened cheesecloth, discarding solids. If you want a stronger flavor, boil rapidly, uncovered. Depending on how long you cook and reduce this, you will have 4 to 6 cups of stock.

DARK, RICH MEATY STOCK

For an even darker, richer stock, coat the onions, eggplant, garlic, celeriac, carrots, and parsnips in olive oil and roast at 375 degrees in a preheated oven for about 20 minutes or until the vegetables give off an aroma and start to turn golden or light brown. Be careful not to burn them.

▶ 2 tablespoons olive oil

2 cups chopped onion

1 1/2 cups eggplant skins and outer flesh, seeded, core discarded

2 tablespoons shoyu

1 whole head garlic, split horizontally

1 cup chopped dark green, tough outer leaves of leeks

1 1/2 cups chopped celeriac (celery root, or knob celery), or 2 cups chopped celery stalks

1/2 cup chopped celery leaves

3 cups peeled and chopped carrots

1 cup chopped parsnips

1 1/2 cups mushroom stems (about 1/3 pound)

1 1/2 cups scrubbed potato skins (optional)

2 to 3 cups chopped green chard stems (or leaves and stems)

1 cup washed lentils or presoaked pinto beans (optional)

2 tablespoons fresh thyme leaves, or 2 teaspoons dried

1 tablespoon fresh rosemary, or 1 teaspoon dried

1 tablespoon chopped fresh sage leaves, or 1 teaspoon dried

1 bunch parsley leaves and stems

2 bay leaves

Heat the oil in a large stockpot and add the onion, eggplant skins, and shoyu. Cover and cook over medium-low heat until tender; do not let the onion brown.

Add 8 to 10 cups of water and all the other ingredients. Bring to a boil, lower the heat, cover, and simmer for 30 minutes, then cook uncovered for an additional 30 minutes to 1 hour. Taste occasionally and remove from the heat when the stock is flavorful. Strain through a colander, then through several thicknesses of cheesecloth, discarding the solids. If you want a stronger flavor, boil uncovered to reduce the liquid. Depending on how long you cook and reduce this, you will have 4 to 6 cups of stock.

RICH SWEET STOCK

3 cups chopped onion

10 garlic cloves, peeled and left whole

1 cup chopped leek, white part only

1 cup chopped celery stalks

1 cup chopped celeriac (celery root, or knob celery), or 1 additional cup chopped celery stalks

3 cups peeled and chopped carrots

2 cups chopped parsnips

2 cups dense, sweet squash such as kobacha, hokkaido, or butternut

1 cup chopped peeled sweet potato or yam (optional)

2 cups presoaked mung beans (optional)

This stock has an orange tinge. The optional yams and mung beans will cloud the stock but add flavor.

1 bunch parsley leaves and stems

1 large or 2 small cinnamon sticks

1 tablespoon fresh summer savory, or 1 teaspoon dried

1 tablespoon fresh rosemary, or 1 teaspoon dried

1 tablespoon fresh marjoram, or 1 teaspoon dried

1/2 teaspoon salt (optional)

Combine all the ingredients with 8 to 10 coups of water in a large stockpot. Bring to a boil, reduce the heat, cover, and simmer for 30 minutes. Uncover and continue cooking for another 30 minutes to 1 hour. Taste occasionally and stop cooking when the stock is sufficiently flavorful. Strain through a colander, then through several thicknesses of cheesecloth, discarding the solids. If you want a stronger flavor, reduce by boiling uncovered. Depending on how long you cook and reduce this, you will have 4 to 6 cups of stock.

ASPARAGUS AND FRESH FAVA
BEAN SOUP WITH SAVORY

Serves 4 to 6

Think about making this soup in April and May when fava beans and asparagus are both recent arrivals at the market. The combination of fresh legume and vegetable makes a simple, seasonal soup that is as light and surprisingly complex as spring itself. I don't recommend substituting dried fava beans in this soup; their intense flavor will overpower the asparagus, adding a bitter winter starchiness.

Though this dish is easy and quick to make, give yourself a little extra time to prepare the fava beans. Crack open the long, ungainly pod, coax the beans to tumble out, and with a small, sharp knife, slit each bean's tough outer skin. With a quick peeling action, your fingers can easily emancipate the beans. It is worth the effort, as the brilliant green, lima-shaped fava has a subtle flavor unmatched by any other legume, fresh or dried.

▶ 2 tablespoons fruity olive oil

1 medium white onion, minced

2 cloves garlic, minced

1/2 cup medium sherry

4 to 6 cups vegetable broth, to taste

2 cups shelled and peeled fresh fava beans (2 pounds pods)

2 cups peeled and coarsely chopped asparagus (2 pounds stalks)

1 tablespoon minced fresh summer savory, or 1 teaspoon dried

1/2 teaspoon freshly grated nutmeg

2 tablespoons cream or kefir (optional)

Salt and ground white pepper to taste

Garnish: 1 tablespoon chopped chives, 1 tablespoon minced fresh savory, fruity olive oil to taste

Heat the olive oil in a small stockpot, add the onion, and sauté about 5 minutes or until translucent; stir in the garlic. Add 1/2 cup water and the sherry and cook down by half. Add the stock, bring to a boil, and add the fava beans; lower the heat and simmer for 2 minutes or until the beans are soft but still bright green. Add the asparagus, savory, and nutmeg and simmer for another 2 minutes. Add cream at the very end and correct seasoning with salt and pepper.

Garnish the soup with chopped chives, savory, and a drizzle of fruity olive oil.

NOTE: This soup can also be puréed, chilled, and served with chopped avocado, chopped pistachios, a dollop of yogurt, and a squeeze of lime. If you plan to purée, however, be sparing about the amount of broth you use, depending on how thick you like your soup to be.

CHAYOTE SOUP
WITH CORIANDER AND CUMIN

Serves 6 to 8

3 tablespoons olive oil

2 large leeks, white and light green parts only, cleaned and cut into thin rounds (about 2 cups)

6 cloves garlic, minced (1 tablespoon)

2 teaspoons ground cardamom

1 teaspoon ground coriander

1/2 teaspoon ground cumin

2 large or 3 medium chayotes, pits removed, flesh chopped (about 5 to 6 cups)

6 cups vegetable broth

3/4 cup fresh coriander leaves, chopped

1 tablespoon fresh lime juice, or to taste

Salt and ground black pepper to taste

Chayote is a light green, pear-shaped squash that grows plentifully in sunny or tropical areas. It has an understated, exotic flavor. The coriander, cumin, nutmeg, and lime add an evocative twist to this otherwise delicate soup.

SPICY TOASTED PUMPKIN SEEDS

1 cup pepitas (green pumpkin seeds)

2 teaspoons shoyu

1/2 teaspoon ground coriander

1/2 teaspoon ground cumin

1/2 teaspoon ground cardamom

1/2 teaspoon powdered chipotle (optional)

Garnish: Kefir, sour cream, or Yogurt Cheese (see page 375)

In a stockpot or large saucepan, heat the olive oil. Add the leeks, cover, and sauté for a few minutes or until they are limp and translucent. Stir in the garlic, cardamom, coriander, and cumin. Allow to cook for a minute, then add the chayotes and vegetable broth. Bring to a boil, reduce the heat, cover, and simmer for 30 minutes. Before serving, add fresh coriander and lime to taste and correct the seasoning with salt and pepper.

Make the pumpkin seeds: Spread the pumpkin seeds out on a baking sheet. Sprinkle with shoyu, then with the spices. Bake at 350 degrees for about 10 minutes or until the seeds are toasted and golden and the shoyu has dried.

Serve the chayote soup with a dollop of kefir topped with a garnish of spicy toasted pumpkin seeds.

HUBERTS CURRIED YAM AND APPLE SOUP
WITH YOUNG THAI COCONUT

Serves 4 to 6

Although you can make this naturally sweet soup without using young Thai coconut, it is far more interesting with it. Young coconut is exactly what it sounds like: meat removed from immature coconuts. This flesh is soft, pliant, almost slippery, quite different from the woody texture of mature coconut. You can buy young Thai coconut in any Thai specialty store. The curry mixture here is one we used in Huberts restaurant when we made this soup. If you have your own favorite curry mixture, by all means use it.

▶ FRESH CURRY POWDER

1 tablespoon cumin seeds

1 tablespoon coriander seeds

1 tablespoon whole cardamom pods

2 bay leaves

1 cinnamon stick

1 teaspoon white peppercorns

1/2 teaspoon fennel seeds

1/2 teaspoon ground turmeric

1/2 teaspoon whole allspice

1/2 teaspoon ground red pepper (cayenne)

2 tablespoons canola oil

1 large onion, chopped (about 1 cup)

3 cups vegetable broth, or more to taste

1 1/4 pounds sweet potatoes or yams, peeled and sliced into 1/2-inch rounds (about 3 cups)

1 1/4 pounds apples (a sweet meaty type like Jonogold, Winesap, Empire), peeled, cored, and sliced thin (about 3 cups)

2 cups Thick Coconut Milk, or more to taste (see page 376), or use canned unsweetened coconut milk

Salt and ground black pepper to taste

Garnish: 1 1/2 cups young Thai coconut, julienned; 2 apples peeled, sliced, and julienned; 1 cup whipped cream, sour cream, or kefir

Make the curry powder: Grind the first 10 ingredients together in a coffee or spice grinder until reduced to a fine powder. Set aside.

Heat the oil in a large saucepan. Add the onion, cover, and sauté for 6 to 8 minutes or until the onion is golden. Add 1 teaspoon of the curry powder, cook for a minute, and add 1 cup of the vegetable broth. Bring to a boil and add the sweet potatoes and apples; simmer uncovered until they are soft. Remove the sweet potatoes and apples with a slotted spoon and purée them in a food processor.

Heat 2 cups of coconut milk and the remaining 2 cups of broth in a large saucepan. Stir in the vegetable purée. Taste and add salt and pepper. Add more of the coconut milk or broth depending on the taste and thickness you prefer. Add julienned slices of young coconut to each bowl before ladling in broth. Serve with a julienne of apple atop a dollop of whipped cream.

Serves 4

In this soup, eggplant is roasted dengaku style — brushed with hoisin sauce, which adds a sweet smokiness to the eggplant as it cooks. The eggplant is then puréed and whisked into a light miso-flavored broth that is embellished with Chinese black mushrooms. Fresh shiitake may be used, but the broth will be less earthy in flavor.

Try to choose small to medium eggplants for this soup. White eggplants, which are less bitter, are best, but are not always easy to find.

▶ 16 dried black or shiitake mushrooms

1/2 cup sherry

3 pounds small or medium eggplants

1 tablespoon olive oil

2/3 cup hoisin sauce

3 to 4 cups vegetable broth (including mushroom liquid)

3 tablespoons Roasted Garlic (see page 373), or 2 teaspoons minced garlic

1 tablespoon mellow white miso

Garnish: 1 cup watercress leaves

Rinse the dried mushrooms in cool water to dislodge any dirt or sand. Cover with room-temperature water for about an hour, or hot water for half an hour. (Hot water will draw out flavor from the mushrooms and should be avoided if you have time. If you do use hot water, save the liquid for the soup.) Gently squeeze out any excess water from the softened reconstituted mushrooms. Remove and discard the stems, which are too tough to use. Slice the caps into thirds, place in a bowl with the sherry, and set aside.

Preheat the oven to 375 degrees.

Cut the eggplants in half lengthwise and arrange on a baking sheet. Rub all over with a light coating of olive oil. Brush the cut surfaces with the hoisin sauce. Bake for 30 minutes or until the pulp is soft and the skin is black and shiny. When the eggplant is cool enough to handle, scoop out the pulp and put it through a strainer fine enough to separate out the seeds. You should have about 4 cups of roasted eggplant meat.

Bring 3 cups of broth to a slow simmer. Whisk in the garlic and miso. Add the mushrooms and sherry and simmer for 10 minutes. Stir or whisk the eggplant purée into the soup. Continue cooking for another 5 minutes, letting the liquid reduce to the desired thickness. (Add more broth for a thinner soup.) Garnish with watercress leaves right before serving.

Serve with garlic bread and yogurt, if desired.

FENNEL SOUP
WITH FENNEL TAPENADE

Serves 4 to 6

4 large or 6 medium bulbs fennel

1/4 cup olive oil

1 cup shallots, whole, peeled

3 cloves garlic, sliced

1 cup white wine

6 cups vegetable broth

1 tablespoon Pernod

Salt and ground black pepper
to taste

FENNEL TAPENADE

2/3 cup sliced fennel

1 clove garlic, minced

1 anchovy fillet

2/3 cup lightly toasted walnuts,
skins rubbed off

1/3 cup freshly grated Parmesan
cheese

1 tablespoon Pernod

4 to 6 slices crusty country
bread, toasted and brushed with
olive oil

Instead of a traditional onion soup with its gooey strings of melted cheese, try this fennel alternative, complete with a slice of crusty bread spread with a wonderful fennel tapenade. Though the soup is delicious without it, the tapenade adds an unusual variation on the theme of bread soup. As the tapenade melts, it also thickens the soup.

Cut the fennel bulbs in quarters, discarding the feathery stems. Slice very thin. Measure 1 packed cup and set aside for steaming.

In a heavy saucepan, heat the olive oil and slowly sauté the shallots and remaining fennel until the fennel is soft. Add the sliced garlic and cook for 1 minute. Add the wine and cook down by half. Add the broth and Pernod and cook for another 10 minutes. Season with salt and pepper.

For the tapenade, steam the reserved cup of sliced fennel until just tender; pat dry. Combine the fennel, minced garlic, anchovy, walnuts, Parmesan, and Pernod in a food processor and process until the mixture has a pastelike consistency.

Ladle the soup into bowls. Spread a piece of the toast with fennel tapenade and float on top of each bowl of soup.

GLASS NOODLE SOUP
WITH TOFU DUMPLINGS

The mai fun rice sticks used in this soup are some of the thinnest noodles you can find, and come packaged in bundles that look like thin white scribbles. They need not be cooked and can be prepared merely by soaking them in hot water for about 10 minutes. Glass noodles made from rice have a more vermicelli-like and less slippery texture than glass noodles made from mung beans.

▶ 10 ounces firm tofu, cut into
   1/2-inch slices

1/2 cup sake

1/4 cup shoyu

2 cloves garlic, crushed, plus 1 1/2
teaspoons finely chopped garlic

2 teaspoons finely chopped fresh
ginger

1 bundle mai fun rice sticks, about
8 ounces, or any other glass
noodle

6 cups vegetable broth

1 tablespoon nam pla fish sauce

1/2 cup chopped cilantro leaves

1 teaspoon flour

1 egg white

1/3 cup finely chopped scallion,
both white and green parts

Marinate the tofu slices in the sake, shoyu, crushed garlic, and 1/2 teaspoon of the ginger for 30 minutes.

Place the rice sticks in a bowl and pour boiling water to cover. Leave for 10 minutes, or follow directions on the package if thicker noodles are used.

Bring the vegetable broth to a simmer. Add 1 teaspoon each of the chopped ginger and garlic. Add the nam pla and cilantro.

Put the tofu slices in a food processor with the flour, egg white, scallions, and the remaining 1/2 teaspoon each of ginger and garlic, and process quickly. Remove and roll into 1-inch balls. Poach the dumplings gently for 1 minute in the simmering vegetable broth, until they expand and float to the top. Add the noodles, simmer for 3 to 5 minutes, and serve.

ICE HOUSE SOUP

▶ 4 cups Yogurt Cheese (double recipe, see page 375), or 1 1/2 quarts (6 cups) plain yogurt, or 3 cups kefir or low-fat sour cream

1 (16-ounce) plastic bag of sauerkraut, or canned sauerkraut

1 quart buttermilk

1/4 cup aquavit or good vodka

3 cucumbers, seeded and chopped, or processed quickly in food processor

3/4 cup finely chopped fresh dill

1 1/2 teaspoons coriander seed

1/2 teaspoon fennel seed

1/4 teaspoon anise seed

Salt and freshly ground white pepper to taste

Imagine Russian noble ladies in long white lace dresses, strands of pearls around their necks, sitting in stiff-backed chairs on the patios of their summer dachas, bringing silver spoons to their lips and sipping chilled white soup served from tureens just rushed from the ice house. Imagine the welcome warmth of a Russian summer, the sight of green leaves returning to a land known for its snow and bitter winters. Cold soups were a rarity even in the aristocratic households of prerevolutionary Russia, yet this favorite, known as chlodnik (also spelled "khlodnik"), was special enough to have survived the revolution.

Like all royalty, chlodnik insists upon what is rich. In soup terms this means sour cream, which I have replaced here with a quick version of "yogurt cheese," yogurt that is drained so that water and whey drip from it, leaving a thickened curd that can easily be substituted for sour cream. With any luck, Ice House Soup will continue to survive upheavals, including a low-fat revolution.

Make yogurt cheese.

Drain and squeeze the sauerkraut. Measure the juice; you should have about 1 1/4 cups. (Reserve the kraut for another use.)

Combine the buttermilk, aquavit, and sauerkraut juice in a large bowl or tureen.

Unwrap the ball of yogurt cheese. It should be thick and have the consistency, depending on how long you have hung it, of sour cream or kefir. Add the yogurt to the buttermilk mixture and whisk to combine. Add the cucumbers.

Grind together the coriander, fennel, and anise seeds. Season the soup with 1 teaspoon of the mixture, or to taste. Add salt and white pepper.

The Ice House Soup can be placed in the freezer and quickly chilled, then served in chilled bowls. At Huberts, we garnished the soup with red and orange nasturtiums and purple garlic chive flowers.

MINESTRONE WITH
BUTTERNUT SQUASH AND BARLEY

Here are my rules for preparing minestrone: Use your favorite seasonal vegetables, use fresh beans if they're available, cook your pasta separately, and have a superb aged cheese on hand to grate into the soup before serving it.

Of course, in matters of soup, I never hesitate to bend rules, especially my own. Minestrone is one of the most forgiving of all culinary icons. This version uses butternut squash, fresh tomatoes, and barley — no string beans, no carrots, no beans, no potatoes, no pasta.

▶ 4 cups peeled, seeded, and cubed butternut squash

2 cups peeled, seeded, and chopped fresh tomatoes (4 medium tomatoes), or 1 (28-ounce) can

1/2 cup pearl barley

6 to 8 cups vegetable broth

12 cloves garlic, minced

1 teaspoon freshly grated nutmeg

1 tablespoon fresh thyme leaves, or 1 teaspoon dried

1/2 cup sherry

Salt and ground white pepper to taste

Cut the squash into 1-inch pieces. Chop the tomatoes into 1/2-inch pieces. If you are using canned tomatoes, drain and seed them before you chop them.

Wash the barley. Bring the vegetable broth to a light simmer in a medium stockpot. Pour in the barley and garlic and cook, partially covered, for 45 minutes or until the barley is almost tender.

Add the squash and tomatoes. Simmer for 5 minutes. Add the nutmeg, thyme, and sherry and cook covered for 30 minutes more or until the squash melts into the soup.

Season with salt and pepper. Serve with grated Parmesan or sharp white Cheddar cheese.

ROADSIDE PUMPKIN SOUP

▶ 2 tablespoons olive oil

1 cup chopped onion

2 strips soy bacon, coarsely chopped, or 2 tablespoons soy bacon bits

6 to 8 cloves garlic, minced

2 cups Sauvignon Blanc or other dry white wine

6 cups loosely packed and measured cubed pumpkin meat

4 cups loosely packed and measured cubed sweet potatoes

1 large cinnamon stick

1 tablespoon ground cardamom

1 teaspoon ground coriander

1 teaspoon garam masala

4 to 6 cups vegetable broth

3 tablespoons chick-pea miso

1 large roasted red bell pepper, or 1/4 cup red pepper purée

It had rained all day in Rhinebeck, New York, but late that dark October afternoon threatening clouds gave way to a silver sky. Sunlight poured over the hills and led the way as I drove along. Weatherwise, it was a glory moment, certain not to last. In the car the children discussed Halloween. The subject was jack-o'-lanterns, and as we passed a roadside stand with crates filled with bright orange pumpkins, they screamed the car to a halt. Off to the side, I spied a table old as the shingles on a New England roof that was piled high with white Lumina pumpkins, prized for their sweet flavor and dense meat. The farm stand promised something for each of us: jack-o'-lanterns for them, soup for me.

As the children tumbled out, each claiming the biggest, funniest pumpkin, the sky suddenly opened up again, throwing an eerie spotlight on the moon-colored Lumina. White pumpkins bathed in translucent rays of light may evoke heaven-sent flavor, but frankly any pumpkin will do for this soup, especially if you eat it by the leering light of newly carved jack-o'-lanterns. Don't resist adding the roasted pepper purée at the end. Like silver skies, the flavor is a glory moment to be savored.

Heat the oil in a large saucepan and sauté the onion until golden. Add the soy bacon and garlic. Stir in the wine and boil until reduced by half. Add the pumpkin, sweet potatoes, cinnamon stick, cardamom, coriander, and garam masala. Cover the vegetables by 2 inches with vegetable broth, about 4 cups, depending on the size of your pumpkin and potato chunks. Simmer, covered, for 30 minutes.

Dissolve the chick-pea miso in 1/4 cup of hot water and add to the pumpkin and sweet potatoes. Cook for another hour. Though this soup can be puréed, the texture is more interesting and varied if you let the pumpkin and sweet potatoes melt into each other through long cooking. Add more vegetable broth for a more liquid soup.

For roasted pepper purée, make sure the pepper is seeded. Put the roasted pepper into a food processor and process until puréed. You should have about 4 tablespoons from 1 large pepper. Though red pepper purée is often drizzled on top of soup for a decorative effect, I prefer to add the purée to the soup for enrichment of flavor and color. Serve this soup with orecchietti and top with grated Cheddar cheese. Serve with crusty country bread.

SALAD SOUP WITH LEMON BULGUR

▶ 3/4 cup olive oil

10 cloves garlic, minced
(2 tablespoons)

8 cups washed and cut lettuce,
such as Boston, Bibb, romaine,
iceberg

6 cups vegetable broth

1 cup white wine

1 1/4 tablespoons fresh thyme
leaves, or 1 1/8 teaspoons dried

1 teaspoon fresh marjoram, or
1/3 teaspoon dried

1 teaspoon ground cumin

1/2 cup plus 1/4 cup fresh lemon
juice (4 to 6 lemons), or to taste

Salt and ground black pepper
to taste

3 cups cooked bulgur, warmed

1 1/2 cups chopped scallions,
whites and greens

2 cups peeled, seeded, sliced
cucumber

1 1/2 cups small yellow cherry
tomatoes, or peeled, seeded,
chopped regular tomatoes

This summer soup is a wonderfully light first course or, with an addition of tofu or beans, a perfect hot-weather entrée. If you like more broth, add more stock and adjust your seasonings. Cherry tomatoes are a welcome addition to this dish, especially if you can get the small yellow ones. Any lettuce or combination of lettuces will do. If you use iceberg, combine it with other greens for more flavor and a better overall texture.

Heat 1/2 cup of the olive oil in a stockpot and sauté 8 of the minced garlic cloves with the lettuce. If you need to add liquid, add 1/4 cup vegetable broth. Cover the pot until the leaves have wilted. Add the white wine and boil uncovered until reduced by half. Stir in the thyme, marjoram, and cumin. Add vegetable broth; continue to cook on medium heat, partially covered, for 30 minutes. Add 1/2 cup lemon juice. Simmer for 15 minutes. Adjust seasoning with salt and pepper.

Combine the bulgur, 1/4 cup of olive oil, 2 cloves of garlic, the remaining 1/4 cup of lemon juice, scallions, and cucumber.

Place a portion of bulgur and some of the tomatoes in each bowl before you ladle in the soup. I have also added the bulgur and tomatoes to the broth, but then the soup must be heated through and served immediately, as the bulgur will absorb a great deal of the broth if it sits too long.

Serve with crusty bread and a good cheese — fontina, Cheddar, or chèvre.

TAMARIND ONION SOUP WITH BUMBU

Serves 6

This Eurasian soup is what happens when a French onion soup meets a spicy Thai broth — no cheese, but lots of ground almonds, coconut, tamarind, and lime. Bumbu is a combination of spices and ground nuts that thicken and enrich the soup. Tamarind is available in many forms: fresh, dried, canned. I use tamarind paste because it is much easier to find and lasts a long time. You will find it in Asian or Indian markets. For a substitute, use fresh lime.

▶ BUMBU

1/2 cup lightly toasted sesame seeds

1 cup lightly toasted almonds or macadamia nuts

1 teaspoon ground coriander

1/4 teaspoon ground cumin

1/4 teaspoon dried chili powder, or 1/2 teaspoon finely minced jalapeño

1/2 tablespoon chopped fresh ginger

6 cloves garlic, minced

1 tablespoon tamarind paste, or to taste

1/4 cup boiling water

6 cups thinly sliced onions

1/4 cup olive oil

1 tablespoon sugar

3 cups Thick Coconut Milk (see page 376), or 2 cups unsweetened canned

3 to 4 cups vegetable broth

2 tablespoons fresh lime juice, or to taste

1/2 cup chopped fresh cilantro

Make the bumbu: Pulverize the sesame seeds in a food processor. Add the almonds and process again. Add rest of the spices and garlic and mix into a paste. Set aside.

Dissolve the tamarind paste in the boiling water, letting it stand for about 15 minutes to soften. Stir or mash the tacky paste with the back of a spoon until it has dissolved. Strain out the pulp through a fine strainer and use only the liquid. Set aside.

In a stockpot, sauté the onions in the olive oil, turning them often so that they cook evenly. When the onions are wilted and golden, add the sugar, raise the heat slightly, and gently caramelize the onions, still turning often, and being careful not to burn them.

Add the bumbu to the onions. Mix well. Add the tamarind liquid, coconut milk, and enough vegetable broth to total 6 or 7 cups. You want a soup thick with onions, with enough stock to cover by at least 2 inches.

Partially cover and simmer for 1 hour. Adjust seasoning at the end by adding lime juice and cilantro.

TAPIOCA SOUP
WITH GARLIC AND SAGE

Serves 4 to 6

▶ 12 to 18 large cloves garlic, peeled

6 cups vegetable broth

1/2 cup cleaned and chopped leeks, white part only

1/2 cup diced parsnips

1 tablespoon olive oil

3 tablespoons tapioca (see Note)

2 tablespoons chopped fresh sage leaves

3 tablespoons heavy cream, or 1/4 cup nondairy substitute such as rice milk or soy milk

Salt and freshly ground white pepper to taste

While some dishes remind us of our past, this one is my past. When my husband and I started out in the restaurant business we were less in the habit of inventing dishes than we were of using cookbook recipes that we thought were delicious and, in culinary terms, timely. As we were new restaurateurs some of "our" best ideas came from Simone Beck's Simca's Cuisine, *especially a favorite chicken soup thickened with tapioca and flavored with garlic.*

Simca is said to have inspired Mastering the Art of French Cooking *which she coauthored with Julia Child and Louisette Bertholle. Her great strength was her authentic and intuitive understanding of French home cooking. Her love of food and entertaining at home shine through everything she has written, and in her own cookbook, recipes and menus were joined to stories about dinners she had cooked for friends. Soupe de Bramafam, along with two or three other of Simca's dishes, remained our customers' favorites for years. A decade after they were taken off the menu, Huberts' guests continued to request them.*

After we received our third star, and long after we had been in the habit of inventing our own original dishes, I had the opportunity to meet Simone Beck at James Beard's house. She was teaching a class in his kitchen to promote her newest book. Simca was quite old by then, and though tall, thin, and still stately, her eyesight was very poor, and she depended upon her assistant to help her teach.

I had brought along my dog-eared, food-stained, and much treasured copy of her Simca's Cuisine *for her to sign after class. I approached her first to express my gratitude and then to explain how important and inspiring her book had been in the development of our restaurant. I was paying homage, laying my accomplishment down at the table of the master. I gushed with appreciation; I thanked her for launching us. Through Coke-bottle lenses, she looked at me uncomprehendingly. Her ice-blue eyes, magnified, seemed impenetrable. Either she could not hear me or my English made no impact. I had the sinking realization that nothing I had just said made any sense to her.*

Her assistant kindly stepped in, and even the august Beard tried to explain, but Simca seemed thoroughly stumped. "She says she started a restaurant using some of your recipes," Beard thundered slowly and kindly.

"Soupe de Bramafam in a restaurant?" Simca asked, looking around at the several of us, perplexed. "But why?" she asked as though we were playing some trick on her. "Why would you serve that in a restaurant?" Behind her Gallic accent, I detected, instead of pride, a slight distaste. At heart, Simca was interested in home cooking. The notion that her cookbook had affected a generation of professional cooks seemed farfetched. Such cooking was not intimate, not significant.

Whether you cook at home or for a restaurant, this dish all comes down to what tapioca and garlic can do in a soup. Simca probably wouldn't bristle at the substitution of a vegetarian stock, nor the removal of chicken, egg yolks, and cream, as long as you prepare this version of tapioca soup for people you care about.

With your palm down against the wide, flat end of a knife blade, press down on the garlic cloves to crush and break them open. Heat the broth in a stockpot and simmer the garlic for 35 minutes, uncovered. Remove the garlic with a slotted spoon and process or beat it into a smooth paste. Whisk the garlic paste back into the simmering broth.

In a separate pan, sauté the leeks and parsnips in the olive oil until softened and add to the broth.

Add the tapioca and cook, stirring often, until the tapioca is translucent and soft and the soup is lightly thickened.

Add the chopped sage. Continue cooking for 5 minutes. Stir in the cream and correct the seasoning with salt and pepper.

NOTE: Tapioca comes in different sizes: large pearl, small pearl, and quick-cooking small grains. Whether you like a large or small pearl depends on your taste. I have used all sizes for this recipe with success. The simplest to use is the quick-cooking, as the larger pearls require soaking and a longer cooking time. Follow the directions on the box of whatever kind you use.

3

SANDWICHES AND BURGERS

SANDWICHES AND BURGERS

SANDWICHES

SANDWICHES

CONTENTS

Most people think of a vegetarian sandwich as having cheese, avocado, sprouts, and tomato. Now that's a good sandwich, but there are other possibilities.

BEET SANDWICH
WITH RED ONION AND RICOTTA CHEESE

Makes 3 or 4 sandwiches

▶ 1/2 cup balsamic vinegar

1 tablespoon honey, diluted in 2 tablespoons boiling water

2 tablespoons light sesame oil

3 whole cloves

Salt and ground white pepper to taste

3 medium beets (about 2 cups sliced)

6 to 8 slices pumpernickel bread

1 cup ricotta cheese or chèvre

Thinly sliced red onion

Bibb lettuce leaves

This is like eating a great borscht sandwich. A quick marination makes for a less intensely pickled beet that doesn't surrender its beety taste to brine. Pickling the beets is easy, and if you use them while they are still warm, this sandwich is at its best. A good pumpernickel bread is especially delicious, and if it has raisins, all the better. Fresh ricotta makes for a simple sandwich spread, but if you are not a ricotta fan, try a slice of chèvre or fromage blanc instead.

Prepare a marinade by combining the vinegar, 1/4 cup of water, honey, sesame oil, and cloves. Bring to a simmer, adjust the seasoning with salt and pepper, then remove from the heat. Peel and slice the beets into thin rounds. Steam briefly, but do not overcook. The beets should still be hard at the center. While the beets are hot, place them in the marinade and let them stand for at least 30 minutes.

Remove enough beets for your sandwich. Pat dry. Spread 1 piece of pumpernickel bread with ricotta cheese. Place pickled beets on top of the ricotta, add very thin slices of red onion and a lettuce leaf, and cover with a second piece of bread.

Offer honey mustard and fruity olive oil at the table.

CHICK-PEA SANDWICH
WITH AVOCADO AND ARUGULA

Makes 2 sandwiches

Bean spreads make easy and delicious sandwiches that travel well. They are as convenient to use as peanut butter and have almost no fat. They can be flavored with spices, curry, or sautéed onions and moistened with your favorite sauce or a soft cheese like ricotta, cottage, or fromage blanc.

▶ 1 cup cooked chick-peas

2 tablespoons Thai peanut sauce

1 tablespoon Tahini Sauce (see page 119)

1 clove garlic, minced

4 slices whole wheat or sesame bread or pita

Avocado slices

1 Kirby cucumber, thinly sliced, skin on

Arugula, watercress, or pepper cress

Mash the chick-peas or process in a food processor with the Thai peanut sauce, tahini, and garlic. Spread on half the bread slices, top with avocado, cucumber slices, and arugula.

KIMCHI, CHEDDAR, AND
SUN-DRIED TOMATO SANDWICH

- ▶ 4 ounces sharp Cheddar or fontina cheese
- 1/2 cup kimchi, chopped fine
- Thin slices of sweet Maui onion
- 2 small baguettes or hearty sandwich rolls, or 4 slices fresh rye bread
- 2 tablespoons sun-dried tomato purée

Here is a sandwich for those who love pungent, spicy flavors.

For each sandwich, arrange 2 ounces of sliced cheese, kimchi to taste, and onion slices on a baguette. Spread one side of each sandwich with sun-dried tomato purée.

ROASTED GARLIC AND BRAISED TOFU
ON SOURDOUGH BREAD

Makes 2 sandwiches

Roasted garlic adds depth of flavor to other dishes, but by itself it makes a great sandwich spread. Marinated baked tofu is available in supermarkets and natural food stores, but you can also make your own very easily.

▶ 2 or 3 heads Roasted Garlic (see page 373), or 2 tablespoons roasted garlic purée

4 slices walnut-raisin sourdough bread

2 to 4 ounces Baked Marinated Tofu (see page 173)

Garnish: Roasted red bell pepper strips

Squeeze roasted garlic onto a piece of walnut raisin sourdough bread. Top with slices of marinated baked tofu and cover with a second slice of bread.

Serve garnished with roasted red pepper strips.

GRAPE, ARTICHOKE, AND GOAT CHEESE SANDWICH

Makes 4 sandwiches

- ▶ 1 pound seedless green grapes: ripe, sweet, firm, about 16 for each sandwich

- 4 to 8 ounces mild goat cheese: fresh, not aged

- Sliced brioche or other soft, sweet bread

- Sugar to taste (optional)

- 2 to 4 fresh artichoke bottoms, sliced in full rounds if possible

My father, Edward, loved grape sandwiches. As an engineer and former military man, he believed the construction of a proper sandwich required forethought and strategy. He was proudest of his grape sandwiches. With precision, he buttered both pieces of bread and sprinkled them with sugar, then meticulously sliced the grapes in half and placed them flat side down in rows so neat they resembled little soldiers, dressed in green, belly up, in full surrender, ready to be eaten.

By itself or with the addition of goat cheese and artichoke hearts, this is a very cheerful and light sandwich.

Slice the grapes in half lengthwise. Spread goat cheese on a slice of bread. Sprinkle very lightly with sugar if desired. Place grapes, flat side down, on the goat cheese. Cover with artichoke slices and the other slice of bread. Repeat with remaining ingredients.

TEMPEH BLT
WITH MANGO MAYONNAISE

Makes 2 sandwiches

A little bit of tempeh goes a long way, and its nutty flavor is especially satisfying on a sandwich. Cut the tempeh into thin slices so that it is rich instead of overbearing, and it will fry into a crispy texture that is deliciously reminiscent of bacon. You can dress this up with arugula and tomato, though I often substitute a nice slice of mango for the tomato.

This is great on sourdough walnut bread.

▶ 6 ounces tempeh

2 tablespoons whole wheat flour

2 teaspoons canola oil

4 slices sourdough bread

Mango mayonnaise

Arugula or romaine lettuce leaves

Thinly sliced tomato or fresh mango

Salt and ground black pepper to taste

MANGO MAYONNAISE

1 cup firm mayonnaise

1/2 cup chopped fresh mango, or skinned nectarine

2 tablespoons fresh chopped coriander

1 teaspoon ground cardamom

1 teaspoon fresh lime juice

1/2 teaspoon lime zest

Cut the tempeh into 1/4-inch slices. Dust lightly with whole wheat flour. Heat the oil in a sauté pan and cook the tempeh slices until golden brown on both sides.

Make the mayonnaise: Combine the mayonnaise, mango, coriander, cardamom, lime juice, and zest in a bowl.

For each sandwich, spread one slice of bread with mango mayonnaise to your taste. Cover with tempeh, arugula, and tomato slices, and salt and pepper. Top with a second slice of bread and serve.

SEITAN STEAK SANDWICH
WITH PEPPERS AND ONIONS

▶ **6 ounces seitan scaloppine (see page 210)**

1/2 cup sliced onion

2 tablespoons shoyu

2 tablespoons red wine

1/4 teaspoon red pepper flakes

1 tablespoon olive oil

1 clove garlic, minced

1/2 cup sliced roasted bell peppers

1 tablespoon capers, rinsed in hot water to remove brine (optional)

Baguette

This sandwich should be served on a baguette or a crusty roll. The best seitan is made locally and sold fresh in natural food stores, but it is also available frozen in packages. Or it is easy to make yourself.

Slice the seitan into steaks. Marinate the seitan and onions in a mixture of the shoyu, red wine, and red pepper flakes for 20 to 30 minutes.

Heat the oil in a sauté pan or on a cast-iron griddle. Cook the onion until golden, add the garlic, heat through, and remove. Grill the seitan on either side over a medium-high flame until it is nicely browned or there are grill marks.

Serve the seitan steak with onion and roasted peppers on a length of sliced baguette with a sprinkling of warm capers.

BURGERS

CONTENTS

Vegetarian burgers are the unsung heros of new vegetarian cooking, for you can pack a lot of flavor and nutrition into the little patties. Foodwise, burgers are part of the American vernacular, culturally indigenous and tough enough to outlast our fickle food-style fads. They are quick and easy, and you can really put your hands around one. In recent years, for purposes of health and variety, we have expanded the classic burger boundaries to include chicken, turkey, venison, and now even garden burgers. On the horizon, no doubt, are breakfast burgers: oatmeal patties on a sesame seed bun.

For vegetarian burgers, chewy texture or bite may add to eating satisfaction, but any further resemblance to meat's taste or texture is unnecessary. Basically, any combination of grains, beans, tofu, or vegetables that sticks together long enough to fashion into a patty and sauté and then be stuck between the top and bottom of a bun is burger material. Vegetable burgers are also one of the simplest ways of combining all the elements that make a whole protein. For that reason a host of classic vegetarian cookbooks have presented variations on a standard veg-burger theme containing mushrooms, soybeans, nuts, eggs, and rice or oats. In this old-fashioned formula grains, beans, and nuts are the foundation, vegetables and seasonings add distinctive flavor, and binders such as eggs, tofu, or bread crumbs help the patty hold together. Since most burgers are sautéed, use a nonstick pan for the easiest preparation.

In *The Vegetarian Compass* cooked grains or rice is added to a burger to help give it a shape, especially if the grains are slightly ground in a food processor or mill before they are worked into the burger mixture. Egg whites have been included in these recipes for body, but you can cook burgers without them, as cooked broken grains will do the same job. Beans in a burger add substantial protein, color, and meatiness. Nuts contribute richness, depth of flavor, and the taste-feel of fat. Tofu adds protein and if frozen, defrosted, and crumbled before it is used, its texture closely resembles that of ground beef. Texturized vegetable protein is another great source of protein and texture. Tempeh — steamed, crumbled, and sautéed in a good oil flavored with garlic or chili or wine and herbs — lends a special fermented, gamy quality to a burger. Vegetables add lightness and character. Carrots and parsnips will offer sweetness, and onions or shallots will add depth and round out the flavor of your burger. Greens like chard or collards, when chopped fine, will bring an earthy, slightly mineral quality, while mushrooms, especially wild ones, will add more earthy, hearty tones.

Vegetable burgers are easily prepared when made from refrigerated leftovers. If your tastes lean toward exotic burgers, add exotic flavors; shake the spice tree of your choice. Though I am fascinated by the Chinese art of preparing mock meat and fake fish dishes, I am not exactly a proponent of using Marmite or Savorex to make grains and vegetables meatlike. I prefer that ingredients taste like themselves. Finally, since burgers have a lot in common with pâtés and loaves, if a flavor pleases you as a burger, you may want to consider using it in these other forms. Season vigorously and remember that a burger has the added flavor advantage of being browned and eaten with such fun toppings as cheese, tomato, avocado, onion, and sprouts.

TEMPEH BURGER

This is as simple as a burger gets. When combined with rice and sage, the flavor and texture of the tempeh base are delicious.

▸ 1 tablespoon canola oil

1/3 cup minced onion

2 tablespoons shoyu

1 teaspoon sugar

1/4 cup white wine

1 1/2 to 2 cups cooked brown rice

8 ounces tempeh

1 teaspoon minced garlic

1 teaspoon freshly grated nutmeg

1 1/2 teaspoons ground sage

1 teaspoon summer savory

1 egg white (optional)

Salt and ground black pepper to taste

2 tablespoons whole wheat flour

Heat the oil in a small skillet and simmer the onion, shoyu, and sugar until golden brown. Add the wine and cook down until almost all the liquid has evaporated.

Place the rice in a processor and process for about 15 seconds or long enough to break the grain.

Slice the tempeh into thin slices and steam for 10 to 15 minutes. Place the tempeh in a mixing bowl and mash with a fork or a hand-held food processor for about 5 seconds.

Add the browned onions, garlic, nutmeg, sage, savory, rice, egg white, salt, and pepper. Form into patties and dust lightly with whole wheat flour. Sauté in a nonstick skillet until golden brown on both sides.

Serve on buns with jalapeño Cheddar cheese, sliced tomatoes, sprouts, and onion.

SUMMER BURGER

1 cup quinoa, cooked

1 cup steamed greens, leaves only: chard, spinach, kale, collards

1 tablespoon olive oil

1 tablespoon butter

1/3 cup finely minced leeks, white part only

1/2 cup finely crumbled tofu

1/2 cup ricotta

2 egg whites

1 teaspoon lemon zest

1 teaspoon freshly grated nutmeg

1/4 cup chopped chives

1 tablespoon fresh lemon thyme, if available, or fresh thyme leaves, or 1 teaspoon dried

2 tablespoons unseasoned bread crumbs, if necessary

1 tablespoon whole wheat flour, if necessary

Canola oil

Quinoa is a very light grain, perfect for a summer burger on a hot day. Your favorite combination of greens will do, but make sure the leaves have been patted or squeezed dry before you chop them. If your burger is too moist to hold together, try adding bread crumbs and/or a little whole wheat flour.

Place the quinoa in a food processor and process for 1 or 2 seconds, long enough to break or split the grain.

Squeeze out any excess liquid from the greens and chop them fine.

Heat the olive oil and butter in a small skillet and sauté the leeks for 5 minutes or until golden.

Place the tofu in a cloth or kitchen towel and squeeze excess water out.

In a large mixing bowl, combine the quinoa, greens, leeks, dry crumbled tofu, ricotta, egg whites, lemon zest, nutmeg, chives, and thyme. Mix well and shape into burgers.

If the burgers do not hold their shape well, you may wish to make them smaller, or add bread crumbs and/or flour to your taste.

Sauté in canola oil until golden brown on both sides. Serve on buns with shavings of aged pecorino cheese.

SHIITAKE HAZELNUT BURGER

This burger has some similarity in taste to pâté. It is rich, earthy, and meaty. Although I use shiitake mushrooms here because of their ready availability, any wild mushrooms may be substituted, including porcini, chanterelle, and portobello. To prevent having mushrooms soak up more oil or fat than you care to eat, try steaming them whole before you mince and lightly sauté them. Be sure to cook the liquid out of the mushrooms before you incorporate them into the burger mixture. A mixture that is too moist falls apart easily while cooking and does not hold its shape in the bun.

▶ 1 tablespoon olive oil, or as needed

1/2 cup minced onion

1 cup minced steamed shiitake mushrooms

1/4 cup black beans, well cooked and mashed or lightly processed

1/2 cup firm tofu, crumbled

1/2 cup hazelnuts, toasted and ground

1 cup brown rice, lightly processed to break or split grain

1 or 2 egg whites

2 teaspoons dried thyme

3/4 teaspoon ground marjoram

1/2 teaspoon grated nutmeg

1/2 teaspoon ground cinnamon

2 tablespoons Thai peanut sauce (optional)

Salt and ground black pepper to taste

Whole wheat flour

BRAISED ONION RINGS

2 cups very thinly sliced red onion

1 teaspoon dark or red miso

1/2 cup red wine

1 tablespoon balsamic vinegar

1 tablespoon fruity olive oil or, for a different flavor, toasted sesame oil

Heat 1 tablespoon of olive oil in a small skillet, add the minced onion and mushrooms, and sauté until the onions are tender and the mixture is dry, 5 to 8 minutes. Remove from the heat.

In a mixing bowl, combine the beans, tofu, ground hazelnuts, and rice with one of the egg whites. Add the onion-mushroom mixture and the seasonings. Mix well to combine; add another egg white if necessary for the ingredients to stick together.

Shape into burgers and dust with whole wheat flour. Oil a nonstick skillet and place over medium-low heat. Sauté the burgers until golden brown on both sides.

Meanwhile, make the braised onion rings: Put the onion in a small saucepan with the miso, red wine, vinegar, and olive oil. Cover and braise for 10 to 15 minutes, adding a little water if the mixture becomes dry. Uncover and continue cooking for a few minutes or as long as it takes the liquid to cook out, leaving the onion sizzling in sauce.

Serve the burgers on buns and topped with the onion.

MACADAMIA WHITE BEAN BURGER
WITH FRESH FIGS AND ONIONS

Makes 4 to 6 burgers

▶ 4 fresh green figs, sliced into rounds

1 small onion, sliced into rounds

1/2 teaspoon sugar

1 1/4 teaspoons ground cumin

1 teaspoon cider vinegar

1 cup cooked and cooled pearl barley

1/2 cup cooked white beans, such as navy

1/2 cup lightly toasted macadamia nuts, crushed

1/2 cup chopped cooked cauliflower florets

For this burger, try to use fresh steamed cauliflower. Frozen cauliflower will yield too much water unless you squeeze it dry after you steam it.

2 tablespoons finely chopped sun-dried tomatoes in oil

1/2 cup crumbled firm tofu

2 egg whites

1 teaspoon chopped fresh basil

Salt and ground black pepper to taste

Canola oil

Combine the sliced figs and onion. Sprinkle with the sugar, 1/4 teaspoon of the cumin, and the vinegar. Toss the compote gently and let stand.

Put the barley in a food processor and process for just a few seconds, long enough to split the grain. Lightly mash or quickly process the beans. Combine the barley and beans, macadamia nuts, cauliflower, and chopped dried tomatoes, tofu, egg whites, remaining teaspoon of cumin, and the basil. Mix well. Correct the seasoning and add salt and pepper to taste.

Shape into patties. Sauté in canola oil, using a nonstick pan if possible.

Serve on hamburger buns with the fig and onion compote.

ROASTED EGGPLANT
WALNUT KASHA BURGER

The ingredients in this dish yield a very rich and substantial burger. If your mixture seems too moist, add more kasha.

▶ 1 medium eggplant (1 to 1 1/2 pounds)

Olive oil

1 head garlic (12 to 20 large cloves)

Branches of fresh rosemary, plus 1 1/2 teaspoons chopped fresh rosemary leaves, or 1/2 teaspoon dried

1 to 1 1/2 cups cooked kasha

1/2 cup cooked pinto beans, mashed or processed

1/2 cup lightly toasted walnuts, skins rubbed off as much as possible, then crushed

2 egg whites

2 tablespoons chopped black olives

1 1/2 teaspoons fresh marjoram, or 1/2 teaspoon dried

Salt and ground black pepper to taste

2 to 4 tablespoons bread crumbs

Whole wheat flour

Preheat the oven to 375 degrees.

Cut the eggplant in half; rub all over with olive oil. Place on a baking sheet, flat side down. Poke the skin in a few places with a fork or knife.

Remove and reserve 2 cloves from the head of garlic. Rub the head with olive oil and place on the baking sheet with the eggplant. Rub several branches of rosemary with olive oil and place over the vegetables. Bake for 30 minutes to 1 hour, depending on the size and width of eggplant. The eggplant is done when it is very soft to the touch.

Remove, cool, and when the eggplant is easy to touch, scrape the pulp out with a spoon. If possible, put the eggplant through a fine-mesh strainer to remove seeds. One pound of eggplant should yield 1 cup of usable pulp.

When the garlic is cool, pop each garlic clove out of its paper jacket. You should have 1 to 2 tablespoons.

Place the kasha in a food processor and process just long enough to break or split the grains. Peel and mince the 2 cloves of reserved raw garlic.

Combine the eggplant, mashed roasted garlic, pinto beans, walnuts, kasha, egg whites, chopped olives, chopped rosemary, and marjoram. Season to taste with salt, pepper, and the freshly crushed garlic. Add bread crumbs if necessary. Mix well and shape into burgers. Dust with whole wheat flour and sauté until golden brown.

Serve on a bun. These are delicious served with a side of chèvre topped with kalamata olives and capers and drizzled with a good fruity olive oil.

MILLET–CHICK-PEA BURGER WITH HOT AND SWEET THAI CUCUMBERS AND CARROTS

Makes 4 to 6 burgers

For this recipe work with each ingredient separately, transferring it from the food processor to your mixing bowl before you process the next ingredient.

▶ 1/4 cup carrot slices, steamed until soft

1/2 cup parsnip slices, steamed until soft

1 cup cooked chick-peas

11/2 cups cooked millet

1/2 cup lightly toasted unsalted cashews

1 egg white

1 tablespoon tahini

1/4 cup chopped shallots, sautéed and cooled

1 teaspoon freshly grated nutmeg

1 tablespoon chopped fresh savory, or 1 teaspoon dried

1 tablespoon chopped fresh rosemary, or 1 teaspoon dried

1/4 cup chopped chives or finely chopped scallion greens

1 teaspoon lemon zest

Salt and ground black pepper to taste

Whole wheat flour

Hot and Sweet Thai Cucumbers and carrots (see page 70)

Mash or quickly process separately (see headnote) the carrots, parsnips, and chick-peas. Process the millet only until the grain just splits or breaks. Crush or quickly process the cashews.

As each ingredient is processed, transfer it to a large mixing bowl. Add the egg white, tahini, shallots, nutmeg, savory, rosemary, and chives. Add the seasonings and mix thoroughly to combine.

Shape into patties, dust with flour, and sauté until golden brown. Serve in buns topped with cucumbers and carrots in Thai vinaigrette.

HOT AND SWEET
THAI CUCUMBERS AND CARROTS

▶ 1 large, thick "soup" carrot, peeled

3 Kirby cucumbers

1 tablespoon honey diluted in 1 teaspoon boiling water

1/4 cup fresh lime juice

1/2 teaspoon white vinegar

1/4 teaspoon chopped jalapeño

2 cloves garlic, minced

1 teaspoon nam pla fish sauce (optional)

Cut the carrot into thirds so that each round is about 3 inches long. Using a vegetable peeler or a cheese plane, slice each piece lengthwise into strips. The bigger and thicker the carrot, the wider the strips will be. Cut the cucumbers the same way, leaving the skin on. Put the carrot and cucumber strips in a serving bowl.

In a small mixing bowl, combine the honey, lime juice, vinegar, chile, garlic, and nam pla. Whisk together. Pour the vinaigrette over the carrots and cucumbers and marinate for at least 1 hour before serving.

4

PÂTÉS AND TERRINES

PÂTÉS AND TERRINES

CONTENTS

Think of pâté or terrine, and you naturally think of company — everyone dipping into deeply colored crockery, spreading something luxurious or unctuous on bread and crackers. This is food made for good times, friends, front porches, picnics, and dinner parties — in short, the gravy times of life.

But these spreads can also find a welcome place in your everyday cooking repertoire. Vegetarian pâtés or terrines should be considered as ingredients, as starting points or as additions to other dishes. They can be used in sandwiches or soufflés, or to heighten the flavors of gratins or casseroles. They can be spread on tofu steaks or big juicy red tomatoes before broiling. They can be used to stuff potatoes, or whisked into soups as thickeners and flavor enhancers.

COMPASS PÂTÉ

Makes about 3 cups

- 1/2 pound fresh porcini mushrooms, or 2 cups sliced, to yield 1 cup steamed and chopped
- 1 1/2 tablespoons toasted sesame oil or olive oil
- 3/4 cup raw chopped onion
- 1 teaspoon granulated sugar
- 1 1/2 teaspoons shoyu
- 1/2 cup crumbled tofu
- 3/4 cup lightly toasted walnuts, loose skins rubbed away
- 1/3 cup lightly toasted sunflower seeds
- 1/3 cup sliced carrots
- 1 tablespoon tahini
- 3 tablespoons Parmesan cheese
- 2 to 3 tablespoons chopped fresh dill
- Salt and ground black pepper to taste
- 1 to 2 teaspoons brown sugar, or less to taste (optional)

When we have company, I serve this pâté before dinner, along with roasted red peppers and yogurt cheese. We sit around the living room, nestled deep into armchairs and the old feather-stuffed couch I inherited from my mother. The food on the coffee table is colorful and inviting. Invariably, the conversation turns to vegetables. Misty-eyed remembrances of great eggplant dishes, towering yam creations, and stories of hungrily gobbled greens begin to fill the room. Then my guests turn to one another and swear they would eat more veggies if only they tasted like this pâté. The air heats up as partners dare each other to start cooking vegetarian food first. It's at that point that I get up to serve the dinner.

Steam the whole mushrooms about 3 minutes or until they are limp and cooked through. Pat dry. Slice or chop them coarsely, then mince in a food processor or by hand. Remove to a mixing bowl.

Heat the oil in a small skillet and sauté the onion until wilted. Add sugar to caramelize, then add the shoyu to darken. If the shoyu sizzles, remove the pan from the heat and toss the onion to evaporate the liquid without burning or blackening the onion. Place the onion in the food processor; pulse briefly until the onion is minced, being careful not to purée it. Add the onion to the mushrooms.

74

THE VEGETARIAN COMPASS

Put the tofu into the food processor and pulse once or twice, until it is crumbled and mealy. Add to the mushroom mixture.

Combine the walnuts and sunflower seeds and pulse until the nuts are chopped fine into coarse crumbs, but not into nut butter. Add to the mushroom mixture.

Put the carrots and tahini in the food processor and pulse long enough to finely grate the carrots. Add to the mushroom mixture, along with the Parmesan cheese.

Fold the ingredients together and mix well. Add chopped dill to taste and season the pâté with salt and pepper, if necessary. Depending on the quality of your ingredients, you may wish to add a sprinkle of brown sugar to round out the flavor of the overall mix, but add it conservatively. This pâté should have a rich mellow flavor, not necessarily a sweet one.

Mold the pâté onto a plate; chill. Serve with crusty country bread, olive and walnut sourdough toast, or crackers.

PÂTÉ QUICK

▶ 1 tablespoon olive oil

2/3 cup chopped onion

1/2 teaspoon sugar

1/4 cup white wine

1/4 cup coarsely grated carrots

1/4 cup grated parsnips

2 tablespoons dark rum

1/4 pound tofu (2/3 cup chopped)

1/4 cup cooked rice or couscous

1 clove garlic, minced, or more
to taste

3 ounces steamed tempeh

1 teaspoon grated fresh ginger

This delicious simple spread is easy and quick to make. It has the luxurious taste of rich pâté, but is lighter in color, calories, and fat.

1 teaspoon shoyu

1 1/2 teaspoons tahini

1/2 teaspoon ground sage

1/2 teaspoon ground rosemary

1/2 teaspoon ground cardamom

Salt to taste

Ground red pepper (cayenne)
to taste

Heat the oil in a small heavy skillet, add the onion, and cook over low heat, stirring occasionally, for about 5 minutes or until softened. Stir in the sugar and cook a few more minutes to caramelize. Add the wine and boil until reduced completely. Add the grated carrots and parsnips and the rum and reduce completely.

Transfer the mixture to a food processor. Add the tofu. Pulse until mealy. Add the rice, garlic, tempeh, ginger, shoyu, and tahini. Pulse until the mixture is a soft spreadable paste. Add the sage, rosemary, and cardamom. Season with salt and cayenne to taste.

Mold onto a plate or pack into a serving bowl. Excellent with crusty bread, crisp toast, or crispy rice crackers.

RUTABAGA AND CARROT MOUSSE

This recipe uses agar-agar and kudzu, two unusual ingredients that can turn a delicious purée into a lovely mousse that needs no baking and no eggs.

Agar-agar is a seaweed gelatin, a pure plant product. Use 1 tablespoon of agar-agar to replace 2 tablespoons of gelatin, an animal product. Kudzu is made from the root of the kudzu plant, and is used as a starchy thickener much like arrowroot or cornstarch. It comes packaged in small rocklike pieces that dissolve easily and quickly in cool liquid. Both ingredients work together to lend the mousse a smooth texture more subtle than that formed by gelatin and cornstarch.

A variety of nondairy milks are available in natural food stores. Although I am not a great fan of soy milk, it is delicious here. If you prefer, use almond milk or rice milk in place of dairy.

Remember to turn on the food processor before you add the liquefied agar-agar and kudzu to the purées to ensure a smooth blend. Work quickly after that to pour the mixture into the mold.

▶ 1/2 cup steamed sliced carrots

1/2 cup steamed sliced parsnips

1/2 cup steamed rutabaga chunks

1/2 cup crumbled tofu

1 teaspoon vegetable bouillon powder

1 1/2 teaspoons fresh lemon juice, or more to taste

2 cloves garlic, minced

1/4 teaspoon freshly grated nutmeg

1/4 teaspoon ground allspice (optional)

Ground red pepper (cayenne) to taste

1 tablespoon kudzu dissolved in 1 tablespoon cool broth, milk, or water

2/3 cup soy milk, almond milk, rice milk, or regular milk

3 1/2 tablespoons flaked agar-agar

Brush a 3-cup mold very lightly with canola oil. Chill in the refrigerator while you prepare the mousse.

In a food processor, purée the carrots, parsnips, rutabaga, and tofu. Add the bouillon powder, lemon juice to taste, garlic, nutmeg, allspice if desired, and cayenne. Leave the mixture in the processor; set aside.

Remove the prepared mold from the refrigerator. Put the kudzu in a small measuring cup and dissolve it in a tablespoon of liquid, using a spoon or your finger to melt the kudzu.

Bring the soy milk to a simmer in a small saucepan and sprinkle the agar-agar on top; let it simmer, stirring constantly with a spoon or balloon whisk, for about 1 minute. Stir the kudzu again with your finger to make sure it hasn't settled in the liquid and add it to the soy milk. Stir with a spoon until the liquid thickens. Immediately pour the entire mixture into the processor *while it is turned on and running*.

Pour into the mold as soon as the ingredients are combined. Chill for at least 1 hour or until the mold seems set.

To release the mousse, dip the mold in a pan of very hot tap water for a second or two and run a sharp knife around the sides. Invert a serving plate over the top of the mold and turn them both over together.

Serve with crudités such as red bell pepper slices and endive leaves, or with toast and crackers. This is also wonderful when topped with Roasted Red Pepper and Cashew Sauce (see page 367).

PISTACHIO AND FAVA CROSTINI

This is a simple but remarkable preparation. Shelled pistachios are available in Middle Eastern stores and many natural food stores. The fresher the better for this springtime spread.

▶ 1 cup cooked unpeeled fresh fava beans (1 pound in the shell)

2 tablespoons fruity olive oil

1 or 2 cloves garlic, minced

1 to 2 teaspoons Pernod, or to taste

Salt and ground black pepper to taste

2 cups shelled, unsalted pistachios, lightly toasted, dry, loose skins rubbed off

1/4 to 1/3 cup grated Romano cheese

1 teaspoon dried savory (optional)

Fruity olive oil

Use a food processor or a hand masher to mash the fava beans. Leave some texture; do not purée them. Add the olive oil, garlic, Pernod, and salt and pepper.

Place the pistachios in a food processor and pulse until the nuts are coarsely crushed, but nowhere near a paste. Add the nuts to the fava beans. Stir in the Romano cheese and, if you wish, the savory.

Chill, drizzle with olive oil, and serve spread on crusty bread, brioche toast, or fennel slices.

TERRINE OF GREENS

Makes 1 terrine

▶ 1/2 cup good cognac

4 ounces pitted prunes

2 tablespoons olive oil

1 cup cleaned and chopped leeks, both white and green parts

2 cloves garlic, minced

6 ounces tempeh, steamed for 20 minutes, then crumbled

1 teaspoon shoyu

1/2 cup chopped parsley

2 1/2 to 3 pounds steamed chard leaves, squeezed dry and chopped fine to yield 2 cups

2 tablespoons vegetable bouillon powder

1/2 cup grated Parmesan cheese

2/3 cup cooked rice

2 whole eggs plus 2 egg whites

1 1/2 cups milk or soy milk

1/2 cup all-purpose flour

2 tablespoons fresh thyme

1/2 teaspoon freshly grated nutmeg, or to taste

Salt and ground black pepper to taste

Pounti, from the Auvergne, is a demi-creature, half terrine, half pie. Traditionally, it is made from chard or spinach. Peasant fare, pounti was often prepared without meat, an item few peasants could count on having with regularity. This version of pounti is made with chard and tempeh and stuffed with pitted prunes soaked in cognac.

Warm the cognac in a small saucepan and soak the prunes for about 1 hour.

Preheat the oven to 350 degrees.

Butter an 8-cup terrine or 9-inch loaf pan and set aside.

Heat 1 tablespoon of the olive oil in a small skillet, add the leeks, and cover the pan. Cook over low heat until wilted but not brown. Stir in the garlic. Transfer to a mixing bowl.

Sauté the crumbled tempeh in the remaining olive oil until golden brown. Add shoyu to darken. Remove from the heat and add the tempeh to the leeks. Add the parsley, chard, crumbled tempeh, bouillon powder, Parmesan cheese, and rice.

In another bowl whisk together the eggs, egg whites, and milk. Add the flour and beat until it forms a smooth batter. Pour the batter over the greens and mix well. Stir in the thyme and nutmeg. Adjust the seasoning with salt and pepper.

Pour half the chard mixture into the terrine. Drain the prunes and arrange them over the chard. Pour the rest of the chard mixture on top. Drizzle with olive oil and bake uncovered for 45 minutes to 1 hour or until the mixture shrinks from the sides of the terrine and the top is golden brown. If the top is browning too quickly, cover lightly with foil.

Cool. Serve warm or cold, sliced, with crusty garlic bread.

TERRINE OF ROASTED VEGETABLES IN ASPIC

▶ 3 1/2 cups cooked vegetables, such as:

- 1 cup roasted red bell pepper slices

- 1/2 cup roasted Japanese eggplant pulp

- 1/2 cup roasted garlic cloves

- 1 cup steamed and chopped curly kale

- 1/2 cup steamed and chopped broccoli

- 1/2 cup sliced avocado

1/2 cup canola oil

1/2 cup fruity olive oil

3/4 to 1 cup cider, raspberry, or balsamic vinegar

4 to 6 cloves garlic, minced

1 tablespoon sugar, or to taste (optional)

Salt and ground white pepper to taste

1/2 cup white wine

5 tablespoons agar-agar

1/4 to 1/2 cup kefir, or to taste (optional)

1/4 cup avocado purée (optional; see Note)

1/2 cup chopped parsley or cilantro (optional)

The aspic in this terrine is essentially a jellied vinaigrette. Use your favorite vinaigrette, or try this one. The recipe includes three variations: garlic vinaigrette; a vinaigrette with a creamy addition of kefir, or yogurt cheese; and, last, a vinaigrette with kefir and a delicious addition of avocado purée. All three variations will jell with the amount of agar-agar suggested.

You will need about 3 to 3 1/2 cups of roasted vegetables, depending on what you choose. If you have vegetables left over, use them for garnish, or make more vinaigrette to cover. If you decide to use some of the roasting juices in the vinaigrette, make sure they are not bitter in flavor and keep the ratio of agar-agar to liquid the same: 2 tablespoons per cup of liquid.

Chill a 6- to 8-cup mold (preferably glass) in the freezer for at least 30 minutes. Arrange the vegetables in the mold. Replace in the freezer to chill briefly while you make the aspic.

In a saucepan, combine the canola oil, olive oil, vinegar, minced garlic, sugar, salt, and pepper. Add the white wine. Bring the mixture to boil, then lower the heat to a simmer. Add the agar-agar and stir continuously for 2 to 3 minutes until the agar-agar is completely dissolved. (Simmering longer will not hurt its ability to jell.) The aspic may be used as is, or you can add kefir and/or avocado purée.

82

If desired, add the kefir and avocado purée and stir until completely dissolved. (If you need to keep the vinaigrette warm, simply place it in a larger pot of hot or boiling water.)

Remove the chilled terrine from the freezer. Sprinkle with parsley or cilantro at the last minute and pour the warm aspic over the vegetables. Chill at least 1 hour or until the aspic is firm.

To unmold, briefly dip the terrine into hot water and run a sharp knife around the sides. Invert a serving plate over the top of the mold, turn them both over together, and give the mold a few taps.

Serve slices of aspic on top of Bibb lettuce, accompanied by warm broad noodles or crusty bread.

NOTE: If you intend to add avocado purée, use only 1/4 cup of kefir.

GRAINS

CONTENTS

GRAINS

AMARANTH CAVIAR

The taste of this amaranth caviar will depend on the nature of the black olives and mushrooms you use. Kalamata olives will provide a good tang, whereas oil-cured black olives will add a saltier, more resinous quality. Canned water-packed olives will lend color and texture but not much taste. As for mushrooms, use fresh porcini, shiitake, or morels if they are available. In a pinch, Chinese black mushrooms may be used, but the result is a chewier, less velvety spread.

▶ 1 cup amaranth

1 teaspoon toasted sesame oil

2 cups hot vegetable broth

2/3 cup minced shallots

2 tablespoons olive oil

1/2 cup pitted black olives, minced

1 cup mushrooms, steamed whole, patted dry, minced

2 cloves garlic, minced

1 tablespoon minced chives or scallion greens

1 teaspoon chervil

1 tablespoon fresh lemon juice, or to taste

2/3 cup pine nuts, toasted and chopped fine

Salt and ground black pepper to taste

In a nonstick saucepan or skillet, sauté the amaranth in the sesame oil until the grains turn golden, but do not let them "pop." Add the broth. Simmer gently, covered, for 35 to 45 minutes or until done.

In a separate pan, sauté the shallots in the olive oil. Stir in the olives, mushrooms, and garlic and remove from the heat.

When the amaranth is cool, add the shallot-olive-mushroom mixture. Stir in the chives, chervil, lemon juice, and pine nuts. Mix well and season to taste with salt and pepper.

Spread on crackers or sourdough toast.

AMARANTH WITH RICE AND BARLEY

▶ 1 cup brown rice

3/4 cup pearl barley

1/2 cup amaranth

3 cloves garlic

1 tablespoon fresh ginger cut into thick matchsticks

1 tablespoon toasted sesame oil

4 cups water or vegetable broth

Because amaranth is so crunchy, I like to add it to other grains for texture. This particular combination with rice and barley is my all-time favorite.

Combine the rice, barley, and amaranth in a saucepan. Peel the garlic and smash lightly with the side of a heavy knife or cleaver. Add the garlic, ginger, sesame oil, and water to the grains. Simmer, covered, for 45 minutes to an hour. Let stand, still covered, for at least 15 minutes so that the grains finish cooking by steaming.

AMARANTH WITH GREEN RATATOUILLE
AND BLUE CHEESE

Serves 4

Because of its size, amaranth has often been compared to the tiny poppy seed. Yet nutritionally it is a giant compared to most other grains. The cultivation of amaranth can be traced back to ancient peoples, who viewed it as a staff of life because it was so easy to grow and store.

▶ 1 cup eggplant cubes, with skin on

Salt

1 cup chopped beet greens, watercress, or arugula

1 cup broccoli florets or chopped broccoli raab

1/4 cup olive oil, plus additional for serving

1/2 cup diced onion

1 1/2 cups dry amaranth grain

3 cups hot vegetable broth

2/3 cup chopped artichoke hearts, fresh or in oil

4 cloves garlic, sliced

2/3 cup chopped roasted red bell peppers

1/2 cup chopped fresh basil

1/4 cup plus 2 tablespoons chopped fresh oregano

1 teaspoon lemon zest

1/4 teaspoon red pepper flakes

3/4 cup crumbled blue cheese or Gorgonzola

Place the eggplant cubes in a colander, sprinkle with salt, and let stand for an hour. Rinse the salt off and squeeze the eggplant dry by wringing it in your hands. Steam briefly, just until the eggplant softens. Do not overcook or the eggplant will "melt" and lose its shape, which will make sautéing very difficult. Steam the beet greens and broccoli just until both turn bright green.

Heat 1 tablespoon of oil in a nonstick skillet and sauté the onion 4 or 5 minutes. Remove with a slotted spoon. Sauté the amaranth in the oil remaining in the pan for under a minute, long enough to brown the grain, but not to "pop" it. Return the onions to the pan with the amaranth. Add the hot vegetable broth, cover, and cook for 30 minutes or until the grain is tender. It should be slightly crunchy but not starchy when fully cooked. Cover and keep warm.

Heat the remaining 3 tablespoons of oil in a sauté pan; add the eggplant, greens, broccoli, artichoke hearts, garlic, and roasted peppers; sauté for 5 minutes or until tender. Stir in the basil, 2 tablespoons of oregano, the lemon zest, salt, and red pepper flakes. Remove from the heat. Fold the crumbled cheese into heated vegetables.

Pack the amaranth into a ramekin and unmold onto individual plates. Spoon vegetables on top. Sprinkle with the remaining 1/4 cup of chopped oregano. Serve with cruets of oil and vinegar and lemon wedges on the table.

CREAMED BARLEY AND
FRESH CRANBERRY BEANS WITH FENNEL

Serves 4 to 6

You may have seen them at the vegetable stand — extravagantly colored, long pink and white pods. Inside them are cranberry beans, white beans the size of pintos, with the same pink striations as their pods. They don't appear often, but when they do, you should cook them, especially with creamed barley, which tastes a little like a grainy risotto.

CREAMED BARLEY

1 tablespoon olive oil

1 cup cleaned and sliced leeks, white part only

1 1/2 cups pearl barley

3 cups vegetable broth

1 teaspoon freshly grated nutmeg

2 to 4 tablespoons cream

▶ CRANBERRY BEANS

2 tablespoons olive oil

2 cups sliced raw fennel

2 sprigs rosemary

2 cloves garlic, minced

1 cup white wine

2 cups vegetable broth

2 cups shelled fresh cranberry beans (about 2 pounds in the shell)

Cook the beans: Heat the 2 tablespoons of oil in a saucepan, add the fennel, and sauté over medium heat until softened, about 5 minutes. Add the rosemary and garlic. Pour in the wine and boil until reduced by half.

Add the vegetable broth and the beans, and bring to a simmer. Cover and simmer gently for 30 to 45 minutes or until the beans are tender. Keep warm.

Meanwhile, prepare the barley: Heat 1 tablespoon of oil in a saucepan, add the leeks, and cook for 4 or 5 minutes, until translucent. Stir in the barley and vegetable broth. Cover and simmer for 45 minutes, until the barley is tender. Add the nutmeg and cream, and stir to combine.

Place a serving of barley in the center of each plate. Ladle cranberry beans on top. Serve with thinly sliced pecorino or freshly grated Parmigiano-Reggiano cheese.

BARLEY WITH MARSALA WINE AND SEITAN

2 tablespoons olive oil

1/2 cup chopped onion

1/2 cup chopped celery

1/2 cup chopped carrots

1/2 cup chopped rutabaga

2/3 cup marsala wine

2 teaspoons fresh thyme leaves, or
1 scant teaspoon dried

1 1/2 cups pearl barley

2 3/4 cups vegetable broth, or as
needed

1 cup chopped "quick" seitan
(see page 202)

I like barley with "quick" or "scaloppine" seitan, which holds up very well under braising. If you prefer your barley mixed with another grain, try equal amounts of barley and brown rice.

In a saucepan, heat the olive oil and sauté the onion, celery, carrots, and rutabaga for 5 to 6 minutes, until softened. Add the marsala and boil until reduced by a third. Stir in the thyme. Add the barley and broth and bring to a simmer. Add the seitan. Simmer, covered, for 35 to 45 minutes or until the barley is soft but not mushy. Add more broth if the mixture boils dry.

BUCKWHEAT GROATS AND SOBA NOODLES

Serves 4

In this recipe, buckwheat noodles lighten the stalwart buckwheat groats. The nutty, hearty groats and the simple, smooth noodles provide a classic marriage of texture and taste. Use either buckwheat groats, which are raw, lighter in color, and subtle, or kasha, darker groats that have been dry-roasted for a toastier flavor.

For dramatic visual contrast add toasted black sesame seeds, either alone or with sweet, briny hijiki seaweed.

▶ 1 tablespoon olive oil or toasted sesame oil

1 cup chopped onion, preferably sweet Maui or Vidalia

1 teaspoon sugar

1 cup buckwheat groats or kasha

1 egg white, beaten

2 cups hot vegetable broth

1 package buckwheat noodles, udon, or soba

2 cups sugar snap peas or snow peas, strings removed, or shelled green peas

1/3 cup black sesame seeds (optional)

1/3 cup black hijiki seaweed (optional)

1 tablespoon mirin, or 1 teaspoon sugar dissolved in 1 cup hot water (optional)

Heat the oil in a saucepan and sauté the onion for 5 minutes. Add the sugar and continue cooking over medium heat to caramelize lightly, being careful not to burn. Remove from the heat.

In a bowl, combine the buckwheat groats with the egg white, stirring to mix well. Let stand for 5 minutes while you preheat a cast-iron or stainless steel skillet. Without oil, toast the groats in the dry pan, while stirring, for about 3 minutes, until the grains are separate. Transfer the groats to the saucepan with the onion. Add the hot vegetable broth and simmer, covered, until the groats are fluffy, about 15 minutes. Remove from the heat and let steam, covered, for 10 minutes.

Meanwhile, cook the buckwheat noodles until tender but still firm and refresh under cold water. Chop into bite-size pieces. Steam the snap peas until they begin to change color.

In a small skillet over medium heat, dry-toast the black sesame seeds for about 1 minute, being careful not to burn. Soak the hijiki in hot water and mirin. Let stand until the hijiki softens, about 20 minutes. Drain and chop.

When the buckwheat groats are done, fluff with a fork and gently fold in the snap peas, noodles, and hijiki. Sprinkle each serving with black sesame seeds.

BULGUR WITH CAULIFLOWER
AND COCONUT MILK

▶ 2 to 2 1/2 cups Thick Coconut Milk
(see page 376)

2 tablespoons dark rum, or to taste

1 cup bulgur

2 cups cooked orzo (rice-shaped
pasta)

2 cups small cauliflower florets,
without stems

2 teaspoons toasted sesame oil

1/4 teaspoon chile powder, or
1/2 teaspoon minced jalapeño

1 1/2 teaspoons ground cardamom

1 teaspoon grated nutmeg

Salt and ground black pepper
to taste

Sugar (optional)

This dish is a study in contrasts, in both texture and flavor. Don't leave out the coconut milk, which really makes the dish. Make your own coconut milk if possible; if not, use a canned variety but make sure you choose an unsweetened brand.

Combine the coconut milk and rum in a saucepan and heat but do not boil. Place the bulgur in a large bowl and pour 2 cups of the hot coconut milk over the grain. Let this stand for 45 minutes to an hour or until the liquid is absorbed and the grains are slightly soft. If you need more liquid, add it to the bulgur 1/4 cup at a time. Or place the bulgur in a steamer and steam gently for 2 to 3 minutes, until softened.

Cook the orzo according to package directions. Refresh under cold water and drain. Steam the cauliflower until it is tender but still firm, 6 to 8 minutes. Put the orzo and cauliflower in a mixing bowl and toss with the sesame oil and chile powder.

When the bulgur is done, add the orzo and cauliflower florets. Season with cardamom and nutmeg and toss. Adjust the seasoning with salt, pepper, and, if desired, a light sprinkling of sugar and additional rum. Serve warm or at room temperature.

BULGUR AND FRESH WHITE BEANS
WITH GARLIC-GINGER VINAIGRETTE

Serves 4

This is a very pretty dish, especially if you catch the season just right and can prepare it with yellow tomatoes and yellow peppers and fresh cannellini beans, which are light yellow to white in color. Fresh cannellini are available for a brief time during late spring and early summer. Fresh fava, cranberry, and limas will also do for this dish. Although this is good chilled, I prefer to serve it warm or at room temperature, because I think the beans taste better that way. The vinaigrette sauce is creamy, spicy, exotic, and slightly sweet.

▶ 1 cup medium bulgur

2 cups boiling water

2 tablespoons vegetable bouillon powder

1 cup shelled fresh cannellini beans (1 pound in the shell)

1/2 cup chopped red onion

1 cup chopped yellow bell peppers

1 cup yellow cherry tomatoes or chopped yellow tomatoes

1/2 teaspoon minced jalapeño, or to taste

1/2 cup finely chopped fennel or celery heart

1 cup chopped parsley or cilantro leaves

GARLIC-GINGER VINAIGRETTE

1/4 cup olive oil

1/4 cup canola oil

2 cloves garlic, minced

1 teaspoon freshly grated or minced fresh ginger

2 tablespoons kefir

1/2 cup fresh lemon juice

1 teaspoon sugar

1 teaspoon ground coriander

1 teaspoon ground cumin

Salt and ground black pepper to taste

Place the bulgur in a bowl and pour over it a mixture of the boiling water and bouillon powder. Let this stand for 45 minutes to 1 hour, until the liquid is absorbed and the grains are slightly soft. Meanwhile, steam the beans for 20 to 30 minutes or until tender.

Toss the bulgur with the onion, peppers, tomatoes, jalapeño, fennel, parsley, and beans.

Combine the ingredients for the vinaigrette and pour over the grain and vegetables. Toss gently. Adjust the seasoning with salt and pepper. You might want to make extra vinaigrette, to serve alongside the bulgur. Serve at room temperature.

BULGUR WITH KALE AND GREEN PAPAYA

▶ 1 cup medium bulgur

2 cups boiling water flavored with 2 tablespoons vegetable bouillon powder

2 cups very finely chopped steamed kale

1 1/2 cups peeled, seeded, finely chopped green (unripe) papaya

1/2 cup fresh lemon juice (juice of 3 or 4 lemons)

1/2 cup fresh lime juice (juice of 4 or 5 limes)

2/3 cup olive oil

1/3 cup canola oil

3 cloves garlic, minced

1 1/2 teaspoons sugar, or to taste

1 teaspoon powdered coriander

1 teaspoon powdered cumin

Salt and ground black pepper to taste

A vegetarian cookbook without a version of tabbouleh seems sacrilegious. Having no desire to buck tradition, I offer this recipe. I rarely get around to serving bulgur hot, because it is so delicious cold. It stands up to vinaigrettes heroically and never loses its grainy texture.

Try green, unripe papaya for this. It is a wonderful addition: crisper than cucumber and slightly fruity. Finely chopped kale takes the place of parsley here for a heartier tabbouleh.

Place the bulgur in a serving bowl and pour the hot bouillon over it. Let this stand for 45 minutes to 1 hour until the liquid is absorbed and the grains are slightly soft. Meanwhile, prepare the kale and papaya.

Add the finely chopped kale and green papaya to the bulgur.

Whisk together the lemon juice, lime juice, olive oil, canola oil, garlic, sugar, coriander, and cumin. Pour about 2/3 cup of the dressing over the bulgur, kale, and green papaya. Toss until thoroughly mixed.

Let stand for at least 2 hours before serving. Just adjust the seasoning with more of the dressing, salt, and pepper.

Serves 4 to 6

This was a popular dish at Huberts restaurant. Wait until your sheet of grits has cooled and solidified before you make your cutouts, or your cakes will fall apart.

▶ 2 1/2 cups milk

2 1/2 cups plus 1/2 cup vegetable broth

1 cup grits

1 teaspoon salt, or to taste

1/2 cup grated Romano or pecorino cheese, plus extra

2 drops Tabasco

1/2 pound fresh wild mushrooms: shiitake, chanterelles, morels, oysters, etc., wiped clean and trimmed

2/3 cup chopped red onion

2 tablespoons clarified unsalted butter or canola oil

1/2 cup white wine

2 to 4 tablespoons heavy cream

1/2 cup flour for dusting

2 tablespoons canola oil

Garnish: Freshly grated Romano or pecorino cheese, fresh thyme, 1/2 cup thinly julienned black radish with skin on

Bring the milk and 2 1/2 cups of the vegetable broth to a boil. Stir in the grits and salt. Cook, covered, for 20 to 25 minutes. Add the grated cheese and Tabasco.

Butter an 18 × 11 × 1-inch jelly-roll pan. Spread the grits evenly to a 3/4-inch thickness in the pan. Let cool at room temperature or in the refrigerator. When the grits have cooled and solidified, cut out rounds with a cookie cutter, or cut into squares.

Steam the mushrooms for 3 to 5 minutes; cool, then slice. Sauté the mushrooms and onion in the clarified butter for 5 minutes, until the onion is softened. Deglaze the pan with white wine and the remaining 1/2 cup of vegetable broth. Boil rapidly to cook down to 1/4 cup. Add the cream and reduce as needed to thicken the sauce.

Lightly dust the grits cakes with flour; sauté in the oil until golden brown on both sides. Place on individual plates and spoon the mushroom mixture over the grits. If desired, serve topped with freshly grated Romano or pecorino cheese, fresh thyme, and, for drama, some thinly julienned black radish with its skin on, if available.

MILLET WITH CAULIFLOWER, PRESERVED LEMON, AND LEEKS

▶ 1 large yellow crookneck squash, about 10 to 12 ounces

1 tablespoon olive oil

1 cup chopped leeks, white and light green part only, about 2 leeks

1/2 cup white wine

1 cup millet

6 cloves garlic, peeled

1/2-inch round slice fresh ginger, sliced in 4 strips

2 cups boiling vegetable broth

1 tablespoon chick-pea miso, or mellow white miso

1 preserved lemon, pulp removed, rinsed, rind cut into 4 to 6 slices (see page 109)

2/3 cup chick-peas, cooked al dente

1 cinnamon stick

The preserved lemon is very pretty among the yellow grains of millet and also provides a most exotic taste and perfume. This dish can be made with or without chick-peas, which I suggest adding if you want to serve it as a main dish.

Cut the squash in half lengthwise. Remove and discard the pulpy interior, leaving the yellow skin and some firm flesh. Cut the shell into thin strips and then cut crosswise to dice into small cubes. You should have about 1 cup.

Heat the oil in a heavy saucepan, add the leeks, and sauté over high heat until they begin to brown. Add the white wine and boil until reduced by half. Add the millet, with the whole garlic cloves, ginger, hot broth, and miso. Bring to a simmer. Add the preserved lemon, cooked chick-peas, and cinnamon stick. Cover and simmer for 45 minutes to 1 hour or until the millet is tender. Let stand, covered, for another 15 minutes. Serve hot.

POLENTA WITH PUMPKIN, QUINCE, AND FROMAGE BLANC

Serves 4

This is a wonderful accompaniment to an entrée dish that has a good deal of sauce. I prefer to bake the pumpkin meat for a richer flavor, but steamed pumpkin will do just fine if you add another tablespoon of cornmeal. If you choose not to use milk, vegetable broth is also acceptable. It is hard, though, to find a substitute for the aromatic quince, which is available during the fall and very early winter. You might try a firm Chinese apple, found frequently in fruit markets.

▶ 1 1/2 cups milk

2 tablespoons creamy peanut butter

1/2 teaspoon freshly grated nutmeg

1/2 teaspoon ground cardamom

1/4 teaspoon ground cinnamon

1 cup cornmeal, fine white or yellow

1 cup chopped baked pumpkin, kabocha, hokkaido, butternut, or other pumpkin-squash (see Note)

1 cup chopped steamed quince (see Note)

1/2 cup finely chopped pitted dates

4 to 6 ounces fromage blanc or fresh chèvre

Heat milk and 1 1/2 cups of water in a large saucepan over medium heat, but do not boil. Add the peanut butter and whisk to dissolve. Add the nutmeg, cardamom, and cinnamon. Pour the cornmeal into the liquid slowly and steadily while you whisk it into the hot milky broth. Keep stirring over low heat until the cornmeal thickens considerably and pulls away from the sides and bottom of the pot. The finer the cornmeal, the quicker your cornmeal will be cooked. Remove from the heat and add pumpkin meat. Whisk into the cornmeal. Add a little more boiling water, if necessary, to make a smooth creamy consistency, not too stiff. Fold in the quince and dates.

Serve while hot, with a dollop of fromage blanc or chèvre on top of each serving.

NOTE: To bake pumpkin or winter squash: Cut in quarters, remove seeds, rub cut surfaces with canola oil, and sprinkle with brown sugar. Bake 1 hour or until pumpkin meat is soft. Scoop out 1 cup for this recipe.

Peel and cut quince into fourths, remove pits, and steam briefly until just fork tender. Do not overcook. Chop into bite-size chunks.

HASH BROWN POLENTA WITH KALE

▶ 1 1/2 cups milk

2 tablespoons light miso

1 cup medium to fine yellow or white cornmeal

1 teaspoon ground rosemary, or 2 teaspoons or more finely chopped fresh rosemary

1/4 cup finely grated Parmesan cheese

Salt and ground black pepper to taste

1/2 cup flour for light dredging (optional)

1 tablespoon canola oil

2 cups chopped kale

1 tablespoon olive oil

1/2 cup chopped onion

2 tablespoons soy bacon bits (optional)

There seem to be about as many recipes for making perfect polenta as there are salamis in Genoa. People have been cooking the versatile dish for centuries, using such available grains as buckwheat and millet, then switching to corn when it became available after the discovery of the New World. Among the controversies involved in the preparation of polenta are such irreconcilable differences as the correct proportions of cornmeal to liquid, the right use of hot or cold water or milk, the manner by which grains should be poured to avoid lumps, as well as the direction in which they ought to be stirred. I have tried to be politic in my preference for a recipe that combines water, milk, and miso for a creamy texture and satisfying flavor, but if you have a great polenta recipe, use it here for your hash browns. I promise, my feelings won't be hurt; at heart, I am a polenta pacifist.

Heat the milk and 1 1/2 cups of water in a large saucepan over medium heat, but do not boil. Add the miso and whisk to dissolve. Pour the cornmeal into the liquid slowly and steadily while you whisk it into the hot milky broth. Keep stirring until the polenta thickens considerably and pulls away from the sides and bottom of the pot, about 25 minutes. (The finer the cornmeal, the quicker your polenta mix will cook. Add more cornmeal by the tablespoonful, if you feel you must.) Add the rosemary and Parmesan cheese. Season with salt and pepper to taste.

Lightly oil a Pyrex or stainless steel baking pan and pour the polenta out, spreading it to the desired thickness, usually about 3/4 inch to 1 inch thick. Let this cool naturally or refrigerate it. When the polenta is firm and cool to the touch, cut into 1-inch chunks. Lightly dust with flour. Heat the canola oil in a skillet and gently sauté the chunks over medium-low heat until they turn golden brown. Keep turning so all sides are nicely colored.

Meanwhile, steam the kale for 10 minutes or until tender. Heat the olive oil in a small skillet and sauté the onion over high heat until golden brown.

In a serving dish, mix the kale with the onion and the optional soy bacon bits for a smoky flavor, if desired. Season with additional fresh rosemary, salt, and pepper to taste. Combine with the browned polenta and serve.

QUINOA AND RASPBERRIES FOR DINNER

Serves 4

▶ 1 teaspoon honey, or as needed

1 cup quinoa

4 cups raspberries

1 pint cream, or 2 pints yogurt

Honey (optional)

Brown sugar (optional)

When I was a child, my mother served fruit for dinner in the summers, big bowls of cherries and berries and platters of melons paired with pots of creamy sour cream, yogurt, and ricotta cheese. As I look back on it, all that was missing from her summertime table was a grain. None seems more suitable than quinoa. Light in texture and taste, when quinoa is cooked, the germ spirals out into a little curlicue, giving it a comical cartoon shape. Like all comic superheroes, despite its gentle outside, it packs a powerhouse wallop. Quinoa's protein value is comparable to that of milk. I like it with light, crunchy vegetables like Jerusalem artichokes or jicama, but it is also perfect with fruit, for summer dinners.

Bring 2 cups of water to a boil in a saucepan; add 1 teaspoon of honey and the quinoa. Simmer for 10 to 15 minutes or until the liquid is absorbed. Let stand for 10 to 15 minutes; fluff with a fork.

Serve in bowls topped with generous servings of raspberries. Offer cream that is lightly whipped or plain, yogurt, and honey or brown sugar if desired.

NOTE: A pleasant variation would be to use a lightly brewed raspberry-flavored fruit tea in place of water, or to add a few tablespoons of sweet sherry or rum to the cooking liquid.

TEFF WITH BARLEY AND BROWN RICE

1 cup diced rhubarb (1/2-inch pieces)

1/2 cup currants

2 tablespoons rum

2 tablespoons honey

1 teaspoon balsamic vinegar

2 tablespoons light sesame oil

3 cups chopped red chard leaves

3 cups vegetable broth

1/2 cup teff

1/2 cup pearl barley

1/2 cup brown rice

1 slice fresh ginger

3 whole cloves garlic, smashed

This dish offers several contrasts. The tiny teff grain provides crackle to the barley and brown rice. The rich, meaty flavor of the red chard is cut by an offering of sweet, tart rhubarb sauce.

In a small nonreactive saucepan, combine the rhubarb, currants, rum, honey, and vinegar. Simmer until the rhubarb has softened but has not yet lost its shape. Set the sauce aside.

Heat the sesame oil in a large heavy saucepan and sauté the chard for 4 to 5 minutes. Add the broth and bring to a boil. Add the teff, barley, brown rice, ginger, and garlic. Cover and simmer for 45 minutes to 1 hour. Since these grains vary, check to see whether you need to add a little more broth and add sparingly. Let stand 10 minutes before serving.

Serve the grains with the rhubarb sauce on the side.

RICE

RICE

CONTENTS

Rice is so incredibly versatile: It can be steamed, braised, fried, molded into loaves and cakes, or wrapped inside leaves. Many clever things to eat can be nestled in it: fruits, nuts, vegetables, tofu, beans. It can be served hot or cold or prepared with other grains or rices, wild and sticky. It can be moistened and brought to life with stock, wine, miso, juice, milk, or cream. Rice can take center stage as an entree, or share the spotlight as a side dish to accompany meals. It can sop up sauce or sit dry and sober on a plate.

In *The Rice Book* Sri Owen writes: "The cultivation of rice is one of humanity's best claims to possess some kind of collective wisdom." Rice is at the heart of much of the world's history, language, literature, and culture, representing the timeless and essential dignity of man's quest to satisfy belly and spirit through food. These are my favorite ways of celebrating rice.

DIRTY RICE WITH SEITAN

▸ 2 tablespoons oil

1/4 cup diced shiitake mushrooms

1/4 cup diced seitan (see page 202)

1/4 cup diced unpeeled eggplant

1/4 cup diced celery

2 tablespoons shoyu

2 cloves garlic, sliced

2 cups brown rice

3 1/2 to 4 cups hot vegetable broth, as needed

1/2 cup diced red bell peppers

Dirty rice is a Southern specialty. It is rice "dirtied" with bits of browned meats or crackling in it, the idea being to lend a simple rice dish more flavor and zest. This version uses diced vegetables and bits of crisply fried eggplant and seitan. A good substitute for seitan bits would be diced teriyaki tofu or aburage.

Heat the oil in a large pot and sauté the mushrooms, seitan, eggplant, and celery with the shoyu until caramel colored. Stir in the garlic and the rice. Add the vegetable broth, cover, and cook for 45 minutes or until the rice is tender and the liquid is absorbed. Remove from the heat. Add the diced red peppers and let the rice steam, covered, for 15 minutes.

This can be served as an entrée or as a side dish.

RISOTTO WITH PRESERVED LEMONS
AND SPICY GREEN OLIVES

Serves 4 to 6

It is in the American culinary nature to fall in love with the flavors of distant lands. When, in 1973, Paula Wolfert first included a recipe for preserved lemons in her classic book Couscous and Other Good Foods from Morocco, *culinary borders opened to the Near East. Paula's exhaustive research was legendary. A stickler for detail, she was to Moroccan cooking what Diana Kennedy had been to Mexican cuisine.*

After the publication of her book, you couldn't have a conversation with food writers or serious eaters without the subject of preserved lemons coming up. Had you tried them? Did you like them? Had you eaten them with couscous? The strange and transformed lemon flavor seemed to separate serious gourmands from those only halfheartedly committed to their Cuisinarts and KitchenAids. The idea of needing several weeks to prepare a single ingredient gave kitchen time a new meaning in food circles.

Paula introduced us to couscous, bisteeya, harissa, and other exotic tastes, but it was the preserved lemon that encouraged the spate of new interest in other foreign cuisines and exotic flavors that followed. The eating culture of the seventies ventured past Julia Child's French kitchen into the realm of Turkey, Afghanistan, Korea, Thailand, and beyond. Interest in cuisine-vérité opened kitchen doors to worlds of foods never before examined so exactingly, as the food writer became part reporter, part anthropologist, and part historian.

My own paean to this special piece of cookbook history is a simple risotto of preserved lemons, spicy cracked olives, and crisp tempeh. The olives can be bought already prepared in any good Italian specialty store but I include a recipe, just in case. I also include a recipe for preserved lemons, but frankly, all roads lead to Paula's original.

▶ 1 cup small tempeh cubes

1/4 cup flour

2 tablespoons canola oil

6 to 8 cups vegetable broth

1 tablespoon fruity olive oil

1 medium onion, chopped fine

2 cloves garlic, minced

2 cups arborio rice

1 tablespoon preserved lemon rind (see page 109)

1/2 cup pitted spicy green olives (see page 109)

1/2 teaspoon ground turmeric (optional)

1/4 cup chopped scallions or chives

Before beginning the risotto, fry the tempeh cubes: Lightly dust them with flour and sauté in canola oil until crisp and golden brown. Drain on paper towels.

To make the risotto, bring the vegetable broth to a boil, then keep it covered and at a low simmer on a back burner as you continue to use it to cook the rice. Heat the olive oil in a large heavy saucepan over moderate heat.

Add the onion and garlic and cook for 5 minutes, until soft but not browned. Add the rice and sauté gently for about 3 minutes. Add 1 cup of broth. The broth will sizzle as the rice drinks up the liquid. Keep the rice uncovered throughout the entire cooking process and use a medium heat. You will be stirring constantly and you will need to see when the rice is thirsty enough to absorb its next cup of broth. Add 1 cup of hot broth at a time, stirring constantly with a wooden spoon or spatula, lifting the rice up over the liquid, letting the rice absorb each cup of liquid before you add the next. After the rice has absorbed about 3 cups of the broth and seems halfway cooked, add the lemon and olives. If you like a slightly yellow rice, stir in the optional turmeric. Continue adding broth, 1/2 cup at a time. You will use between 6 and 8 cups, depending on your handling of the rice and your control of the heat.

The whole process of stirring and tending your risotto should take 20 to 25 minutes. When it is done, the risotto should be creamy looking with a thick soupy consistency. The rice should be tender yet have some bite at its center. It is said that when risotto is properly done, each grain appears to have a white eye at the center, similar to a fine pearl.

When the risotto is done, gently fold in the fried tempeh. If it crumbles in the risotto, all the better. Sprinkle the risotto with scallions or chives. Serve with grated aged Parmesan cheese.

PRESERVED LEMONS

Wash the lemons with a Teflon pot scrubber or stiff-bristled vegetable brush. Place them in a nonreactive bowl; cover with warm water and let soak for 3 days, changing the water at least once each day. Cut the lemons into 4 parts, leaving the quarters connected at the bottom so lemons can be reshaped. Salt the inside and outside of each lemon and reshape them.

Place the lemons in a 1-pint sterile mason jar. Push the lemons down to fit them in the jar, salting and adding the spices between them. If the lemons don't make enough juice to cover themselves, add fresh lemon juice—not water or oil—to cover. Leave a little air space on top and close the lid tightly. Turn the jar upside down each day.

The lemons will be ready after 3 to 4 weeks. Rinse each lemon as you use it to remove the salt and any harmless film that may have accumulated. Generally, only the peel is used and the flesh is scooped out and discarded.

▶ 6 small smooth-skinned lemons

1/4 cup salt

1 cinnamon stick

8 cardamom seeds

Fresh lemon juice, if needed

SPICY GREEN OLIVES

If you cannot find good pitted olives, crack large green olives by pressing down on each olive with the heavy or broad end of a knife or spatula. Sprinkle red pepper flakes and garlic over the olives and toss in olive oil. If possible let the olives marinate overnight.

▶ 1 cup large green olives, pitted

1/2 teaspoon red pepper flakes

1/4 cup olive oil

MASALA KHICHRI
WITH FRIZZLED ONIONS

Serves 4 to 6

▸ 1/2 cup lentils, preferably Le Puy

4 to 4 1/2 cups vegetable broth, or as needed

2 cups brown basmati rice

1 cinnamon stick

1/4 teaspoon chopped jalapeño

2 cloves garlic, minced

1 teaspoon freshly ground cardamom seeds

1 1/2 cups Thin Coconut Milk (see page 376)

3 tablespoons canola oil

2 cups finely sliced onion, cut into very thin rounds

1/4 cup chopped flat-leaf parsley

Khichri is a dish that combines rice and lentils. Here I use fragrant basmati rice with Le Puy lentils, a flavorful legume that holds its shape and will not melt into the rice.

Pick over the lentils; rinse and drain them. Simmer in 2 cups of the broth, covered, for 30 to 45 minutes or until they are tender. Do not overcook. Though the lentils should be tender they should retain their shape and not split. Drain the lentils but save any broth to use for the rice. Keep the cooked lentils covered so that they do not dry out.

Bring the remaining 2 1/2 cups of broth to a boil. Add the rice, cinnamon stick, jalapeño, garlic, and cardamom. Bring to a simmer and add the coconut milk. Simmer, covered, for 30 to 40 minutes, until the rice is tender.

Combine lentils, rice, and any reserved broth. Let stand covered for 15 minutes before serving.

Meanwhile, heat the oil in a sauté pan. Add the onion, in small batches if the pan is small, and cook over high heat until brown and crisp. Drain on paper towels.

Serve the masala khichri with a generous portion of frizzled onion on top.

Serves 4

Rice that is flavored with the sweetness of dried fruits and the crunchiness of lightly toasted nuts makes a great accompaniment dish. Dried fruits that I have used in rice with success include golden raisins, chopped apricots, peaches, prunes, and papaya. Dried fruits will drink up extra water as they reconstitute, so for every 1/2 cup of dried fruit you use, add an extra tablespoon of water. Cut the fruit into small, bite-size pieces. For nuts, I like to cook with blanched almonds, walnuts, or hazelnuts, lightly toasted and with as much of their bitter-tasting skins rubbed off as is possible. To keep them from turning soggy, I fold the nuts into the cooked rice just before serving. This is a good all-around recipe that can be used for rice with any dried fruit and nut combination.

▶ 1/2 cup chopped shallots

1 tablespoon canola oil

2 cups brown rice

2 tablespoons shoyu (optional)

4 cups plus 1 tablespoon vegetable broth (see Note)

1/2 cup chopped dried apricots

1/2 cup chopped hazelnuts, lightly toasted, loose skins rubbed off

In a large heavy saucepan, sauté the chopped shallots in the canola oil until golden, about 8 minutes. Stir in the rice and shoyu. Add the broth and bring to a boil. Add the chopped apricots. Lower the heat to a gentle simmer and cook, covered, for 45 minutes or until the liquid is absorbed and the rice is tender. Let the rice stand for 10 to 15 minutes. Just before serving, stir the rice with a fork and fold in the nuts.

NOTE: If you use shoyu and canola oil, use only 4 cups of cooking liquid.

PAN-TOASTED RICE WITH ORZO

- ▶ 1 tablespoon toasted sesame oil

- 1/2 cup finely minced onion

- 2 tablespoons shoyu

- 1 cup long-grain brown rice

- 2 cups hot vegetable broth

- 1 cup orzo, whole wheat if available

- 1 tablespoon clarified butter

- 2 tablespoons miso

- 2 cups boiling water

This is a healthy alternative for those of us who harbor a secret love of Rice-A-Roni, that satisfying combination of rice and noodles. The secret is in browning both rice and noodles so that each contributes a nutty flavor to the dish. Orzo is a rice-shaped pasta that glides over the tongue and combines well with rice, and is available made from either white or whole wheat flour. For an especially flavorful dish, I use dark miso to flavor the orzo and I control the amount of water used.

Heat the oil in a saucepan and sauté the onion and 1 tablespoon of the shoyu until almost golden, about 7 minutes. Add the rice and continue sautéing until both are golden. Add the hot broth and simmer, covered, for 45 minutes or until the rice is tender and the liquid is absorbed. Let stand for 15 minutes more.

Meanwhile, in another saucepan, sauté the orzo in butter and the remaining tablespoon of shoyu until golden brown. Add the miso and 2 cups of boiling water. Boil, uncovered, adding more water as necessary, until the orzo is tender. Drain and add to the rice, using a fork to mix in the orzo and fluff the rice.

SWEET RICE AND DATES
WITH BRAISED SAVOY CABBAGE AND KIMCHI

Serves 4 to 6

Sweet rice is an acquired taste, more because of its texture than its flavor. It is also known as sticky or mochi rice because the gummy Japanese dessert cakes known as mochi are made from it. In this dish, the smooth sweet rice and dates contrast with cabbage and kimchi, the pungent Korean pickled cabbage available in Asian grocery stores or Korean fruit markets. Some kimchi comes packed in spicy chile oil. If so, omit any extra oil when you sauté the fresh and pickled cabbages together. This dish can be made entirely with sweet rice, or you can use more brown rice than sweet rice for a firmer texture. I like a little barley in this dish, but if you do not, simply make up the amount with brown or sticky rice.

▶ 1 tablespoon olive oil

1/2 to 3/4 cup kimchi, finely chopped, to taste

3 1/2 cups chopped savoy cabbage

4 cups vegetable broth

1 cup Japanese sweet rice (sticky rice or mochi rice)

3/4 cup short-grain brown rice

1/4 cup pearl barley (optional)

1/2 cup chopped seedless dates

2-inch piece of lemongrass, or 1 teaspoon lemon zest

GARNISH

1 cup sweet navel orange rounds or slices, white pith removed

1 cup sweet grapefruit slices, white pith removed

1/2 cup chopped seedless dates

1/2 teaspoon ground cardamom

1/4 teaspoon freshly grated nutmeg

1/4 cup finely chopped cilantro

1 tablespoon sugar, if necessary

Heat the oil in a skillet and sauté the kimchi and savoy cabbage, adding a few tablespoons of water if necessary, for 8 minutes or until the edges are lightly browned.

In a large saucepan, bring the broth to a boil and add the rice, barley, dates, lemongrass, and cabbage mixture. Simmer, covered, for 45 minutes to 1 hour or until rice is tender. Let stand for 15 minutes.

Meanwhile, in a serving bowl combine the oranges, grapefruit, chopped dates, cardamom, nutmeg, and cilantro. Taste and add sugar if desired. Place on the table and serve as a garnish to the rice.

WILD RICE MIX WITH DRIED CHERRIES, PISTACHIOS, AND COLLARDS

- ▶ 4 cups vegetable broth
- 1 cup brown rice
- 1 cup wild rice
- 1 tablespoon toasted sesame oil
- 1 cup chopped collard greens
- 2/3 cup dried cherries
- 2/3 cup lightly toasted pistachios, skins rubbed off

This is a fine holiday dish when something especially festive is called for. The best dried cherries come from Washington; use Bing, Rainier, or even Columbia River tart varieties. Pistachios are available without skins, but it might take work to hunt them down. If you can't find them, toast shelled pistachios lightly in your oven, and the skins will rub off between your fingers or palms. To make this an entrée dish, add a cup of chopped browned seitan with the pistachios.

Bring the broth to simmer in a large saucepan and add the rice. In a separate small skillet, heat the oil and cook the collards over low heat for 10 minutes. Stir the collards and cherries into the simmering rice and continue to cook, covered, for 45 minutes to 1 hour or until the rice is tender. Lightly crush the pistachios and fold them into the rice before you serve it.

Serves 8 to 10

This is an unabashedly rich dish, and I make no apologies for it. My cousin the forensic scientist gave me this recipe, and it is to die for.

▶ 4 cups vegetable broth

2 cups brown rice

1 pint reduced-fat sour cream, or substitute Yogurt Cheese (see page 375) or kefir

1/4 cup mild green salsa, any good brand

9 ounces Monterey Jack cheese, shredded

6 to 9 ounces canned diced mild green chilies, any good brand

Salt and ground black pepper to taste

Bring the broth to a simmer in a saucepan. Add the rice, cover, and cook over low heat for 45 minutes or until tender. You should have 6 cups of cooked rice. In a large mixing bowl combine the sour cream and the cooked rice. Add the salsa and shredded cheese. Since chilies may differ between brands, taste as you add the chopped chilies. The dish should be comfortably spicy, not overwhelming. Season with salt and pepper.

Pack this into a casserole dish and bake uncovered at 325 degrees for 30 minutes until slightly browned at the edge and bubbly. This dish goes well with broiled or baked fish, and black beans.

FRUIT SUSHI

▶ 1 cup milk or Thin Coconut Milk
(see page 376)

1/2 cup white rice

1/2 cup Japanese sweet rice
(sticky rice or mochi rice)

3-inch piece lemongrass, or peel
from 1/2 lemon

1/2 teaspoon lemon zest

2 teaspoons sugar

1 teaspoon ground cinnamon

1 teaspoon wasabi (Japanese
green mustard)

2/3 cup kefir or Yogurt Cheese (see
page 375)

Here is a dish based on a simple idea, but it has a lovely result. I like these sushi as appetizers or hors d'oeuvres, or for light summer dinners. The nori is a delicious and simple touch. If you are skilled at making nori rolls, you might cut them into slices, drape the fruits over each round, and serve the sushi that way.

2 cups prepared fruit: mango,
papaya, peach, nectarine, melon,
strawberries, raspberries

Nori seaweed sheets cut into
3-inch squares, or kept in large
sheets if you make rolled sushi

Bring the milk and 1 cup of water to a simmer in a saucepan. Add the rice, lemongrass, zest, sugar, and cinnamon. Cover and cook over low heat for about 45 minutes or until the rice is tender and the liquid is absorbed. Turn off the heat and let the rice stand for 10 to 15 minutes. Allow it to cool before you start to shape it.

Dissolve the wasabi in 2 tablespoons of kefir and then fold this mixture into the rest of the kefir. Set the sauce aside.

Prepare the fruit by slicing it into flat and even pieces that will fit or drape over the sushi mounds as neatly as possible. If you plan to use peaches or nectarines, poach them first in boiling water for 30 to 45 seconds and then remove the skins.

To make the sushi, shape 2 tablespoons of rice into a mound. Drape and press onto the top of the rice one or more slices of mango, peach, nectarine, melons, sliced strawberries, or raspberries. Place the entire sushi onto a nori square. Repeat with the remaining rice and fruit, and serve immediately with the wasabi-kefir sauce.

CIDER PILAF WITH BRUSSELS SPROUTS, ROQUEFORT, AND APPLE BOURBON SAUCE

Serves 4

I don't often add cheese to grains or rice, but in this recipe the Roquefort contributes its distinctive savor as a perfect complement to the other ingredients. You can make this dish less of a splurge and more of a weekday dish by just offering grated Parmesan on the table for those who would like additional zest sprinkled on top of their rice.

▶ 1 tablespoon olive oil

2/3 cup chopped leeks, white part only

1 1/2 cups brown rice

6 to 8 cloves garlic, sliced fine

2 cups hot vegetable broth

1 cup apple cider

1 cup cooked white beans

12 brussels sprouts, trimmed and cut in half

1 tablespoon fresh thyme leaves, or 1 teaspoon dried

5 Granny Smith apples

1 tablespoon bourbon, or to taste

1 teaspoon sugar

1 cinnamon stick

1/2 cup crumbled Roquefort cheese (optional) or grated Parmesan cheese offered at table

Toasted crushed walnuts

Heat the olive oil in a saucepan, add the leeks, and cook over low heat until golden, about 8 minutes. Add the rice, garlic, hot broth, and cider. Cover and simmer for 25 minutes. Add the beans, brussels sprouts, and thyme. Cook for 20 to 35 minutes more or until the rice is tender and the liquid is absorbed. Let stand, covered, for 10 to 15 minutes.

While the rice is cooking, make the apple bourbon sauce: Peel and chop the apples. Add 2 tablespoons water, bourbon, sugar, and cinnamon stick. Simmer gently until the apples have melted into a sauce. Add a little more water only if necessary.

Just before serving, carefully fold the crumbled Roquefort into the rice with a fork. Serve the rice topped with walnuts, and with apple bourbon sauce on the side.

RICE KIBBEE WITH TAHINI SAUCE

Makes 24 to 36 kibbee, depending on size

▸ 2 cups cooked brown rice

1 cup quick seitan scaloppine, chopped (see page 210)

1/2 cup toasted pine nuts

1 teaspoon ground cumin

1/2 teaspoon ground coriander

1/2 teaspoon dried tarragon

1/2 teaspoon freshly grated nutmeg

1/2 teaspoon ground cinnamon

2 teaspoons sugar

1/4 teaspoon chili powder

1/4 cup chopped fresh flat-leaf parsley, or cilantro if preferred

1 egg white

Salt to taste

Flour for dredging

Canola oil for deep frying

Pita bread (optional)

Tahini sauce (see page 119)

Here, seitan takes the place of meat in this Middle Eastern version of meatballs.

Place the rice in a food processor and process just long enough to break or split the grain. Transfer to a mixing bowl. Place the seitan in the processor (seitan should not be wet). Process for a few seconds—only long enough to grind the seitan. Add to the mixing bowl along with the pine nuts.

Add the cumin, coriander, tarragon, nutmeg, cinnamon, sugar, chili powder, parsley, and egg white. Season with salt to taste. Mix until thoroughly combined.

Shape into balls or patties. Arrange on a baking sheet without touching and allow the balls to dry while the oil is heating.

Fill a deep pot one-third full of oil and gradually heat to 365 degrees on a deep-fry thermometer. Or if you prefer to shallow-fry, heat a generous amount of oil in a skillet.

Cook the kibbee a few at a time until golden. Drain on paper towels. Serve by themselves or in warmed pita bread with tahini sauce.

TAHINI SAUCE

This is most easily made in a food processor or a blender. Combine the tahini, garlic, and juice, and slowly add 1/2 to 3/4 cup of cold water until you have a consistency that is easy to pour, but also will cling to a raw vegetable or piece of kibbee.

▶ 1 cup tahini

2 to 3 cloves garlic, crushed

1/4 to 1/2 cup fresh lemon juice, to taste

RICE SALAD WITH CHIPOTLE DRESSING

▶ 4 cups freshly cooked rice

1 cup cooked black beans or black-eyed peas

1 3/4 cups freshly cut corn kernels

1/3 cup chopped red onion

1/2 cup chopped fresh cilantro

CHIPOTLE DRESSING

1/2 cup fresh lime juice

1/2 cup fruity olive oil

3 cloves garlic, minced
(1 teaspoon)

1 1/2 teaspoons sugar

1 teaspoon Chipotle Purée
(see page 370)

2 tablespoons kefir, Yogurt Cheese
(see page 375), or low-fat sour
cream

1 teaspoon ground coriander

Salt and ground black pepper
to taste

Garnish: Avocado and red bell
pepper slices

Combine the warm rice, beans, corn, onion, and cilantro in a serving bowl.

Combine the ingredients for the dressing: lime juice, oil, garlic, sugar, chipotle purée, kefir, coriander, salt, and pepper. Mix well until the kefir is dissolved. Pour the dressing over the rice salad and mix.

Serve garnished with slices of avocado and crunchy red pepper.

PASTA AND NOODLES

CONTENTS

The last restaurant my husband and I owned and ran was called Onda. Like our first venture, it was housed in an old, wood-paneled bar, but the similarities ended there, for Onda featured Italian and Thai dishes. Our customers were often amused by this pairing, and when curious dinner guests asked me what the two cuisines had in common, I offered the simplest answer: They were united by the noodle.

This chapter features the universal noodle as it slips and slides across geographic and cultural borders. Over the years, noodles have captured the American imagination. Although Italian pasta was our first love, as we came to appreciate the foods of Europe, the Far East, and Asia, we discovered plates full of noodles came not only from China and Japan, but from places that stretched as far away in our imaginations as Thailand and Vietnam. Nowadays supermarkets carry not only a wide array of standard Italian pastas but noodles made from vegetable starches like mung bean and yam, as well as wheat, rice, and buckwheat varieties.

Anything that crosses borders so easily should be simple to prepare, and it is in that spirit that I offer the recipes in this chapter.

RIGATONI IN SESAME AND SHOYU
WITH STEAMED VEGETABLES

Serves 4 to 6

- ▶ 2 cups carrots, cut into rounds and steamed

- 2 cups young leafy greens: collards, kale, or bok choy leaves, chopped and steamed

- 1 medium yellow crookneck squash, sliced and steamed

- 1/2 pound sugar snap peas, strings removed and steamed

- 1 (16-ounce) box rigatoni, cooked al dente and drained

- 2 to 4 tablespoons toasted sesame oil, to taste

- 2 cloves garlic, crushed

- 1/3 cup shoyu

- Lemon wedges (optional)

- Gomashio (toasted sesame seed salt; see page 374) (optional)

This is my favorite light dish for warm weather. It is easily assembled and simple yet rich in flavor. Prepare the noodles by themselves, or toss with vegetables. Any combination of seasonal vegetables will do, though I especially like a selection of young carrots, greens, yellow crookneck squash, and snap peas. Steam each vegetable separately and take care not to overcook.

Bring a large pot of salted water to a boil while you prepare the vegetables. Steam each vegetable only until tender, and keep them warm.

Boil the rigatoni according to package directions until tender but still firm. Drain and place in a large bowl.

Combine the sesame oil, garlic, and shoyu and toss with the warm cooked noodles. Add the vegetables. Adjust the seasoning and add more sauce if needed. Squeeze a little fresh lemon over your dish if desired, and top with gomashio.

FRESH LO MEIN NOODLES
WITH THAI SAUCE AND TOMATOES

Serves 4

Freshly made wheat noodles, which are commonly known as lo mein, are sold in Asian specialty stores. Because they are curlier and longer, and have a firmer bite than most freshly made Italian pasta, I often use them in place of fettuccine or spaghetti. Here, lo mein noodles are tossed with fresh tomatoes and peanut sauce for a dish that borrows from two cultures: Italy and Thailand.

▶ 1/4 cup toasted sesame oil

3 scallions, finely chopped greens only, about 1/2 cup, or 1/4 cup chopped fresh chives

1 clove garlic, minced

2 cups peeled, seeded, chopped tomatoes

1/2 cup white wine

1 1/2 teaspoons ground coriander

1/2 teaspoon ground cinnamon, or to taste

1/3 cup Thai peanut sauce, available in supermarkets and natural food stores

1 (16-ounce) package fresh lo mein noodles

1/2 cup toasted crushed hazelnuts, skins rubbed off, or substitute peanuts

1/2 cup chopped cilantro or flat-leaf parsley (optional)

Heat the sesame oil in a wok or a large saucepan and add the scallions and garlic. Sauté for 1 or 2 minutes and stir in the tomatoes. Bring to a boil, add the wine, and boil until the liquid is reduced by half. Season with ground coriander and cinnamon. Add the Thai sauce and boil to reduce slightly.

Bring a large pot of salted water to a full boil and add the noodles gradually. Stir constantly to keep from sticking. When the water returns to a full boil, add 1 cup of cold water. Continue cooking until the noodles are tender (test by tasting them), adding cold water each time the pot boils (3 or 4 times). Drain and rinse under cold running water to remove surface starch.

Add the cooked and drained noodles to the sauce and toss over low heat until combined and heated through. Top each serving with crushed hazelnuts and cilantro.

HUBERTS GOAT CHEESE LASAGNE

▶ 1 tablespoon olive oil

1 cup chopped onion

1/2 cup wild mushrooms, steamed and sliced

1 tablespoon flour

1/4 cup vegetable broth

1/2 cup sun-dried tomatoes, reconstituted and chopped

1 cup milk

6 ounces crumbled aged goat cheese, any mold or rind removed

1 pound fresh pasta sheets

2 cups ricotta cheese

1/4 cup grated Parmesan cheese

1/2 cup fresh artichoke hearts, cooked and sliced

This favorite lasagne can be made with or without wild mushrooms and fresh artichoke hearts. It is good either way.

Butter or oil a 13 × 9 × 3-inch lasagne pan. Preheat the oven to 400 degrees. Put a large pot of salted water on to boil.

Make the goat cheese sauce: Heat the oil in a saucepan, add the onions, and cook for 5 minutes, until softened but not browned. Stir in the mushrooms. Sprinkle the flour over the onion-mushroom mixture and stir to combine. Add the broth and stir over low heat until the sauce thickens. Add the sun-dried tomatoes and slowly pour in the milk. Stir to incorporate into the sauce, then add the goat cheese and cook over low heat for another 2 minutes.

Boil the pasta sheets until barely tender; drain and separate them.

Line the bottom of the prepared pan with pasta and spread with one-third of the ricotta, then with one-quarter of the goat cheese sauce. Sprinkle with 1 tablespoon of Parmesan. Repeat the layers, scattering the artichoke hearts over the middle layer, so that you have 4 layers of pasta and 3 of filling. Top with remaining cheese and sauce, cover with foil, and bake for 30 minutes. Remove the foil and bake another 15 minutes or until bubbly. Let stand for 10 minutes before serving.

PENNE WITH TOMATO SAUCE

Everybody's got a red sauce. This one's mine.

I developed this sauce with my children in mind. I like a chunky sauce, but of course children, suspicious creatures that they are, prefer a thin, smooth topping with no mysterious lumps. Rather than take all the adventure out of family cooking, though, every so often I like to slip a little TVP (texturized vegetable protein) into the sauce, just to get back at them.

If you haven't already discovered the difference between organic canned tomatoes and regular ones for your sauce, you will find organic ones are much sweeter, with no bitter aftertaste.

▶ 2 tablespoons olive oil

1 cup finely chopped onion

1 tablespoon sugar, or more to taste

2 cups full-bodied red wine

1 large cinnamon stick

2 (16-ounce) cans organic tomatoes

4 cloves garlic, minced

1/2 to 2/3 cup pitted kalamata olives

1 tablespoon fresh thyme leaves, or 1 teaspoon dried

1 tablespoon fresh oregano, or 1 teaspoon dried

1 tablespoon fresh marjoram, or 1 teaspoon dried

Salt and ground black pepper to taste

1/2 cup TVP (optional)

1 (16-ounce) package penne

Grated Parmesan cheese

Heat the oil in a large nonreactive saucepan and sauté the onion over medium heat for about 5 minutes, until softened. Add the sugar and stir until melted and caramelized. Add the red wine and boil to reduce by at least half. Add the cinnamon stick.

If you prefer a smooth sauce, place the tomatoes and their juice in a blender and blend until completely smooth. If you prefer a chunky sauce, add tomatoes from the can and crush them with your fingers. Stir in the garlic, olives, thyme, oregano, and marjoram. Adjust the seasoning with salt and pepper to taste. Add TVP if desired.

Simmer, covered, for at least 2 to 3 hours. If you prefer a thicker sauce, uncover for the last hour and let the sauce reduce naturally. Remove the cinnamon stick.

Bring a large pot of salted water to a boil. Add the penne and cook according to package directions until tender but still firm. Drain and remove to a large serving dish. Serve the sauce over the penne with freshly grated Parmesan cheese.

MOUNTAIN SPRING NOODLES
WITH BROWN SUGAR

Serves 4

▶ 12 ounces good-quality rice stick noodles, preferably wide enough for the sauce to cling to

2 tablespoons toasted sesame oil, or more to taste

2 tablespoons clarified unsalted butter, or more to taste

1/4 to 1/2 cup raw brown crystallized sugar (see Note)

I do not remember the name of the town, but it was famous throughout mainland China for the rice noodles a local factory made from an especially pure spring water that poured down from a nearby mountain. Our oldest son, Matthew, fluent in Chinese after his junior year abroad in Taiwan, proudly translated the menu. We all ordered the same thing: mountain spring noodles with brown sugar.

Opalescent in color and meltingly light in texture, the noodles were unlike any I had ever tasted, and I have never since discovered a dish like this on any other menu. The restaurant was like so many in rural China, large and bare as a factory loft, its wooden floors dark and worn, mismatched chairs scattered all about the room near round tables large enough to seat families of twelve or fifteen. Ambience is not everything, though, and we three were tired from traveling. After our son ordered, we sipped tea and took in the busy, clattering scene. The din stopped once we bent our heads to eat, and we realized that many eyes were on us. The diners' faces expressed the time-honored hope that foreign guests would honor what they appreciated in their homeland.

Soak the rice stick noodles in warm water for about 20 minutes or until they soften; the time will depend on their thickness. Drain.

Bring a pot of water to a boil. Immerse the soaked noodles in boiling water for a few seconds, long enough to heat through and soften a little more. Do not overcook. Drain.

Toss the warm noodles with sesame oil and butter. Sprinkle with sugar to taste before serving.

If you want to serve this with greens, try a simple peppery arugula salad.

NOTE: If possible, use turbinado, demerara, or Hawaiian sugar, which will soften but not melt too quickly and will keep its crystalline shape and slightly crunchy texture long enough for you to taste it on the warm noodles.

GLASS NOODLES WITH LEMON

This version of a simple recipe was first prepared for me by Irene Quo, wife of General C. C. Quo, and one of our country's first great Chinese cookbook authors. She had an aristocrat's appreciation of a simple native dish.

Use the thinnest bean thread noodles you can find. Bean threads will cook up transparent, hence the name glass noodles. This dish can also be made with thin rice stick noodles, which are translucently white in color when prepared. Serve cool or at room temperature, since the noodles are meant to be refreshing.

▶ 8 to 12 ounces thin bean thread noodles

2 tablespoons toasted sesame oil

2 tablespoons shoyu, or more to taste

1 to 2 tablespoons fresh lemon juice, or more to taste

1/2 cup chopped cilantro

1 cup chopped avocado, ripe but firm enough to hold its shape

1 cup freshly grated daikon

1 1/2 teaspoons mirin

2 teaspoons ponzu sauce, or additional fresh lemon juice

Soak the noodles in warm water for about 20 minutes, or until they soften. Drain.

Bring a pot of water to a boil. Immerse the soaked noodles in boiling water for a few seconds, long enough to heat through and soften a little more. Do not overcook. Drain and transfer to a serving bowl.

Toss the warm noodles with sesame oil, shoyu, and lemon juice. Sprinkle with cilantro and avocado. In a separate bowl, toss the daikon with the mirin and ponzu sauce and serve a pinch of this daikon salad on the side of each plate.

PERCIATELLI WITH BROCCOLI RAAB

▶ 1 pound broccoli raab, trimmed

2 to 4 tablespoons olive oil

2 to 3 cloves garlic, minced

1 cup chopped roasted red bell peppers

1/3 to 1/2 cup pitted, chopped black kalamata olives

1/2 cup good white wine

1/4 cup vegetable broth

1 (16-ounce) package perciatelli

6 ounces chèvre, cut into chunks

Salt and ground black pepper to taste

1/3 to 1/2 cup lightly crushed toasted walnuts, loose skins removed

Perciatelli is a hollow spaghetti, and though it generally likes a sauce, I like it with this flavorful topping of broccoli raab, roasted red bell peppers, black olives, walnuts, and chèvre.

Bring a large pot of salted water to a boil. Immerse the broccoli raab, then remove at once with a slotted spoon to a colander. Allow it to cool; chop into bite-size pieces. Do not drain the water.

Heat the olive oil in a large skillet and sauté the broccoli raab for 5 minutes or until wilted. Add the garlic, roasted peppers, and black olives. Pour in the wine and boil until the liquid is reduced by half. Add the vegetable broth and reduce slightly. Cover and keep warm.

Return the water to a full boil and cook the perciatelli according to package directions until tender but still firm. Drain and transfer to a large serving dish. Add the chèvre to the hot pasta and toss; add the broccoli raab, peppers, and olives. Sprinkle with crushed walnuts and serve. Offer thinly sliced or grated Parmesan cheese at the table.

PASTA WITH RICOTTA
AND BAKED ACORN SQUASH

Serves 4

This satisfying combination is the essence of a calm and simple vegetarian meal.

▶ 2 small to medium acorn squashes, cut in half

1 tablespoon canola oil or melted unsalted butter

2 tablespoons honey, or more to taste

1 (16-ounce) package bowtie noodles or other short pasta

1 pound ricotta cheese

Salt and ground black pepper to taste

Preheat the oven to 375 degrees. Rub the inside of the squash halves with oil or butter. Spread the honey evenly in the cup of each squash. Arrange the squash cut side up on a baking sheet; bake for 1 hour or until tender.

Bring a large pot of salted water to a boil and cook the bowties according to package directions until tender but still firm. Drain and place the noodles in a large bowl. Toss with the ricotta cheese. Season with salt and pepper. Scoop out the baked squash and fold lightly into the pasta.

Offer shaved or grated Parmesan at the table.

BEANS

CONTENTS

BEANS

BLACK-EYED PEAS AND CHANTERELLES
IN CHAMPAGNE VINAIGRETTE

Serves 4

I like to combine black-eyed peas with any one of champagne's many forms. The effervescent flintiness of a good champagne, whether for drinking or cooking, lifts the mineral and earthbound flavor of the legumes. This particular dish uses champagne vinegar in a warm salad.

▶ 3 cups cooked black-eyed peas

1 cup diced cooked yellow squash

6 ounces chanterelles, stems removed, steamed

2 cups cooked, squeezed dry, and chopped kale

1/3 cup fruity olive oil

1/3 cup champagne vinegar

2 tablespoons fresh lemon thyme

1 clove garlic, minced

1/2 teaspoon honey

Salt and ground black pepper to taste

In a mixing bowl, combine the black-eyed peas, squash, chanterelles, and chopped kale.

In a separate bowl, combine the olive oil, champagne vinegar, lemon thyme, garlic, honey, salt, and pepper. Whisk until thickened. Pour over the vegetables and toss gently. Serve at room temperature, or chill and adjust seasoning before serving. Serve with crusty country bread and olive oil, and offer additional vinaigrette on the table.

BLACK-EYED PEAS
BRAISED OVER SAUERKRAUT

1 pound fresh sauerkraut

2 tablespoons olive oil

8 to 10 pearl onions

6 cloves garlic, minced

2 cups Gewürztraminer wine

2 to 3 cups vegetable broth

1 cup dried black-eyed peas, already soaked

2 tablespoons fresh thyme leaves, or 1 scant tablespoon dried

1 bay leaf

1/2 teaspoon ground allspice

3 or 4 apples, peeled, cored, cut in halves or quarters depending on size of apple

For the best flavor, try to find sauerkraut that is packaged, without additives, in a glass jar or a plastic bag or container. Late-harvested Golden Delicious apples are good in this dish, as are other mellow, sweet varietals.

Drain the sauerkraut and reserve the juice for something else. Squeeze the sauerkraut dry.

Heat the olive oil in a large nonreactive saucepan and sauté the onions until golden. Add the garlic and sauerkraut and heat through. Add the Gewürztraminer, bring to a simmer, and boil rapidly to reduce by half. Add the vegetable broth and bring to a simmer.

Stir in the black-eyed peas, thyme, bay leaf, and allspice, and simmer slowly for 30 minutes before adding apples. Simmer for a total of 45 minutes to an hour, or until the beans are tender.

Serve with brown rice, barley, or broad noodles like pappardelle.

BEAN SALAD
WITH CHICORY, LIME, AND SAGE

Serves 4 to 6

It isn't often that I prefer dried herbs to fresh, but now that there are organic, nonirradiated dried herbs available I find I use them more often, as their flavor holds truer to that of their fresh counterparts. A bean salad like this one is a perfect place to exploit the pungent accents of dried herbs. Ground sage and rosemary do well together here. Though I would use equal amounts of each if including fresh herbs in this dish, let the sage come through a little more than the rosemary if using dried, for more of a flavor dynamic.

Try to use only the inner leaves of chicory, which add more tang and less bitterness to the salad. Frisée will also work, or a peppery, slightly bitter leaf, such as arugula.

▶ 3 cups cooked navy beans, drained

3 cups heart of chicory leaves or frisée

1 cup chopped roasted red or yellow bell peppers

1/3 cup olive oil

1/3 cup fresh lime juice

1/4 teaspoon Chipotle Purée (see page 370)

1 tablespoon fresh sage, or 1 teaspoon dried

1 tablespoon fresh rosemary, or 1/2 teaspoon dried

2 to 3 cloves garlic, minced

2 teaspoons tamari

Freshly ground white pepper (optional)

Garnish: Sliced avocado

Place the beans and chicory in a bowl large enough to toss the salad. Scatter the peppers on top.

Combine the olive oil, lime juice, chipotle purée, sage, rosemary, and garlic. Pour over the beans. Drizzle with tamari and season with pepper. A nice garnish with this is sliced avocado, served with a sprinkling of lime juice and tequila.

BLACK BEANS IN MOLE COLORADO

▶ 1/2 cup dark rum

1 cup pitted prunes

1/2 cup lightly toasted skinned hazelnuts, ground

1/2 cup lightly toasted blanched almonds, ground

1/4 cup lightly toasted sesame seeds, ground

1 to 2 heads roasted garlic, to yield 2 tablespoons roasted garlic purée, plus 2 cloves raw garlic, minced

1/2 to 1 teaspoon Chipotle Purée (see page 370)

1/2 teaspoon ground allspice

1/2 teaspoon ground cinnamon

1 teaspoon ground cardamom

1 teaspoon ground coriander

1 tablespoon fresh oregano, or 1 teaspoon dried

1 tablespoon fresh marjoram, or 1 teaspoon dried

1/2 teaspoon ground annatto

1 cup chopped leeks, white and pale green parts

1/2 cup chopped celery

1/2 cup chopped carrots

2 tablespoons olive oil

1 1/2 cups red wine

2 cups vegetable broth

1 cup dried black beans, presoaked

1 cinnamon stick

1 ounce semisweet chocolate, or to taste

Mexico is a land of sauces, and one of its most complex is mole (MOH-lay). Traditionally, mole is made from a combination of chilies, dried fruit, nuts and seeds, and sometimes chocolate. One persistent Eurocentric legend about the origin of mole poblano concerns sixteenth-century Puebla nuns who faced the difficult task of entertaining a visiting archbishop when their larder was bare. Prayers were answered through heavenly inspiration; everything edible in and around the convent was impetuously toasted, ground, and blended into a brick-colored pastelike sauce that was, Deo gratias, finished with a peccadillo's worth of chocolate — not meant to overpower the sauce but merely to round out the flavor and add a heavenly depth of character.

Although moles are traditionally served with poultry and meat, I find them delicious sauces in which to cook beans. The nuts and seeds thicken the sauce while chilies and spices flavor it. I prefer to use black beans in mole, but any dark, meaty bean such as pinto or anasazi would also be a good choice.

Warm the rum in a small saucepan and soak the prunes for at least 30 minutes.

Mix together in a processor the hazelnuts, almonds, and sesame seeds. When these are ground, add half the soaked prunes, the garlic purée, and chipotle purée, and grind again into paste. Add the allspice, ground cinnamon, cardamom, coriander, oregano, marjoram, and annatto.

Heat the oil in a large heavy saucepan and sauté the leek, celery, and carrots until limp. Add the remaining prunes and the red wine. Boil rapidly to reduce the wine by half. Add the vegetable broth and beans and bring to a simmer. Stir in the nut-seed-prune-chile mixture. Add the cinnamon stick. The sauce should be like a brothy pea soup at this point, easy to stir.

Simmer, covered, for 45 minutes to 1 hour, until the beans are almost tender. Uncover. Add the chocolate and cook for 30 minutes more, letting the sauce reduce and thicken so that you can see the bottom of the pot when the sauce is stirred and moved with a spoon.

Remove the cinnamon stick. Serve with brown rice, tortillas, salsa, and guacamole.

BEAN PIZZA

▶ 1/4 cup olive oil

1 cup chopped radicchio

2 cloves garlic, minced

1 1/2 cup fresh tomatoes, peeled, seeded, and chopped

1/8 teaspoon ground cinnamon

2 tablespoons chopped fresh basil, or 1 tablespoon dried

1 tablespoon fresh oregano, or 1 teaspoon dried

1/4 cup kalamata black olives, pitted

2/3 cup cooked dried beans, white or pink

Salt and ground black pepper to taste

1/4 cup vegetable broth, if needed

Pizza Dough (see page 141)

1/4 cup grated Parmesan cheese

1/2 cup shredded mozzarella cheese, or more to taste

These days everything lands on a pizza, so why not beans? This is a simple radicchio, tomato, and bean topping; another possibility would be the Cannellini Bean Pesto (see page 155).

Heat the oil in a nonreactive saucepan and sauté the radicchio until wilted. Add the garlic, tomatoes, cinnamon, basil, oregano, and olives. Simmer for 5 minutes or until the tomatoes cook through and turn color. Add the cooked beans and salt and pepper to taste. If you need a little liquid, add some vegetable broth. Allow the topping to cool while you preheat the oven to 350 degrees.

Fit the dough onto an oiled baking sheet and spread the topping evenly to within 1/2 inch of the edges of the pan. Sprinkle with the cheeses. Bake for 15 to 20 minutes or until the cheese is golden and the crust starts to brown. Slice and serve hot.

PIZZA DOUGH

The following is my favorite pizza dough recipe, from Judith and Evan Jones's wonderful The Book of Bread.

▶ 1 tablespoon active dry yeast

1/4 cup nonfat dry milk

1 tablespoon coarse salt, or
2 teaspoons table salt

1/4 cup olive oil

2/3 cup coarsely ground whole
wheat flour

2 to 2 1/2 cups white flour,
preferably unbleached

Cornmeal

Dissolve the yeast in a large bowl with 1/2 cup of warm water. Stir the dry milk and salt together with 1 cup of warm water until dissolved, then pour over the yeast. Add the olive oil, whole wheat flour, and about 2 cups of the white flour, stirring to mix, then turn out on a floured surface and let rest while you wash out and oil the bowl.

Knead the dough until smooth, adding more flour as necessary — about 6 to 8 minutes. Return the dough to the bowl, cover with plastic wrap, and let rise until doubled in volume.

Preheat the oven lined with baking tiles or stone to 450 degrees (see Note).

To make 9-inch pizzas, divide the dough in quarters (if you don't want to make 4 pizzas immediately, freeze remaining dough). To make two 18- to 20-inch pizzas, divide the dough in half.

Start stretching the piece of dough you are working with by kneading a bit first, then flattening it out and coaxing it out from the center toward the edges. It will be bouncy and resistant, so you must work at it, pulling lightly and stretching, concentrating on the areas that remain thick, twirling it over your fist the way they do in pizza parlor windows. The important thing is to get it as thin and even as possible.

Sprinkle either a paddle or a cookie sheet with cornmeal. Place the stretched dough for one pizza on top of the cornmeal, patting it into a round of the desired circumference. Now spread on the filling, leaving a 1/2-inch border. Your oven and tiles or baking stone should be piping hot now. Open the oven door and with a quick gesture (as though you were pulling the tablecloth out from under a table setting), slide the pizza off the paddle onto the tiles. Bake just about 12 minutes, a little more if it isn't quite as brown at the edge as you want.

NOTE: If you do not have a baking tile or stone, we have found the next best thing is to bake on a heavy black baking sheet.

REFRIED BEANS WITH TRUFFLES

▶ 3 cups cooked dried pinto beans, in their broth

1/4 to 1/3 cup fruity olive oil, to taste

3 tablespoons Roasted Garlic purée (see page 373)

Salt and ground white pepper to taste

1/4 cup freshly shaved truffles

If you want Mexican taste with a French flair, consider this delicious dish. Only a true bean lover would consider refried beans with truffles to be delicious rather than sacrilegious. Traditionally, refried beans are mashed and fried in lard. Try a fruity olive oil instead, or, even better, a truffled oil, if you have some in your kitchen.

Lightly mash the beans by hand.

Heat 2 tablespoons of olive oil in a heavy skillet. Add 1 cup of pinto beans. Mash and fold the beans over in the oil. Add 1 tablespoon of roasted garlic and fold into the mashed beans.

Add another tablespoon of oil. When the mashed beans begin to sizzle, add another cup of beans and another tablespoon of garlic. Mash and fold them in. Repeat the process a third time, or until the beans and garlic and oil are mixed. Mash and fold until the beans are thick and creamy. Add salt and pepper to taste.

Gently fold in the truffles. Place in a serving dish. Drizzle a little oil and grate some truffle over the refried beans.

Serve this as an appetizer with pan-toasted tortillas or crusty bread, or try it with gnocchi sprinkled with a little aged Parmesan. This is also delicious served with crumbled feta cheese and chopped red onion.

FAVA CROSTINI

Fava beans are great on their own, but this dish features asparagus and avocado folded in. Because this is a delicate summer spread, use only fresh herbs to flavor it. This crostini also makes a delightful sandwich.

▶ 2 1/2 pounds fresh fava beans
(2 cups shelled)

4 to 6 stalks asparagus
(2/3 cup chopped)

2 tablespoons olive oil, plus
additional as needed

2 tablespoons minced onion

1 clove garlic, minced

2 tablespoons grated Parmesan
cheese

2/3 cup ripe avocado cut into small
chunks

1 teaspoon fresh lemon juice, or
more to taste

1 teaspoon fresh summer savory

Salt and ground black pepper
to taste

Shell the beans; you should have about 2 cups. To remove the bitter skins, cover the shelled beans with boiling water for 30 seconds, then drain and plunge into cold water. Slide a thumbnail along a bean to open the skin, then squeeze to release the bean.

Steam the beans or boil them in a generous amount of salted water for 20 to 30 minutes or until tender. Drain them and set aside.

Peel the asparagus, cut into pieces, and steam for 5 to 8 minutes or until tender. Chop the pieces and measure 2/3 cup. Set aside.

Heat 2 tablespoons of olive oil in a skillet, add the onion, and sweat for 3 to 5 minutes or until golden. Add the minced garlic and cook for 30 seconds or long enough to cook it through.

Add the fava beans.

Mash the fava and onion with the Parmesan by hand, or put in a food processor and process very quickly. There should be some texture; this should not be a pastelike purée.

Fold in the chopped asparagus and the avocado. The mixture should be chunky enough to sit on the bread nicely. Add the lemon juice, savory, salt, and pepper. Drizzle with good fruity olive oil and stir to combine.

Serve immediately on country bread that has been toasted and brushed lightly with olive oil.

FAVA BEAN SUCCOTASH

▶ 2 cups cooked fresh fava beans
(see Fava Crostini, page 143)

3 ears fresh corn, cooked briefly on
the cob, or 1 cup steamed corn
kernels

1 cup chopped jicama, or
substitute more corn or yellow bell
peppers

1/2 cup chopped red onion

1/2 cup chopped cilantro

1/2 teaspoon minced jalapeño, or
to taste

1/3 cup olive oil

1/3 cup fresh lemon juice

1 teaspoon Dijon mustard

1 teaspoon ground cumin

1 clove garlic, crushed

Salt and ground black pepper
to taste

2 tablespoons kefir or cream

Here is an updated version of classic succotash that features fresh fava beans and a citronette dressing. It is best served as a warm salad, contrasting the silky-textured fava with crisp ingredients like jicama. Don't overcook your corn, and if you must use dried legumes, try black-eyed peas or return to the tried-and-true lima.

In a serving bowl, combine the fava beans, corn kernels, jicama, red onion, cilantro, and jalapeño.

Mix in a blender the olive oil, lemon juice, mustard, cumin, garlic, salt, and pepper. Add kefir when the dressing has thickened and blend again.

Dress the salad and toss. Correct the seasoning with salt and pepper.

FAVA CANNELLONI

My aunt Carrie Genova and I created this recipe one June day after shopping all morning in the Marin County farmers' market, one of the best in the country. We parked my children at the face painter's stand, then went in search of fresh fava. We had waited all year for their arrival, and we knew just what we wanted to do with them!

If you don't want your cannelloni filling to seem monotonous, don't overprocess or purée the fava. If you prefer this dish without a tomato sauce, try a traditional béchamel. I include a recipe for fresh pasta that works well for either ravioli or cannelloni, though these days very good fresh pasta sheets can be bought in Italian specialty stores or pasta shops.

▶ THE FILLING

2 cups fava beans, cooked
(see Fava Crostini, page 143),
drained, lightly mashed

3/4 cup ricotta cheese

1/4 to 1/2 cup grated Parmesan
cheese, to taste

1/2 teaspoon lemon zest

1/2 teaspoon freshly grated
nutmeg

1 teaspoon fresh savory

Salt and ground black pepper
to taste

FRESH TOMATO SAUCE

3 large tomatoes, peeled, seeded,
chopped, or 2 cups drained canned
tomatoes

1/4 cup olive oil

1/4 cup white wine

1/4 to 1/2 cup vegetable broth

1 clove garlic, minced

FRESH PASTA

3 cups all-purpose or semolina
flour

3 eggs, or 4 whites and 1 teaspoon
canola or olive oil

Make the filling: Combine the mashed fava beans, ricotta, and Parmesan in a bowl with the lemon zest, nutmeg, savory, and salt and pepper to taste. Set aside.

Make the tomato sauce: Sauté the tomatoes in the olive oil over medium-high heat for 10 to 12 minutes. Add the white wine and boil to reduce. Stir in 1/4 cup of vegetable broth and the garlic. Simmer for another minute. If the sauce doesn't have enough liquid, add more broth. Set aside.

Make the pasta: Pour the flour into a mound on your work surface. Use a spoon to dig a little crater or cup in the center of the mound. Make sure your cup is big enough to hold 3 eggs. Break the eggs into this cup.

With a fork, begin to mix the eggs into the flour from the inside of the cup, so that as more egg is incorporated, the walls of the cup widen into a shallow bowl.

At first a sticky mass will form. Start working the dough with your hands, lightly sprinkling flour on your hands and on the dough as you go along. Don't worry about any stray sticky pieces that cannot be incorporated. Knead for about 5 minutes, and when the dough has a smooth surface and an elastic texture, roll it into a ball, cover it with a lightly damp towel, and let it rest at room temperature for 30 minutes.

Roll out and follow the instructions on your pasta machine. Or roll out very thin and use a sharp knife to cut sheets for cannelloni (6 inches square) or ravioli (6 by 8 inches).

To assemble and bake the cannelloni: Preheat the oven to 350 degrees.

Cut each pasta sheet into 8 squares, allowing 2 per person. Cook in a large pot of boiling water one or two at a time just until tender. Immediately refresh in ice water to stop the cooking. Spread a damp kitchen towel on a work surface. Place the cooled pasta squares on it.

Spoon some of the filling along the edge of a cannelloni square, being careful not to overstuff. Roll up. Place seam side down in a nonreactive baking dish brushed with olive oil. Heat fresh tomato sauce, pour over the cannelloni, and cover with foil. Bake for 5 to 10 minutes or just long enough to heat through.

GOLDEN LENTIL HALF-MOON TORTELLI

Tortelli are ravioli, shaped like half-moons, that can be made as big or small as you wish. Use small, salmon-colored lentils, known in India as masoor dhal, for this dish. This variety is the smallest lentil available and cooks quickly, in about 20 minutes. Simmer the dhal, covered, in as small amount of liquid as possible so as to make a nice, thick filling. Using a non-stick pan, I have used as little as 1 1/2 cups of water, but be certain to check often that the lentils are not burning. You may find using 2 cups of liquid is easier.

Quark is a fresh cultured curd cheese, but you may substitute farmer cheese or ricotta.

▶ GOLDEN LENTIL FILLING

1 tablespoon olive oil

1 cup red lentils, or masoor dhal, picked over and rinsed

2 tablespoons vegetable bouillon powder

3 or 4 cloves garlic, minced (2 teaspoons)

1 cup Quark, farmer cheese, or ricotta

2 1/2 teaspoons ground coriander

1 teaspoon ground cumin

1/4 cup grated Parmesan cheese

Salt and ground black pepper to taste

Fresh pasta (see page 145)

Egg wash: 1 egg, beaten with 1 teaspoon water

Make the filling: Heat the olive oil in a saucepan and sauté the lentils for a minute over low heat. Add the vegetable bouillon powder and 1 1/2 cups of water. Simmer, covered, for about 20 minutes, stirring often, until lentils completely soften, adding another 1/2 cup water only if necessary. Try to keep the lentils as thick as possible, steaming them in their own liquid without diluting them too much.

The frequent stirring will beat the lentils smooth. Add the garlic. Stir in the Quark cheese. Add the coriander, cumin, Parmesan, salt, and pepper to taste. Set the filling aside.

To assemble the tortelli: Roll the pasta out to sheets 6 inches wide and 12 inches long. Starting at the top and running down the center of a sheet of pasta, place teaspoonfuls of golden lentil filling at 2-inch intervals.

With your fingers or a pastry brush, run some of the egg wash between the mounds of filling and along the edges of the sheet, so that the pasta will seal well.

Fold one side of the pasta sheet to meet the other like a book, covering the mounds of filling in the middle. The filling will run along the spine of the pasta "book." With a round cookie cutter or the rim of a drinking glass, cut out half-moon shapes. Press down with a fork or your fingers to make sure the edges are closed.

Cook a few at a time in a large pot of boiling salted water. The tortelli will rise to the top as soon as they are done. Serve with equal parts clarified butter and olive oil, and freshly grated Parmesan. Makes 12 to 24 tortelli, depending on size.

RICH LENTIL AND BUTTERCUP SQUASH STEW

Serves 6 to 8

This is an easy way to make a great bean stew with exotic flavor that can be assembled in a relatively short time. The lentils do not need to be soaked, and the squash will cook quickly and melt, both thickening the stew and sweetening it.

The tastiest lentils are the French Le Puy variety, mottled in color and smaller than the brown and green lentils most commonly used in our country. Le Puy lentils keep their shape beautifully in any stew and have a distinct flavor and crunchy texture. They can be found in some specialty shops and health food stores. Buttercup squash has a dense, sweet meat, but you can use hubbard, kabocha, or delicata. If these are unavailable a simple butternut will work, too. Don't be nervous about using whole garlic; it melts into the stew, and should a clove find its way onto your plate, it will be delectable.

I have also served the stew on top of bread spread with almond butter and sprinkled with a few drops of fresh lemon juice as an open-faced sandwich.

▶ 1/4 cup olive oil

1 cup chopped onion

1 cup chopped celery

1 bay leaf

16 cloves garlic, peeled and left whole

1 teaspoon grated nutmeg

1 teaspoon ground cardamom

1 1/2 teaspoons crumbled sage

4 cups winter squash cut into 2-inch chunks

6 cups water or vegetable broth

2 cups dried lentils

Heat the olive oil in a large saucepan and sauté the onion and celery for 8 minutes or until golden. Add the bay leaf and garlic and cook for 1 minute. Stir in the nutmeg, cardamom, and sage. Sauté long enough to release the flavor of garlic and spices. Add the squash and the water. Bring to a simmer. Add the lentils and cook at a gentle simmer for 2 hours, or longer. The stew is done when the lentils are soft and the squash and garlic have melted.

LOVE'S CHILI

- 1 large (28-ounce) can whole peeled plum tomatoes
- 1 medium onion, chopped (3/4 cup)
- 2 tablespoons olive oil
- 4 cloves garlic, minced, plus additional if desired
- 1 teaspoon dark brown sugar or honey
- 1/4 cup dark rum
- 2/3 cup red wine
- 1 tablespoon fresh thyme leaves, or 1 teaspoon dried
- 1 tablespoon fresh marjoram, or 1 teaspoon dried
- 1 cinnamon stick
- 2/3 cup TVP (see Note)
- 1 ounce semisweet chocolate
- 1 to 1 1/4 cups cooked kidney beans
- 1/2 teaspoon Chipotle Purée, (optional; see page 370)
- Salt and ground black pepper to taste

It's Sunday afternoon, and the weekend papers are strewn about the living room. You get up to heat yourself a bowl of last night's chili. You think, Should I heat one up for him, too? *Cooking can tell you a lot about the state of your relationship. If you don't care enough to heat up his chili, it's a sure sign that things are not going well. But if you still look forward to cooking for him, there is hope. This chili is a bonafide love barometer. Most telling is whether you care enough to chop the tomatoes into bite-size pieces . . .*

Drain the tomatoes and reserve their juice. Cut the tomatoes in quarters and then again in fours.

In a large heavy saucepan, sauté the onion in olive oil until golden, about 8 minutes. Stir in the garlic. Add the brown sugar and rum; cook for 5 minutes, or until alcohol is reduced. Add the red wine and juice from the tomatoes. Reduce for 5 minutes over high heat.

Stir in the chopped tomatoes, herbs, and cinnamon stick. Reduce the heat. Add the TVP, stir well, and cook for 5 minutes. Cover and simmer for 1 hour, stirring often. Add the chocolate, cooked beans, and chipotle purée. Simmer for another 30 minutes.

Adjust the seasoning with salt, pepper, and garlic.

Serve the chili over rice, or wrapped in warm soft tortillas with avocado slices, chopped romaine lettuce, chopped steamed tomatillos, jalapeños, sliced or grated sharp Cheddar cheese, or low-fat sour cream.

NOTE: Textured vegetable protein is available in health food stores. I have seen it packaged in two sizes: large, about 1/2 inch, and small, about 1/4 inch. I think it adds something special to this chili. It has the chunky texture of chicken and holds up nicely under long cooking.

LIMA BEAN RAGOUT

This dish belongs in the realm of What I Really Feed My Family. It meets several important criteria. The soft Chinese cabbage leaves melt inconspicuously into the stew, the purple sweet potatoes are fun, the cardamom is sweet enough not to be suspect, and the limas are big enough for my seven-year-old to pick out with his fingers. Family success that this dish is, I am still forbidden to place an olive near either of my children's plates.

▶ 2 tablespoons olive oil

2/3 cup chopped onion

1/2 cup chopped carrots

1/2 cup chopped celery

1/2 teaspoon freshly grated nutmeg

1 teaspoon ground cardamom

1 teaspoon fresh thyme leaves, or 1/3 teaspoon dried

1 1/2 cups white wine

1 large peeled, seeded, and chopped tomato

12 kalamata olives

2 cups chopped Chinese cabbage leaves, ribs removed

1 cup peeled and chopped sweet potatoes, purple or orange

6 garlic cloves, peeled and minced

1 tablespoon white miso

6 cups vegetable broth

1 cup dried lima beans, soaked

Heat the oil in a large heavy pot and sauté the onion, carrots, and celery for 5 minutes. Add the nutmeg, cardamom, and thyme. Deglaze with the white wine and boil until reduced by half. Add the tomato, olives, cabbage, sweet potatoes, and garlic. Stir in the miso and vegetable broth. Bring to a simmer. Add the lima beans. Cook uncovered for 1 hour or longer, until the beans are tender.

LIMA BEANS, CHAYOTE, AND BABY BOK CHOY
IN LEMONGRASS RAGOUT

▶ 2 tablespoons olive oil

2 stalks fresh lemongrass, coarsely chopped

1 cup vegetable broth

1 tablespoon white miso

2 cloves garlic, sliced

1 tablespoon chopped fresh savory, or 1 teaspoon dried

2 cups chayote chunks, peeled and seed removed, from 3 small or 2 medium chayotes

2 cups cooked fresh lima beans (2 1/2 to 3 pounds before shelling)

12 baby bok choy, or 3 cups chopped bok choy leaves from 1 large head

Salt and ground black pepper to taste

Garnish: Chopped flat-leaf parsley

This dish combines sweet, buttery lima beans and mild, firm chayote with the tender, savory greens of bok choy, contrasting three unprepossessing flavors and textures in a simple lemon-miso broth. The ragout will be lightest if you use fresh lima beans, which appear in late summer. You will need to shell 2 1/2 to 3 pounds of pods in order to get about 2 cups of fresh limas. The younger the lima, the more buttery and the shorter the cooking time. Young, fresh limas take about 8 to 10 minutes to cook, while older, larger beans take about 15 minutes, sometimes a little more. Chayote turns translucent in cooking and does not melt as quickly as do some other squash. If you can find baby bok choy in your market, use them for this dish. They are about 6 inches long and solid green in color. Use the baby bok choy whole, slicing only the larger ones in half lengthwise down through the root end. If you are using a mature bok choy, use only the leaf and save the ribs for a stir-fry.

Lemongrass always reminds me in appearance of a very stiff scallion. Remove any tough, dry outer leaves. Use the lower third of the stalk sliced in half lengthwise for this dish to add a special lemony flavor and fragrance. A substitute would be about 1/2 teaspoon of lemon zest.

Combine the olive oil, lemongrass, broth, white miso, garlic, and savory in a large heavy saucepan and simmer for a few minutes to release the flavor of the lemongrass and garlic. Add the chayote and lima beans. Cook covered for 5 minutes.

Add the bok choy and cook covered for 3 to 5 more minutes.

Remove the cover and cook down until the liquid emulsifies and thickens a little, making a sauce, about 2 to 3 minutes more. Adjust seasoning with salt and pepper.

Remove the lemongrass. Serve the vegetables over millet or brown rice. Sprinkle chopped parsley over all.

LIMAS AND LEEKS
WITH OREGANO AND GORGONZOLA

Serves 4

Surrender to cow cheese — sometimes it's worth it. This is a wonderful, rich dish that can be made with any freshly shelled beans: fava, lima, or cranberry.

▶ 3 or 4 leeks

2 to 4 tablespoons vegetable broth

2 tablespoons fruity olive oil

1 clove garlic, minced

2 tablespoons cream (optional)

2 cups cooked fresh lima, fava, or cranberry beans (about 2 1/2 to 3 pounds before shelling)

2/3 cup crumbled Gorgonzola cheese

Garnish: 1 tablespoon chopped fresh oregano, or 1 teaspoon dried

Remove the tough, dark green leaves of the leeks, leaving about 1 inch of the pale green part. Cut off the root but be careful not to cut the white bulb. Cut the leeks in half lengthwise and rinse well, letting water run between the layers to let any dirt and sand run off.

Turn a leek half on its flat end and, with a sharp knife, cut it into thin ribbons. Or you may find it easier to quarter the leek lengthwise, then cut the quarters lengthwise into eighths. Rinse the leek strips again.

Steam the leeks for no more than 3 minutes or until they turn a lively bright green and are tender. Drain and set aside.

In a small saucepan, make a sauce with the vegetable broth, olive oil, garlic, and cream. Bring to a simmer and cook for 2 minutes, until the flavor of the garlic is released.

Preheat the oven to 350 degrees.

Spread the bottom of a shallow baking dish with a few tablespoons of sauce, just enough to keep the leeks from sticking. Arrange the leeks and beans in the dish. Lay crumbled Gorgonzola over all and bake uncovered for 5 to 10 minutes or until the sauce has reduced and the cheese has melted but not separated.

Sprinkle with fresh oregano and serve at once.

CHERRY BEER BEANS WITH MOLASSES

- ▶ 16 ounces (2 cups) Grolsch cherry beer

- 1/2 cup dried cherries

- 1 tablespoon fruity olive oil

- 1 cup chopped red onion

- 1/4 to 1/2 cup molasses, to taste

- 1 teaspoon Dijon mustard

- 1/2 teaspoon red pepper flakes, or more to taste

- 1 cup anasazi, pinto, or any light pink bean, soaked

- 1 cup vegetable broth

- 1 slice fresh ginger, about 1/2 inch thick

My grandfather, a proud Alsatian, drove trucks for Dutch Schultz during Prohibition, so the Hubert household was never without brew. Despite the family predilection for it, I came very late to beer, eschewing its bitter taste. When I discovered cherry beer, instead of drinking it, I immediately thought of all the things I could cook with it, and beans were at the top of my list.

Warm the beer in a small saucepan and soak the dried cherries in it for about 30 minutes.

Heat the oil in a large saucepan and sauté the onions for 5 minutes. Add molasses, mustard, and red pepper flakes. Add the beans, vegetable broth, ginger slice, beer, and cherries. Bring to a simmer. Cover and simmer slowly for 1 1/2 hours or until the beans are tender, or bake for 1 1/2 to 2 hours at 350 degrees. Add more liquid if needed. Cook uncovered for the last 10 minutes so that the sauce reduces and thickens somewhat.

Serve with curried rice or over egg noodles.

CANNELLINI BEAN PESTO OVER RIGATONI

Though I am a great fan of the Great Northern bean, I prefer cannellini with pasta, because they are so buttery. For this dish, cook your beans just a little longer than you might ordinarily. I suggest squeezing the kale dry after steaming it so as not to add unnecessary liquid to the sauce.

▶ 1/2 cup white wine

1/3 cup plus 1 tablespoon olive oil

1 bay leaf

1/4 cup sun-dried tomatoes

1 1/2 cups fresh basil leaves

2 or 3 cloves garlic, minced, or as needed

1/2 cup lightly toasted pine nuts or lightly toasted walnuts, as much skin rubbed off as possible

1/2 cup grated Parmesan cheese

1 tablespoon or more vegetable broth, if needed

Salt and ground white pepper to taste

2 cups cooked cannellini beans, or other white beans such as navy or Great Northern

1 cup steamed, squeezed dry, then finely chopped kale leaves

8 ounces (1 package) rigatoni

Bring 1/2 cup of water, white wine, and 1 tablespoon of the olive oil to a boil in a small pan. Add the bay leaf and sun-dried tomatoes. Simmer slowly until the liquid is reduced to less than 1/4 cup; then let the tomatoes stand, covered, to reconstitute. Remove them from the liquid when they are soft and chop them coarsely. Save any remaining liquid.

Place the fresh basil, garlic, nuts, Parmesan cheese, and reconstituted tomatoes in a food processor. While processing, slowly drip the remaining 1/3 cup of olive oil into the container until the pesto has a smooth consistency. If it seems dry, add some of the tomato poaching liquid or a tablespoon of vegetable broth. Adjust the seasoning with garlic, salt, and white pepper.

In a sauté pan, toss the cannellini beans with the chopped kale leaves. Add the pesto. If the mixture is dry, add the rest of the poaching liquid from the sun-dried tomatoes.

Bring a large pot of salted water to a boil. Add the rigatoni and cook according to package directions until tender but still firm. Drain and serve with the pesto.

CANNELLINI AND ESCAROLE

- 6 cups escarole, torn into small pieces

1/4 cup fruity olive oil

---

8 to 10 cloves garlic, sliced

1/4 cup white wine

---

2 cups cooked cannellini beans

1/2 cup vegetable broth or water (optional)

Salt and ground black pepper to taste

I first ate escarole at the home of my oldest friend, Donna Maria DeCreeft. Her father, José, sculpted the Alice in Wonderland statue that stands in New York City's Central Park just above the sailboat pond. When Donna and I played together as children, José would often call us into his studio to sit for him, depending on whether he needed my cheeks and ears or her eyes and nose. After a day of playing and modeling we would sit down to a robust dinner, in which escarole was always present. José lived to within a few short years of one hundred. He carved marble until his death, and his Alice is one of the most beloved (and climbed) sculptures in the world. Need I say any more about the virtues of escarole?

Blanch the escarole in a large pot of boiling water just long enough for the escarole to give up a little of its bitterness and turn a brighter green color. Remove and drain. I like a little liquid in this sauce, so I do not refresh the escarole under cold water, nor do I squeeze it dry. Do so if you prefer a drier dish.

In a medium saucepan, heat the oil and sauté the garlic gently. Do not let it burn. Add the wine and boil to reduce for a minute. Add the escarole and cannellini beans and simmer, covered, for 15 minutes or longer. Add more olive oil and vegetable broth if desired. Taste and correct seasoning with salt and pepper.

VARIATIONS: This dish can be served by itself or over pasta.

For another variation, add 1/8 teaspoon of red pepper flakes and 1/4 cup each of golden raisins and kalamata olives to underscore the assertive flavor of the escarole.

PUMPKIN AND BEAN POLENTA

Here is a wonderful one-pot dish to eat by itself, or to have with soup instead of a sandwich. You can make this recipe without milk by using either rice milk or vegetable broth, or water and vegetable bouillon powder. Polenta sets up as it cools, so anticipate that your mix will be at least one-quarter more solid than it is when you have finished cooking it. Make sure the polenta is stiff enough to hold the pumpkin and beans, both of which should be as dry as possible when folded into it. Use a thick, meaty pumpkin or a less watery squash such as buttercup, hokkaido, or butternut that has been steamed in large slices, cooled, then carefully cut into small chunks.

▸ 3/4 cup cooked and drained white beans

1 tablespoon olive oil

1 clove garlic, minced

1/3 cup white wine

1 teaspoon ground sage

Salt and ground black pepper to taste

2/3 cup steamed pumpkin chunks

1 cup milk or rice milk

2 tablespoons vegetable bouillon powder

1 1/4 cups fine cornmeal, yellow or white

1 cup freshly cut corn kernels

1/4 cup grated Parmesan cheese

Oil an 8-inch springform pan or a Pyrex baking dish. Set aside.

Sauté the beans in olive oil. Add the garlic and white wine. Reduce the wine completely until the beans have absorbed all the flavor and no liquid remains in the pan. Add the sage, salt, pepper, and the small chunks of pumpkin. Adjust the seasoning; set aside.

Heat 3 cups water and milk together in a large saucepan; do not let it boil. Add vegetable bouillon powder.

In a slow, steady stream, pour the cornmeal into the hot liquid, stirring all the while with a balloon whisk. As the cornmeal thickens, add the corn kernels. Stir over low heat until the polenta thickens. If you think your mixture is too loose, slowly sprinkle in a little more cornmeal. The texture should be moist and moving easily in the pot, but it should also be capable of holding vegetables as the polenta sets.

Add the beans and pumpkin, gently folding them in so that the pumpkin doesn't melt too much into the polenta. Do not overblend; the polenta cake should not look homogenous, but studded with beans and pumpkin. Pour out into the prepared pan. Let stand for at least 20 minutes so that the form sets. Slice like a cake and serve with freshly grated Parmesan cheese. This is also good with a light fresh tomato sauce.

WHITE BEAN BRANDADE
WITH FENNEL AND STAR ANISE

▶ 1/4 to 1/2 cup olive oil, to taste

1 cup coarsely chopped shallots

1 teaspoon brown sugar

1/2 cup sliced celeriac

1 cup sliced fennel

1/2 cup sliced parsnips

2 or 3 cloves garlic, minced

3 cups cooked white beans, drained

1/3 cup kefir or Yogurt Cheese (page 375), or 1/3 cup cream

1/2 to 1 teaspoon ground star anise, or 1 teaspoon Pernod, to taste

Salt and ground black pepper to taste

This brandade is gently flavored by ground star anise. The little star-shaped spice, known as eight-angle fennel in Chinese, can be ground in an electric spice mill. It tastes like the fennel it underscores in this simple brandade, but it is sweeter and imparts a slightly exotic flavor.

Heat 2 tablespoons of the olive oil in a small skillet. Add the shallots, cover, and sweat them until soft. Add the brown sugar, raise the heat, and sauté until the shallots caramelize. Cook long enough to heat through, then put the shallots aside.

Steam the celeriac, fennel, and parsnips for 10 minutes or until the vegetables are cooked through. Remove and pat dry if necessary.

Place the fennel, celeriac, parsnips, and minced garlic in a food processor and process until smooth. Add the beans and process again, slowly adding 2 tablespoons of olive oil, or more according to the desired richness. Add the kefir. Mix well and season with ground star anise, salt, and pepper.

Fold in the shallots. Place the brandade in a serving dish and drizzle fruity olive oil over the top.

Serve on toasted country or sourdough bread.

WHITE BEANS IN WHITE MOLE

Allergic to chocolate, but still yearn to know the splendors of a chocolate mole? This dish, no poor cousin to a cocoa bean, has an unusual combination of flavors: savory fennel, briny capers, and bright tomatillos combined with mole's traditional ground nuts, seeds, and dried fruit. The mixture is finished with tahini, to replace traditional sesame seeds, as well as unctuous white chocolate and kefir cheese, a tangy, low-fat, cultured sour cream made with acidophilus.

▶ 1 tablespoon olive oil

1/2 cup chopped white onion

6 cloves garlic, minced

1 cup husked and chopped tomatillos

3/4 cup chopped fennel

1 cup white wine

1 tablespoon capers

1/2 to 1 teaspoon finely chopped jalapeño or Chipotle Purée to taste (see page 370)

1 teaspoon ground cumin

1 teaspoon ground coriander

1 cup blanched, lightly toasted almonds

1/2 cup golden raisins

1 cup presoaked dried white beans or lima beans

2 cups vegetable broth, or as needed

1 tablespoon tahini

1 ounce white chocolate, chopped

2 to 4 tablespoons kefir, to taste, or 3 tablespoons Yogurt Cheese (see page 375)

Heat the oil in a large saucepan and sauté the onion for 5 minutes, until soft. Add the garlic and heat through. Add the tomatillos, fennel, and white wine. Boil to reduce the wine by half. Rinse the capers to remove extra salt and add to the tomatillos. Add the chile, cumin, and coriander.

Pulverize or process the almonds and raisins. Add to the tomatillo mixture.

Stir in the beans with enough broth to cover, about 2 cups. Cook covered for 45 minutes to 1 hour or until the beans are tender. Uncover and continue cooking to reduce the liquid, about 30 minutes. Add the tahini, white chocolate, and kefir, folding gently to dissolve. Adjust seasonings.

Serve with a simple salad of bitter greens such as arugula.

TOFU, TEMPEH, AND SEITAN

TOFU, TEMPEH, AND SEITAN

Vegetarian cuisine is nothing if not varied. Variety is at the heart of creating a vegetarian diet that works for you. Beans and grains are natural ingredients, but tofu, tempeh, and seitan are made by man. Tofu is bland but chameleonlike, capable of taking on whatever flavor it is cooked with. Seitan has much the same quality, taking the flavor of the poaching broth in which it is first made. Tempeh has the most character because it is fermented. Treat these three as you would any sturdy protein: grill, broil, steam, poach, fry, or sauté them. They will accommodate to any technique.

TOFU

CONTENTS

Serves 8

This delicious variation on lasagne features wild mushrooms, tofu, and a fresh tomato sauce flavored with basil and green curry. Thai green curry paste is available in the Asian section of many supermarkets.

- ▶ 3/4 to 1 pound fresh lasagne noodles, enough sheets to form at least 3 layers
- 1 pound mushrooms, wild or button
- 3/4 cup chopped leeks, white and pale green parts
- 3 tablespoons olive oil, plus extra for drizzling
- 2 cloves garlic, minced
- 4 cups peeled, seeded, chopped fresh tomatoes
- 1 to 2 teaspoons sugar, or to taste
- 1 cup vegetable broth
- 1/2 cup white wine
- 1/2 to 1 teaspoon Thai green curry paste, or more to taste, but add slowly depending on product used
- 1/4 to 1/3 cup chopped fresh basil
- Salt to taste
- 2 to 4 tablespoons cream (optional)
- 6 to 8 ounces chèvre, sliced thin
- 1/2 pound tofu, sliced thin
- Grated Parmesan cheese

Lightly oil a 13 × 9 × 3-inch baking dish; set aside.

Cook the pasta in boiling water until it is al dente. Drain, place in a bowl of ice water to stop the cooking, and separate the noodles. Drain again and keep damp by placing in between the folds of a clean kitchen towel.

Clean and stem the mushrooms. Steam in a steamer for 5 minutes or until they are cooked through. Cool and slice.

Sauté the leeks in 1 tablespoon of olive oil until limp. Add the mushrooms and garlic. Sauté until golden. Set aside.

Heat 2 tablespoons of olive oil in a saucepan and sauté the tomatoes with the sugar until softened. Add the vegetable broth and white wine. Cook until the tomatoes meld into a light, fresh sauce. Add the green curry paste, basil, and salt to taste. Finish the sauce by adding a little cream if desired.

Preheat the oven to 350 degrees.

Arrange a layer of noodles in the bottom of the prepared baking dish. Cover with one third of the mushrooms, then with one third of the chèvre and tofu slices. Spoon tomato sauce over all. Repeat the layers until you have 4 layers of noodles and 3 layers of filling. Spread the top layer of pasta with the remaining tomato sauce; sprinkle with Parmesan cheese and a drizzle of olive oil. Cover tightly with foil and bake for 20 to 30 minutes or until the sauce is bubbling, then uncover and let the top layer turn a golden brown. Allow to rest for 15 minutes before cutting into serving portions.

TOFU ENCHILADAS WITH TOMATILLO AND SUN-DRIED TOMATO SAUCE

Serves 2 to 4

The tomato sauce used for this dish is especially piquant thanks to the addition of roasted tomatillos. For roasting, place the vegetables on a grill and remove quickly, or use one of the inexpensive top-of-the-stove roasters being sold these days in cooking sections of department or hardware stores. They are placed above a burner, and use the flames of the burner itself for roasting vegetables. No muss, no fuss, and they work very well for small or cut vegetables like the tomatillo.

▶ SAUCE

1 tablespoon olive oil

1/2 cup chopped onion

1 pound tomatillos, husked, cut in half, and roasted

2/3 cup sun-dried tomatoes reconstituted in olive oil

1/2 cup pitted black kalamata olives

3 cloves garlic, minced

1 teaspoon to 1 tablespoon roasted Chipolte Purée, depending on heat (see page 370), or 1/2 to 1 teaspoon chili powder

2/3 cup white wine

Salt to taste

TOFU ENCHILADAS

1 cup diced tofu

1/3 cup fresh pumpkin seeds, toasted (see Note)

1/4 cup currants

1 clove garlic, minced

1/2 teaspoon ground cinnamon

1 teaspoon oregano

Salt to taste

8 to 12 corn tortillas

1 to 1 1/4 cups grated Monterey Jack cheese made with jalapeño, divided

Preheat the oven to 375 degrees. Lightly oil a shallow ovenproof dish.

Make the sauce: Heat the oil in a saucepan and sauté the onions for 4 to 6 minutes, until golden. Add the tomatillos, sun-dried tomatoes, olives, garlic, and chile purée. Stir in the white wine and boil until reduced slightly. Place in a food processor and pulse about 3 times, enough to chop, but not purée, the ingredients. Add salt to taste. Set the sauce aside.

Make the enchiladas: Combine in a bowl the diced tofu, pumpkin seeds, currants, garlic, cinnamon, and oregano. Mix well; add salt to taste. Place a little sauce in each corn tortilla, divide the tofu mixture between the tortillas, and sprinkle with 3/4 of the cheese. Roll up and arrange the tortillas seam side down in the baking dish. Pour the remaining sauce over the tortillas; cover with foil and bake for 20 minutes or until the sauce is bubbling. Uncover and sprinkle with the rest of the cheese. Heat until the cheese has melted and serve.

NOTE: Taste the pumpkin seeds before you toast them. They must be fresh, not stale or rancid.

POTATO AND MARINATED TOFU GRATIN

Serves 4 to 6

This dish is a favorite of mine. I have used it successfully to feed dinner guests as well as those demanding creatures, my children. Have no fear cooking it, for it is in fact that versatile creature, a gratin: thinly sliced layers of potatoes and tofu that bake while soaking up a flavorful broth. It is best when made with tofu that has been marinated and prebaked, but if you cannot buy baked, marinated tofu and have no inclination to bake it yourself, try the quick marinade on page 172.

▶ 1 1/2 cups finely chopped onion

1 tablespoon olive oil

1 teaspoon sugar

2 tablespoons sherry

8 ounces Baked Marinated Tofu (see page 173, or see quick recipe on page 172)

1 pound potatoes, peeled

1/4 to 1/2 cup freshly grated aged Parmesan cheese (optional)

3/4 cup milk

1 1/2 cups warm vegetable broth

1 tablespoon vegetable bouillon powder or light miso

2 cloves garlic, minced

1 teaspoon freshly grated nutmeg, or more to taste

1 egg white, lightly beaten (optional)

Preheat the oven to 350 degrees. Butter or oil an 8- to 10-inch baking dish.

Sauté the onion in olive oil and sugar over medium-high heat to lightly caramelize it. Add the sherry and cook briefly until the onion soaks up the sherry.

Slice the tofu into thin slices. Slice the potatoes into thin rounds.

Arrange slices of potato in a circular pattern in the prepared baking dish to make one layer. Arrange the tofu slices for a second layer. Sprinkle caramelized onion over all as well as Parmesan cheese, if desired. Repeat and make 2 or 3 layers, depending on the desired thickness and the size of the baking pan.

Combine the milk, broth, bouillon powder, garlic, and nutmeg. Add the egg white if a firmer texture is desired. Pour over the layers. Bake uncovered for 1 hour or until the potatoes are soft. If the potatoes are browning too quickly, cover with foil and uncover closer to the end of cooking.

NOTE: For a nondairy broth, omit the milk and use only vegetable broth with a teaspoon of light miso such as mellow white miso. Or in place of milk use rice milk.

QUICK TOFU MARINADE

1/4 cup shoyu

1 tablespoon honey or brown sugar

1/2 cup sherry or white wine

3 cloves garlic, minced

2 tablespoons toasted sesame oil

1/2 pound raw tofu

In a small saucepan, combine the shoyu, honey, sherry, garlic, and sesame oil. Place over moderate heat and stir until honey is diluted.

Slice the tofu into 1/4-inch slices and place in a shallow baking dish. Pour the marinade over the tofu. Marinate for at least 30 minutes. Pat the slices dry before you use them.

BAKED MARINATED TOFU

Baked tofu, often called teriyaki tofu, is available in natural food stores and some supermarkets throughout the country. It is generally sold in small, thin blocks. It is made from firm tofu that is pressed for greater firmness and then marinated in a soy-based marinade and baked. The store-bought product is excellent, and firmer than what you can make at home. Still, it costs less to prepare your own version, and you can vary the flavor of the marinade. This tofu is great for sandwiches, spreads, pâtés, stews, and gratins, and adds a dense, rich, almost smoky flavor to a dish.

▶ 8 ounces raw firm tofu

1 1/2 tablespoons honey, diluted in 2 tablespoons boiling water

1/4 cup shoyu

1 teaspoon lemon zest

1/3 cup sherry

3 cloves garlic, minced

3 tablespoons minced onion or onion puréed in a processor

2 tablespoons Thai peanut sauce (optional)

2 tablespoons toasted sesame oil

1 tablespoon puréed sun-dried tomatoes

3/4 cup boiling water

Cut the tofu into 1-inch-thick slices and place them in a shallow baking dish, preferably with a nonstick surface.

Combine the rest of the ingredients in a saucepan and bring to a simmer. Pour the marinade over the tofu. If possible, marinate for 2 to 4 hours, turning the slices. Bake at 325 degrees for 45 minutes to 1 hour or until the marinade has thickened on the tofu and any liquid in the baking dish has been absorbed. The tofu is then ready to use.

Serve with rice, or in sandwiches, or chopped for vegetable and grain loaves.

TOFU RAVIOLI

▶ 3/4 cup finely chopped shallots

1 tablespoon olive oil

1 teaspoon sugar

2/3 cup white wine (see Note)

3/4 cup finely chopped cooked
kale, squeezed dry

3/4 cup mashed firm tofu,
squeezed dry

1/2 to 3/4 cup freshly grated aged
Parmesan cheese

1 tablespoon dried sage, or
2 tablespoons chopped fresh, plus
1/4 cup for topping

1 1/2 teaspoons freshly grated
nutmeg, or more to taste

This simple recipe fashions won ton wrappers into ravioli. Use your own pasta recipe if you prefer. The secret is in the stuffing.

1 egg white (optional)

Salt and ground black pepper
to taste

2 packages wonton wrappers or
enough pasta sheets to yield
4 dozen ravioli

Egg wash: 1 egg white beaten with
1 teaspoon water

Butter or olive oil

3/4 cup grated Parmesan cheese

Sauté the shallots in olive oil for 5 minutes or until softened. Add the sugar and stir over medium-high heat to lightly caramelize the shallots. Add the wine and cook down almost completely, until the shallots have absorbed it. Transfer to a small mixing bowl. Add the kale, tofu, Parmesan, sage, nutmeg, and egg white, if a slightly firmer stuffing is desired. Season the stuffing with salt and pepper.

Lay out wonton wrappers on a work surface. Place a scant teaspoon of stuffing in the middle of each. Brush the ends with egg wash, fold over the wonton, and press sides together. The sides may be trimmed with kitchen scissors to form traditional half-moon-shaped ravioli. You should have 3 cups of filling, enough for 4 dozen ravioli if you use a generous teaspoon for each.

Bring a large pot of water to a boil and place the ravioli in, a few at a time. When the ravioli float to the top, they are done.

Toss with butter and fresh sage, or olive oil, garlic, sage, and Parmesan cheese.

NOTE: If you prefer, you may use sherry but omit the teaspoon of sugar.

CHICKEN-BAKED TOFU

Here is a version of a classic tofu recipe worth revisiting not only because it is delicious but also because it is so useful. This simple recipe is for the times when you want to use tofu, but you want it to have its own distinct taste, and not just the standard sesame and shoyu flavorings.

You will need a good vegetable bouillon powder and powdered spices or a prepared poultry seasoning. If you wish, you can also add such vegetable-based seasonings as Spike. When you grow comfortable with this recipe, you will move on to flavoring tofu in other ways you prefer, but the basic technique, which adds a substantial taste and texture to the tofu, is worth knowing.

▶ **1-pound block of tofu, cut into 1-inch slices or chunks**

1 tablespoon canola oil

1 tablespoon ground sage

1/2 tablespoon ground rosemary

1 1/2 teaspoons ground cardamom

Prepared poultry seasoning to taste (optional, or even in place of above spices)

2 tablespoons vegetable bouillon powder

Ground red pepper (cayenne) to taste

Preheat the oven to 350 degrees.

Place the tofu in a shallow pan or mixing bowl. Rub the pieces lightly with canola oil.

Combine the spices, vegetable bouillon powder, and cayenne. Sprinkle onto the tofu and gently rub the spices in. Do not add salt; the bouillon powder is probably salty enough.

Arrange on a nonstick baking sheet and bake for 30 to 45 minutes.

Serve in sandwiches, or use for spreads, sautés, or casseroles, or combine with rice and grains to add flavor, texture, and protein.

BEAN CURD SHEETS STUFFED WITH
TOFU, SPINACH, AND PISTACHIOS

Serves 4 to 6

▶ STUFFING

1/2 cup Madeira

8 to 12 pitted prunes

1/2 cup chopped shallots

1 tablespoon olive oil

3 cloves garlic, minced

1 cup chopped steamed spinach, chard, or watercress

1 cup finely chopped steamed mushrooms

1/2 cup unflavored bread crumbs or cooked brown rice

2/3 cup lightly toasted unsalted pistachios, loose skins removed, slightly crushed

1 large or 2 small to medium egg whites

1/2 teaspoon freshly grated nutmeg

Salt and ground black pepper to taste

10 to 12 ounces tofu

1/4 cup shoyu

1/4 cup plus 1 tablespoon toasted sesame oil

1 teaspoon sugar, or more to taste

1 tablespoon fresh ginger cut into fine matchsticks

3 to 6 sheets yuba, bean curd skin, or dried bean curd sheets
(see Note)

Basting liquid: 1 tablespoon canola oil, 1 tablespoon clarified butter or ghee, 1 teaspoon shoyu

Buddhist teachings require that family members mourn their departed loved ones by abstaining from meat, chicken, and fish for forty days after their relative's death. In response, the Chinese have created a substantial and interesting repertoire of meatless dishes. Unlike the chefs who have developed our New Vegetarian cuisine in the West, the Chinese have traditionally been interested in replicating the meat dishes of which they are most fond, hence the many mock meat, duck, and fish recipes prepared from tofu in Chinese cuisine.

This dish does not try to mock anything, but it does make use of the excellent technique employed in those Buddhist dishes that do — namely, stuffing tofu and topping it with yuba, or bean curd sheets.

The stuffing is prepared with pistachio and prunes, the tofu is marinated in shoyu, and both are wrapped in soy bean sheets, then brushed with oil and soy and baked long enough to heat the dish and crisp the yuba. One way of thinking of the dish is as an all-tofu lasagne without the sauce; another is as a modified mock duck. Either way, it is simpler to prepare than it sounds.

If you feel intimidated by the procedures involved, but want to try the recipe anyway, simply layer the tofu slices and stuffing in a baking dish, cover, and bake for 30 minutes, then top with plenty of Yuba Bacon (see page 180).

Heat the Madeira in a small saucepan, add the prunes, and allow to steep off the heat for 30 minutes to 1 hour. Drain and reserve any liquid. Chop the prunes coarsely.

Preheat the oven to 375 degrees.

Sauté the shallots in olive oil until softened. Add 2/3 of the minced garlic, the spinach, and the mushrooms. Turn into a mixing bowl. Add the bread crumbs, pistachios, egg whites, nutmeg, and chopped prunes. Season with salt and pepper to taste. Set the stuffing aside.

Cut the tofu into thin slices and place in a shallow tray or bowl. Combine the shoyu, 1/4 cup of sesame oil, the sugar, remaining garlic, and ginger. Pour over the tofu slices and let marinate at least 15 minutes.

Soak the yuba sheets in warm water to reconstitute for about 5 minutes or until they soften and turn pale. If you are not ready to use them, place them between the folds of a dampened clean kitchen towel.

For the basting liquid, combine 1 tablespoon of sesame oil, the canola oil, butter, and shoyu. Set aside.

Brush a shallow rectangular baking dish with oil. Arrange slightly overlapping layers of yuba on it to extend about 12 to 14 inches by about 10 to 12 inches. Set one layer of the gingered tofu slices down the center of the yuba sheets. Place some of the stuffing on top, then another layer of tofu, then more stuffing. Finish with a layer of gingered tofu. Fold each side of the yuba sheets over the filling, wrapping them tightly to form a firm log, or roll. Turn the roll over so that the smooth side is on top, and tuck ends under the roll. Brush with the basting liquid. Pour any Madeira prune liquid and tofu marinade into the baking dish and add 1/4 to 1/3 cup of water or broth. There should be enough liquid to cover the bottom of the baking dish. If it evaporates during steaming or baking, add more.

Cover tightly with foil and bake for 20 to 30 minutes, to let the yuba steam, then uncover and baste often with the oil, butter, and shoyu mixture until the yuba turns a golden, crispy brown. The more you baste the yuba, the crisper it will be.

Serve hot.

NOTE: To cover a loaf of about 10 inches you will need sheets about 12 to 14 inches long and 10 to 12 inches wide.

VARIATION: To add more crispness, prepare some yuba bacon on the side that you can serve on top of the dish. Yuba Bacon is easy and quick to make and is always very crisp and satisfying. See the recipe for Yuba Bacon on page 180.

NUT-CRUSTED TOFU SCALOPPINE

▶ 1 pound tofu

1 teaspoon grated fresh ginger

1 clove garlic, minced

1/3 cup shoyu

1 tablespoon Madeira or medium sherry

1 teaspoon hoisin sauce, or 1 tablespoon apple butter (optional)

1 cup crushed lightly toasted tamari nuts: pecans, walnuts, or mixtures of sunflower and cashew or sunflower and almond, for example

1/3 cup all-purpose flour or fine matzo meal

Egg wash: 3 egg whites beaten with 2 teaspoons of water

2 to 3 tablespoons canola oil or equal parts canola oil and butter

Tofu scaloppine is a dish that is fun to eat. Any nut or combination of nuts will do, as long as they are fresh. Here I suggest sunflower seeds and almonds, but I have also made this recipe with walnuts, pecans, and cashews. If you can find freshly roasted tamari nuts, all the better.

Slice the tofu into 8 to 12 pieces, depending on the thickness desired.

In a shallow pan deep enough for marinating the tofu slices, combine the ginger, garlic, shoyu, Madeira, and hoisin sauce. Place the tofu slices in the mixture and let them marinate for at least 15 minutes, turning several times.

In a food processor, pulse the nuts until they are well crushed, mealy but nowhere near paste. Add the flour and mix together. Pour onto a plate.

Pat the tofu slices dry. Brush each one with egg wash, or dip into the egg wash until covered on all sides. Coat with the nut and flour mixture. Place on a platter and chill until firm.

Heat 2 to 3 tablespoons of canola oil, or equal parts canola oil and butter, in a skillet. Sauté each piece of nut-crusted tofu until golden brown on both sides, being careful not to burn.

Serve immediately. Serve plain or with plum sauce, hoisin sauce, apple butter, or Spicy Peanut Sauce (see page 20).

TOFU FLAN WITH SWEET POTATO
AND ROASTED GARLIC

Serves 6

An unusual blend of flavors and textures. The roasted garlic can be puréed with the mixture or used chopped.

▶ 3/4 pound tofu (2 cups chopped)

3/4 pound sweet potatoes, steamed

1/4 cup plus 2 tablespoons cream, milk, or rice milk

1 1/2 to 2 tablespoons dark rum, to taste

1 tablespoon vegetable bouillon powder

Whites of 3 large or 4 medium eggs

1 1/2 tablespoons sugar

1 teaspoon ground cardamom

1/2 teaspoon salt

1/2 teaspoon ground red pepper (cayenne)

12 to 18 large cloves roasted garlic (1/2 cup), chopped

Butter a 2-quart soufflé dish or 6 custard cups. Preheat the oven to 375 degrees.

In a food processor, combine the tofu, sweet potatoes, cream, rum, bouillon powder, egg whites, sugar, cardamom, salt, and cayenne. Pulse until smooth. If necessary, place in a blender and process until the texture is absolutely smooth. Add the roasted garlic.

Pour the mixture into the prepared dish and bake for 25 to 35 minutes or until the custard is firm and the top is golden brown.

Serve with a garlicky spinach sauté garnished with lemon.

YUBA BACON

- 1 cup hot vegetable broth

- 1 tablespoon vegetable bouillon powder

- 2 tablespoons shoyu

- 1/2 teaspoon chipotle powder, or more to taste

- Several sheets of yuba cut into 8 × 2 1/2-inch strips

- 2 tablespoons canola oil

- 1 1/2 teaspoons butter (optional)

I borrowed the original idea for this great little recipe from Bonnie Mandoe, author of Vegetarian Nights. *Thin strips of yuba, or bean curd sheets, are marinated, then sautéed until they develop a crisp, baconlike crunch. Adding a little powdered chipotle chile makes them taste smoky and delicious, perfect for a BLT. Use scissors to cut the yuba into strips.*

I prefer to sauté these in a nonstick pan, and because so little is needed I like to use a little butter with the oil, but oil can be used by itself.

In a pie plate or shallow bowl, combine the vegetable broth, bouillon powder, shoyu, and powdered chipotle chile. Marinate the yuba strips in this mixture for at least 15 minutes, or overnight if desired.

Heat the oil and butter in a nonstick skillet. Sauté a few strips of yuba at a time; do not crowd the pan. Turn the strips when they brown. If you are making a lot of yuba bacon, you may want to change the oil and butter mixture every so often. Place on paper towels to drain. Serve hot.

TEMPEH

CONTENTS

Of all the soy-based, protein-rich products available to vegetarian cuisine, tempeh has the most complex, savory flavor, full of depth and culinary potential. Depending on how it is cooked and seasoned, it can taste meaty, nutty, earthy, smoky, or even sweet.

A little goes a long way, as tempeh is rich and substantial. Unlike tofu, which is known for its bland and chameleonlike nature, tempeh is unmistakably itself. It has a robust, slightly mysterious character, not unlike a perfect Camembert. Its firm texture, slightly nutty flavor, and mushroom aroma call for matching with wine. Tempeh can be found in natural food stores and sometimes in the frozen foods section of a market. It is sold in half-inch-thick cakes.

TEMPEH IN COCONUT MANGO RICE

▶ 1 tablespoon canola oil

1 tablespoon toasted sesame oil

1 (8-ounce) package tempeh, diced

2/3 cup chopped onion

2 cups brown basmati rice

1 cup hot vegetable broth

3 cups Thin Coconut Milk
(see page 376)

3 cloves garlic, sliced

1 cup ripe but firm mango chunks
sprinkled with 1 teaspoon sugar

Heat the canola and sesame oils in a medium saucepan. Add the tempeh and stir until coated. Add the onion and rice and sauté until the tempeh is golden. Stir in the hot broth and coconut milk. Add the garlic slices. Bring to a boil, lower the heat, and simmer, covered, for 30 minutes.

Fold in the mango chunks, cover, and cook another 30 minutes or until the rice is tender and liquid is absorbed. Let the rice stand for 10 minutes before uncovering the pan.

Serve with Ragout of Cabbage in Butter with Star Anise (page 228).

TEMPEH KACANG OVER RICE VERMICELLI

Serves 4

Tempeh has been a staple in the Indonesian diet for centuries. The cultured, fermented soybean cake contains all the essential amino acids and possesses the same quality of protein as poultry. This dish places tempeh in its characteristic Indonesian context: a light peanut sauce with the sweet and sour flavors of coconut milk, lemongrass, tamarind, ginger, garlic, and chile.

▶ 1 (8-ounce) package tempeh, sliced

2 tablespoons canola oil with
1 teaspoon toasted sesame oil

1 (8-ounce) package rice noodles
(see Note)

1/2 cup plus 1/4 cup vegetable broth

2 tablespoons peanut butter

1/2 cup Thin Coconut Milk
(see page 376)

1 tablespoon cognac

1 tablespoon minced lemongrass
(about 3 inches, cut fine)

2 cloves garlic, minced

1 teaspoon fresh ginger cut into
thin matchsticks

1/2 teaspoon ground cumin

1/2 teaspoon ground coriander

1/4 teaspoon shrimp paste
(optional)

1/4 teaspoon Thai red curry paste
(purchased) or Chipotle Purée
(see page 370)

1/2 cup chopped fresh basil

1/2 teaspoon tamarind juice, or
fresh lemon juice to taste

Salt and ground black pepper
to taste

1 tablespoon toasted sesame oil

1 teaspoon shoyu

Steam the tempeh slices for 20 minutes or until tender. Cool and dice. Sauté in the oil until golden. Set aside.

Place the rice noodles in a bowl and pour boiling water over to cover them. Leave for 10 minutes, or longer if necessary.

Heat 1/2 cup of broth in a saucepan. Add the peanut butter and stir until dissolved. Add the coconut milk, cognac, lemongrass, garlic, ginger, cumin, coriander, shrimp paste, and red curry paste; and simmer gently for 10 minutes. Add the basil and tamarind juice. Stir in the tempeh. Season the sauce with salt and pepper.

Heat the remaining 1/4 cup of vegetable broth, the sesame oil, and shoyu in a wok or deep pot. Drain the noodles, add them, and cook until they are soft and the liquid has cooked out. Pour the tempeh sauce over the noodles, toss, and serve.

NOTE: Wider rice noodles that look like fettuccine or linguine, as opposed to the very fine angel hair noodles, will do best in this dish. The noodles should be wide enough to "hold" the tempeh.

TEMPEH SWEETBREADS
WITH WILD MUSHROOMS AND PEAS

Serves 2 to 4

1 (8-ounce) package tempeh

1/2 cup whole wheat pastry flour

2 tablespoons olive oil

1 tablespoon canola oil or light olive oil

1/2 cup white wine or dry sherry

1/2 cup vegetable broth

2 tablespoons heavy cream, or 1/4 cup kefir

1/2 teaspoon freshly grated nutmeg

1 tablespoon chopped chives

Salt and ground black pepper to taste

1/2 teaspoon fresh lemon juice, or more to taste (optional)

1/2 pound sliced wild mushrooms: chanterelle, cremini, shiitake

1 cup fresh shelled peas (about 1 pound in the shell)

1/2 cup chopped shallots

With its rich and unctuous flavor, tempeh has always reminded me of sweetbreads. But unlike sweetbreads tempeh does not need to be soaked, blanched, cleaned, trimmed, or pressed — nor will it send your cholesterol sky-high. I like tempeh in a light version of a wild mushroom, fresh pea, and cream sauce classically associated with sweetbreads. Instead of cream, you can try substituting kefir, a cultured fermented yogurt cheese that can easily be likened in taste, though not in fat content, to crème fraîche.

Cut the tempeh into thin slices. Dust with flour. Heat 2 tablespoons of olive oil in a skillet and sauté the tempeh until golden brown. Transfer to a heated plate and keep warm in a 200-degree oven.

Deglaze the pan with wine and vegetable broth. Boil until cooked down to 1/2 cup of liquid. Stir in the cream. Finish the sauce with nutmeg, chives, salt and pepper to taste, and a squeeze of lemon juice, if desired.

Steam the wild mushrooms until they wilt, being careful not to overcook. Steam the peas for 5 to 10 minutes, just until they turn a bright green. Sauté the shallots in the canola oil until softened. Add the mushrooms and peas. Fold the mushrooms, peas, and shallots into the sauce and spoon the sauce over the tempeh sweetbreads. Serve with broad noodles and greens.

Serves 2 to 4

Yassa is a spicy lemon dish from West Africa, and a perfect showcase for tempeh. Surprisingly, African cuisine uses many of the same elements as Indonesian cuisine, where tempeh is a mainstay. Ginger, peanuts, tomatoes, chilies, coriander, cardamom, and lemon make this a dish that travels well, especially these days, as continents seem to move closer and the world grows smaller.

For an all-out great African meal serve this with a Malay Slaai (see page 368) and an Ethiopian kitfo, collards in feta (see page 221), and rice, of course.

▶ 2 tablespoons canola oil

1 cup minced onion

1/2 cup minced red bell peppers

1/2 cup minced yellow bell peppers

1/2 teaspoon minced jalapeño or other fresh hot chile

3 cloves garlic, minced

3 slices ginger, cut into matchsticks (about 2 tablespoons)

1 cup peeled, seeded, chopped red or green tomatoes

1 bay leaf

1/2 teaspoon ground coriander

1/2 teaspoon ground cardamom

1/2 teaspoon freshly grated nutmeg

2 to 4 tablespoons fresh lemon juice, to taste

1/4 cup chunky peanut butter

1/2 cup Thin Coconut Milk (see page 376)

1 (8-ounce) package tempeh, sliced and steamed for 20 minutes

2 tablespoons olive oil

Heat the canola oil in a nonreactive pan and sauté the onion and minced red and yellow peppers for 5 to 7 minutes, until softened. Add the jalapeño, garlic, ginger, tomatoes, and bay leaf. Simmer for 10 minutes or until the tomatoes begin to wilt and the ginger grows yellow and softens. Remove from the heat. Add the coriander, cardamom, nutmeg, and lemon juice.

Combine the peanut butter and coconut milk in a blender or food processor until thoroughly mixed. Add to the tomato mixture and simmer until the sauce thickens slightly, about 10 minutes.

Sauté the tempeh slices in the olive oil until golden and lightly crusted. Return the sauce to the heat and cook, stirring, over high heat until it thickens. Adjust the seasoning. Spoon over tempeh.

TEMPEH SCALOPPINE WITH SORREL CREAM

Serves 2 to 4

▶ 1/2 cup chopped shallots

2 tablespoons olive oil

1/2 cup dry vermouth or white wine

1/2 cup vegetable broth

2 tablespoons minced fresh sorrel

1 (8-ounce) package tempeh

1/2 cup whole wheat pastry flour

1 tablespoon canola oil or light olive oil

2 tablespoons heavy cream, or 1/4 cup kefir

1 teaspoon freshly grated nutmeg

1 1/2 teaspoons fresh lemon juice

Chopped chives

Salt and ground black pepper to taste

It is very easy to treat tempeh as one might a scaloppine of veal or chicken. Quick-sauté dishes, enhanced by a classic or nouvelle reduction sauce, are the most expedient items in the technical repertoire of any good cook, whether vegan or carnivore. Here, the grassy, piquant flavor of a sorrel sauce provides a natural contrast to the rich flavor of tempeh.

Sauté the shallots in olive oil in a nonreactive pan until softened but not brown. Deglaze the pan with wine and vegetable broth. Cook down to 1/4 cup of liquid. Add the sorrel and stir until it wilts. Set aside.

Cut the tempeh into thin slices. Dust with flour. Sauté the tempeh in canola oil until golden brown. Transfer to a heated plate and keep warm in a 200-degree oven. Don't worry if the tempeh crumbles.

Stir the cream into the sorrel sauce. Finish the sauce with nutmeg, lemon juice, chives, and salt and pepper to taste. Spoon the sauce over the tempeh.

188

PAN-BLACKENED TEMPEH

Tempeh's full flavor holds up well to this spicy seasoning, which Cajun chef Paul Prudhomme made famous with fish. Sauté in slices or even in cubes, if you prefer. Serve this with something cooling, like a daikon salad and rice. Although I prefer to steam my tempeh before I cook it, it isn't necessary for this dish, unless you like a more tender tempeh.

▶ 1 (8-ounce) package tempeh, sliced thin

Olive oil

2 to 4 teaspoons Spice Mixture (see below)

Place a large cast-iron skillet over high heat for 5 minutes or more, until the skillet begins to turn white hot. (You will need to turn on the exhaust fan and turn off the smoke detectors.)

Coat the slices of tempeh with olive oil and season on both sides with the spice mixture. Place the tempeh in the hot pan. The contact between the skillet's hot surface and the tempeh coated in oil and spice forms a sealing layer which blackens as it cooks. Sear briefly on both sides until blackened but not burned.

Serve with rice and Daikon Salad with Ponzu (see page 17).

SPICE MIXTURE

Makes about 1 cup

Combine all ingredients and mix thoroughly.

Store in a glass jar, tightly sealed.

▶ 2 tablespoons sea salt

1 teaspoon ground white pepper

1 teaspoon ground black pepper

2 teaspoons chipotle powder, or to taste

2 teaspoons dried thyme

2 teaspoons dried oregano

2 teaspoons ground cardamom

3 teaspoons onion powder

4 teaspoons garlic powder

TEMPEH RISOTTO
WITH WALNUTS AND SHALLOTS

Serves 4 to 6

▶ 1/2 cup toasted pecans or walnuts

2 tablespoons each canola oil and walnut or hazelnut oil, to make 1/4 cup

1 (8-ounce) package tempeh, cubed

6 cups vegetable broth, or more as needed (see Note)

1/2 cup chopped shallots

1 cup Gewürtztraminer or other white wine

2 cups arborio rice

1/2 to 1 cup grated aged Parmesan cheese, to taste

Salt and ground white pepper to taste

This risotto has an unabashedly robust flavor — sweet, nutty, and rich — and uses golden brown tempeh and aged Parmesan for a savory note.

Toast the nuts, cool, and rub gently between your hands to remove loose skins. Chop coarsely and set aside.

Heat 2 tablespoons of the oil in a skillet. Sauté the cubed tempeh until golden brown. Remove and drain on paper towels. Set aside.

Bring the broth to a boil in a saucepan; lower the heat and keep at a simmer while the rice is prepared. Meanwhile, in a separate pan, sauté the shallots in the remaining 2 tablespoons of oil until golden, about 8 minutes. Add the wine and boil until reduced by half. Stir in the rice and 1 cup of the hot broth. Stir until all the broth is absorbed. Over medium heat, keep adding more broth, a cup at a time, letting the rice absorb each cup of stock before you add the next. Stir constantly, lifting the rice up over the liquid. When the risotto seems about half cooked, add the tempeh and continue cooking. The whole process of stirring and tending your risotto should take about 20 to 30 minutes. Toward the end of cooking, add the broth in 1/2-cup increments. When it is done, the risotto should be creamy looking, with a thick soupy consistency, and the rice should be tender but al dente at the center. Fold in the Parmesan. Taste and adjust seasoning with salt and pepper. Garnish the risotto with the toasted nuts and serve with a green salad.

NOTE: Some people like their risotto well cooked instead of al dente. More stock and more stirring ought to give you your preferred texture. Don't be afraid to try this recipe with different kinds of nuts: macadamia, pine, even hazelnuts as long as they are toasted and crushed.

TEMPEH SCALOPPINE
IN RHUBARB BEURRE BLANC

Serves 4

This sauce was created for Huberts by a cook who insisted it be served over baked brains, which ultimately proved his point that a great sauce will sell anything on a menu. The first rhubarb beurre blanc ever to be served in a New York restaurant, this deliciously quirky sauce is simple to prepare. In this recipe its spunky piquancy balances tempeh's earthy flavor and dense texture.

- 1 cup apple cider
- 2 cups thinly sliced rhubarb
- 1/4 cup white wine
- 1 (8-ounce) package tempeh
- 3 tablespoons fruity olive oil
- 1 cup vegetable broth
- 3 tablespoons minced shallots
- 1/2 teaspoon ground cinnamon
- Salt and ground black pepper to taste
- Sugar to taste
- 2 tablespoons unsalted butter

In a medium nonreactive saucepan, boil the cider until it is reduced down to 1/4 cup. Add the rhubarb and wine and cook over moderate heat until the rhubarb is soft. Push the rhubarb through a strainer or a chinois to strain out any fibrous parts. The sauce can be completed ahead of time up to this point. You should have between 1/2 and 1 cup.

Slice the tempeh thin and steam for 20 minutes. Cool and pat dry. Heat 2 tablespoons of oil in a skillet and sauté the tempeh slices until golden and slightly crusted. Keep warm in a 200-degree oven while you finish the sauce.

Boil the vegetable broth until it is reduced to 1/4 cup. Sauté the shallots in 1 tablespoon of oil until golden, about 8 minutes. Add the reduced broth and the rhubarb sauce. Boil gently until thick and syrupy. Add cinnamon, salt, pepper, and a dash of sugar to taste. Finish the sauce by whirling in small pieces of butter to thicken slightly. Spoon over the tempeh.

TEMPEH DOSA

▶ **DOSAS**
(LENTIL AND RICE CRÊPES)

1/2 cup split red lentils (dhal)

1 1/2 cups uncooked brown rice

2 teaspoons ground cardamom

2 tablespoons granulated sugar

3/4 teaspoon salt

Ground black pepper to taste

1/4 cup plain yogurt

2 tablespoons clarified butter
or clarified butter and canola oil
mixed

TEMPEH FILLING

1 (8-ounce) package tempeh, diced

1/4 cup flour

3 tablespoons olive oil or canola oil

1 cup diced potatoes

1 cup sliced onion

1 teaspoon brown sugar

3 cloves garlic, minced
(1 1/2 teaspoons)

1/2 cup white wine

1 cup roasted red pepper strips

1 teaspoon fresh marjoram

1 teaspoon ground cardamom

1/2 teaspoon ground coriander

I ate my first dosa at an ashram. Friends had taken me there to meet their guru. We had sat cross-legged in the meditation hall, on heated marble floors, listening to the guru speak. All that chanting worked up a curiously strong appetite for worldly sustenance! So, before we went up to receive darshan, or blessing, we made a beeline to the ashram café, known to have a divine kitchen. As it turned out, the guru, whose parents had been restaurateurs in India, had grown up as a restaurant brat, and so the food offered to devotees was of the highest quality.

Dosas are pancakes made from lentils and rice that have been soaked, ground, and fermented together. These are really quite simple to make, but you will need patience to wait overnight for the batter to ferment. The batter does not perform exactly as a wheat batter does, and you may have to lose one or two to practice spreading it out on a cast-iron or nonstick griddle, but it is worth it. The flavor is very unusual, but if you like sourdough, or the flavor of beer or rye, you will love these unusual crêpes. which are a perfect match for tempeh. If you prefer to make a quicker crêpe, one that doesn't involve waiting for a batter to ferment, you can use any simple crêpe recipe, such as the one on page 278.

Traditionally these are made with urad dhal, a yellow dhal that is not always easy to obtain, so I have made them with the easier-to-find split red lentils, also known as masoor dhal.

Filled with diced tempeh, potatoes, roasted red peppers, and onions, the crêpes are a meal in themselves. Use the mango chutney and yogurt cheese as a side dish or, if you prefer, to moisten and flavor the filling. I like to add crushed unsalted pistachios to the batter right before I pour it out onto the griddle, or, alternatively, gomashio, crushed sesame salt.

1/2 teaspoon fresh ginger cut into
small matchsticks

1 1/2 cups Yogurt Cheese
(see page 375)

1/4 to 1/2 cup Mango Chutney
(see page 363), or to taste

Make the dosas: Wash the dhal several times until the water runs clear and then soak it in water at room temperature overnight or for 8 hours. Wash the rice several times until the water runs clear, then soak it also at room temperature overnight or for 8 hours. Soak the beans and rice separately.

Drain and wash the rice again until the water runs clear. Drain and wash the dhal until the water runs clear. Put the rice in a blender or processor and purée, adding 1/2 cup of water. Repeat the procedure with the dhal. Now, combine the dhal and rice mixture. You should have about 2 1/4 to 2 1/2 cups of batter. Let this batter stand covered, at room temperature, overnight, or at least 12 hours. The rice-dhal batter will bubble slightly and have a slightly fermented smell.

Add the 2 teaspoons of cardamom to the fermented mix. Adjust the seasoning with sugar, salt, and pepper. Now add the yogurt and enough water to make the batter slightly runny. I have found the most successful ratio to be equal parts of liquid (including the yogurt) and solids. The thicker the batter, the thicker your crêpe, or dosa. Try a few practice dosas to suit your own taste.

Preheat your griddle over a medium-low flame, butter or oil it, and pour 1/3 to 1/2 cup of batter onto the griddle, depending on how large you like your dosa. These take longer to cook than crêpes made with flour. I give them 1 1/2 to 2 minutes on each side. The dosa should be well cooked, dry, and cohesive before you carefully turn it over and cook it on its other side. Remove with a spatula and place on a warm platter. Keep in a warm oven, covered with a damp kitchen towel to keep from drying out, until you are ready to stuff the dosas with filling. This should make about 8 large or 16 small dosas.

Make the filling: Steam the tempeh for 20 minutes. Remove from the steamer, cool, dredge in flour, and sauté in 1 tablespoon of oil until golden.

Steam the potatoes until they are partly cooked but still somewhat firm. Sauté in 1 tablespoon of oil until golden. Add to the tempeh.

Sauté the onion in 1 tablespoon of oil; add the brown sugar and cook until lightly caramelized. Add the garlic and heat through. Add the white wine and boil to reduce until the onion has completely absorbed the wine.

Combine the tempeh, potatoes, onion, and roasted red peppers. Season the filling with marjoram, cardamom, coriander, and ginger.

Mix the yogurt cheese and chutney. Serve this on the side, or, for a moister filling, add it to the tempeh and vegetable mix.

Spoon 1/2 cup of filling down the center of each large dosa. Roll up, or fold the sides around the filling to form a package. Serve 2 dosas per person.

TEMPEH SAUSAGE

▶ 1 (8-ounce) package tempeh

2 tablespoons flour

1 egg white

4 cloves garlic, crushed, or
2 teaspoons minced garlic

1 1/2 teaspoons brown sugar

1 1/2 teaspoons ground sage

1 teaspoon freshly grated nutmeg

1 teaspoon ground rosemary

1 teaspoon ground cardamom

1/2 teaspoon ground allspice

1/4 cup soy bacon bits (optional)

1/2 teaspoon Chipotle Purée
(optional; see page 370), or 1/4
teaspoon ground chile powder

Salt and ground black pepper
to taste

1 tablespoon canola oil

2 teaspoons butter

This savory mixture can be rolled into sausage links, but I like it best served as thin, crisply fried sausage patties, sautéed in a nonstick pan in canola oil with a little butter. The smoked flavor of soy bacon bits adds an interesting touch, but it is not necessary. A spicy smoked flavor can also be achieved if you add ground chipotle powder.

Cut the tempeh into 3/4-inch slices. Place tempeh in a bamboo steamer and steam for 20 minutes. Transfer to a bowl and mash.

Add the flour and mix well. Add the egg white, garlic, brown sugar, sage, nutmeg, rosemary, cardamom, and allspice. If you wish to add soy bacon bits, you may want to soak them in a few tablespoons of water for about 30 seconds. Added dry, they give a slight crunch to your sausage, something you may actually enjoy. Add the optional chipotle purée and salt and pepper to taste.

The mixture should look crumbly but hold together very well when pressed or rolled into a shape. Fashion into sausage patties. Sauté in the oil and butter until browned and crisp on both sides.

The mixture can also be rolled into a log, wrapped in plastic, and refrigerated. Slices can be cut and sautéed as desired. This freezes very well.

TEMPEH OVER SAUERKRAUT

My father's family came from Alsace, where braising meat over sauerkraut is an established tradition. The savory nuttiness of tempeh is greatly enhanced by pickled cabbage, whose brininess cooks out, leaving an enriched piquancy. Rather than the canned variety, choose a good organic sauerkraut from a natural food store, or one that is freshly made, or sold in plastic bags or jars. The fewer additives, the better. In the fall, small whole lady apples are pretty and delicious additions. Otherwise, any good baking variety will round out the final flavor of this dish with a mellow, satisfying sweetness.

▶ 1 pound sauerkraut

2 tablespoons olive oil

4 cloves garlic, minced

4 juniper berries, crushed

1 cup Riesling or other fruity white wine

1 cup vegetable broth

1 1/2 cups turnip chunks

2 tablespoons chopped soy bacon, or 2 smoky-flavored soy hot dogs, whole

2 bay leaves

1/2 cup coarsely chopped parsley

1 tablespoon fresh savory, or 1 1/2 teaspoons dried

1/2 teaspoon freshly grated nutmeg

1 (8-ounce) package tempeh, cut into 4 equal pieces

2 tablespoons fresh chervil, or 1 tablespoon dried

1 cup peeled and cored apple halves or chunks, or 8 to 10 lady apples

Drain the sauerkraut. Squeeze dry by wringing it out by hand. Reserve the juice. (If the sauerkraut is salty, you may want to rinse it under cold water and then wring dry.)

Heat the oil in a heavy saucepan and lightly sauté the garlic and juniper berries. Add the sauerkraut. Stir until warmed through. Add the Riesling and cook down by half. Add the broth and reserved sauerkraut juice and bring to a simmer.

Add the turnips, soy bacon, bay leaves, parsley, savory, and nutmeg. Simmer for 10 minutes. Add the tempeh, chervil, and apples. Cook covered for 30 to 45 minutes longer.

Serve over broad noodles, potatoes mashed with Roasted Garlic (see page 372) and chèvre, or with Potato Cakes with Roasted Garlic and Tarragon (see page 238).

SEITAN

CONTENTS

MAKING SEITAN FROM SCRATCH

A group of us were gathered in the rectory hall of a small-town church. A group of folding chairs had been set up to face the stage, which was in fact a simple kitchen behind a fold-away screen. Our small crowd settled in as three tall women stood before us, all Seventh-Day Adventists, their hair in nets, their hands crossed in front of their starched aprons. Their open faces were well scrubbed, and they wore the smiles of pious, good-natured, and well-meaning people. I thought guiltily of the Sundays I had missed church, and contemplated how the lure of food had brought me closer to an altar than I had been in months. We were about to hear a lecture-demonstration on preparing seitan gluten — the protein part of wheat — poached in a soy sauce broth. Seventh-Day Adventists are renowned vegetarians and experts in the art of preparing wheat protein. I knew that gluten was made by washing the starch out of wheat flour: A simple dough made from flour and water was repeatedly kneaded and rinsed in water until the starch washed out of the dough and the protein, or gluten, remained, ready to be cooked in a flavored broth. I was here to learn the basics of seitan preparation from these three women, who had cooked it at least once a week all their adult lives.

Ruth, the tallest of the three, called us to attention by banging a spoon against a small copper-bottomed pot. She tightened her apron and marched behind the kitchen counter, her tan cotton skirt rustling at mid-calf. There, she combined three pounds of flour — the higher the gluten content the better — with about three cups of warm water. For several minutes she kneaded the mixture by hand, adding a little water until it resembled dough. We watched and listened as she proclaimed the gluten covenant: protein and fiber without cholesterol or fat.

After watching her knead for five minutes, my wrists were aching in sympathy, so I raised my hand and asked if this initial step could be better accomplished by a KitchenAid with a bread hook. Ruth looked bewildered. Had I unwittingly committed a moral faux pas in this brave new gluten culture, or was it all right to want to make gluten more easily?

Mil, the second good lady, in her light blue short-sleeved pantsuit with its many useful pockets, came to the rescue and said, "Well now, I must admit I've never thought of that."

Louise, our third hostess, sunny in her yellow shirtdress, seemed charmed by such a radical thought as a bread hook, but then realized it was her turn to take over the gluten demonstration, and she hustled the plastic bowl of gooey dough over to the sink.

"All righty then, I hope you all can see what I'm doing," Louise said pertly as she slid the bowl under a faucet that ran and ran and ran water over the ball of dough, which became increasingly tacky as she kneaded it. I thought my fingers would wrinkle and turn prunish in empathy as I watched her push and punch and roll the dough until its starch washed away. I suddenly recalled the county had recently experienced a bad drought, and the image of dry reservoirs came to mind.

I again spoke up. "Is there any way to make gluten using less water?"

Ruth perked up, her finger pressed against her cheek. "Well now, Mil always says that if you soak the dough in water overnight, you need much less time washing it. Don't you always say that, Mil?"

Mil seemed reluctant to fess up to the efficacy of an overnight dough-soak. I couldn't tell what embarrassed her more, basking in the light of all this attention, or admitting to having had a time-saving idea that, to her, may have smacked of laziness.

After ten minutes, Louise turned the kneading over to Ruth and after that, volunteers from the audience were invited, and of course I raised my hand. The kneading went on for over thirty minutes, as we kept stretching and kneading and rinsing the dough, then pinching it between our fingers to dissolve any gritty bits. The gluey gray mass felt just like it looked. Clearly, you either liked kneading gluten or you didn't. It was far more elastic than bread; it had an obstinate nature, and it fought back.

When the kneading was finally done, Ruth took the spotlight again and prepared the broth from soy sauce and vegetable bouillon, explaining that any tasty liquid whose flavor you wanted to impart to the spongy gluten as it cooked would do. My hand shot up again.

"Can you use miso, or garlic, or hey, how about wine?"

You could now hear a pin drop in that hall.

"Wine?" Ruth stroked her long neck, calming herself, while Mil and Louise looked worriedly at each other. *Wine?*

I had begun to get the hang of this gluten thing; it was full of possibilities. I knew I shouldn't be asking so many questions, but now I wanted to find out if things like diced vegetables or currants could be kneaded into the dough before it was cooked, and whether it was possible to fashion different shapes, like thin scaloppine or jelly rolls, out of it.

After the gluten was ceremoniously laid to rest in a large stockpot full of broth, trays of food that had been prepared earlier for the demonstration were placed on the counter, and the audience was invited to eat. We entertained ourselves with tastes of seitan stroganoff, seitan kebabs, and even seitan fudge, chewing on our bits of wheat meat as we watched the roly-poly seitan ball rumble around in the simmering liquid.

A few of us sipped soft drinks and chatted near the stove, weighing the benefits and flavor of seitan against the effort it took to prepare it. Suddenly Ruth summoned our attention by banging on the pot again. This time there was a sense of command, of important announcement and denouement. She cleared her throat, held up a Tupperware container, peeled off the pink top, and showed us the contents by tilting it toward the audience. Inside were piles of very cute looking little scaloppine. She cut them up and passed them around; they were meaty in texture and flavor like the rest of the seitan.

"Now then, *these* are made from *instant* gluten flour. There may be some among you," she announced, looking directly at me with her eyebrows arched, "who don't want to put in the time or effort to make gluten from scratch. Don't let that stop you, because good seitan can also be made from instant gluten flour."

"Now she tells us," a friend whispered in my ear.

She held up a box of instant seitan mix, her smile as righteous as if she were showing us a bad man made good by faith.

"This is for you," Ruth said, handing me the box. "You'll need it. It's easier to work with, and you seem to be the type who likes to experiment."

I have since made gluten many times and in many ways. I still refer to the notes I took in that rectory hall and I have repeatedly found the basic directions of those three good ladies to be indispensable. Whenever I make seitan, I remember the austere kitchen and the three Seventh-Day Adventists, and of course I remember the food, which was delicious. I also remember the gift of encouragement given to me by someone who was not *experimental*, like myself, but who did not stand on ceremony when it came to passing on culinary information. I have been taught a good many things about cooking from a good many people, but I would have to say that of all my teachers, Ruth definitely had my number, at least as far as preparing seitan was concerned.

QUICK SEITAN

It will come as no surprise that I suggest you use an instant gluten flour mix, or what is sometimes called Vital Wheat Flour, the first time you attempt to make gluten. Both can be found in any natural food store.

Seitan is also available in some natural food stores already made. The best seitan is prepared locally and stored in large pots or plastic barrels in soy or shoyu broth. This kind of fresh seitan is really quite excellent. If it has a rancid taste or sour smell, it is past its time, and you should wait until the store gets a new shipment. When it is prepared locally for a store, seitan is generally delivered once or twice a week and kept in a refrigerated section. Ask the store manager to tell you the days it comes in, and you will be able to get it at its freshest. Fresh seitan generally lasts for about one week. Keep it in the refrigerator in water and shoyu and change the water every two days. Seitan is also available in packages, but this variety tends to be sold in small quantities and often has been frozen. If fresh seitan is available, by all means, buy some and try it to see how you like it. Then you won't have to first worry about making the gluten before you can begin to cook with it and enjoy it!

MAKING INSTANT SEITAN

If you are using a seitan or gluten mix that you have bought in bulk or in a package, follow the given instructions. An instant gluten flour, or seitan mix, is made up of glutenous flour that has already had its starches removed, and is then dried and pulverized. You add liquid, knead for about five minutes, and then place it in a broth made up of a soy-based stock.

Adding liquid: If you add a fairly hot liquid to the dry mix, you get a much lighter product. Instead of adding water, try adding a broth. Flavor your broth with herbs, spices, garlic, or even tomato paste.

Kneading: Most mixes will tell you to knead for at least 5 minutes, but I have found that beyond combining, the less kneading the better. I try not to knead more than about 3 minutes, and never more than 5 minutes.

To add other ingredients: You might also consider kneading diced vegetables like carrots, parsnips, and onions into the dough. Do this very early in the kneading process. The vegetables may seem slippery at first, but they will lock into the dough and will stay there while the dough cooks. You can also knead in currants and raisins, nuts, or semi-cooked grains such as millet or kasha, which lend the seitan texture and lighten it.

The broth: The better the broth, the tastier the seitan. Prepare the broth as you would a good soup. I like to start with an excellent vegetable stock, or a high-quality powdered vegetable broth added to water. I add shoyu for color, preferably one that is not too salty. I also like to include garlic, fresh ginger, and wine. Red wine lends a rich flavor and color, while white wine contributes flavor without too obvious a color. You can also add a quartered onion, several stalks of celery, and a few chopped carrots for even more flavor. The vegetables will not interfere with the cooking of the seitan. Be careful about adding additional salt. Usually a powdered broth has salt, as does soy sauce or shoyu. If the broth cooks down, add more liquid. Simmer — don't boil — seitan.

The many shapes of seitan: Here are some techniques for cooking seitan in a number of different shapes that will let you work with it in an interesting range of ways.

LOAF OR LOG: The most obvious way of cooking seitan is as one big mound. In other words, place the entire kneaded shape, or log, into the simmering broth and cook. A log takes about four hours of cooking. Turn it from time to time while it simmers, covered. Preparing one large piece of gluten is good for large family dinners, or making a mock turkey.

PULLS: After you have kneaded the gluten, divide it into 6 or 8 pieces by pulling or cutting. Cook in broth for 2 to 2 1/2 hours, or longer. (You cannot really overcook seitan.) Some find this a more manageable way of making and storing or freezing seitan.

SCALOPPINE: Divide gluten into many small pieces and pull into thinner scaloppine shapes. It is hard to get these too thin, as gluten is very elastic. You can try a heavy rolling pin, too, but don't expect skinny cutlets. Cook in broth for 2 to 2 1/2 hours. Scaloppine are probably more successfully formed by cutting larger pieces after they have been cooked.

JELLY ROLL: An amazing technique created by gluten master Dorothy Bates. Start with your basic roll or log of kneaded gluten. Pull, stretch, and roll out the gluten into a rectangle as close to 8 by 16 inches as possible. Brush both sides of the gluten with canola oil. Wet a yard or so of cheesecloth, then squeeze it dry. Lay it out and place the gluten on the cheesecloth, which will extend beyond the edges of the gluten. Fold the overhanging sides over the gluten and then roll it up like a loose jelly roll. Don't roll this tightly because the gluten will expand when it cooks. Tie kitchen string around the roll to hold the cheesecloth in place.

Cook the roll for 2 to 2 1/2 hours, turning frequently. Cool. Unroll the seitan, and remove the cheesecloth. You now have a perfect shape for stuffing before roasting or braising.

GROUND SEITAN: Place pieces of cooked seitan in a grinder or food processor and grind or pulse until chopped. This is good for use in loaves, burgers, and "meat"balls in spaghetti.

SEITAN CARBONNADE

The northern part of France, which borders on Belgium, is especially proud of its beer. It is no surprise that the favorite local beverage turns up in stews. Here is a classic recipe from the region that uses seitan in place of meat. Braised in beer with caramelized onions, the great chameleon seitan soaks up all the flavors of carbonnade à la flamande. You can experiment with the kinds of beers you like best, whether light Pilsners or heavier, richer brews. Ginger beer produces a spicier dish. I prefer Grolsch, or cherry beer, in this dish. Parsnips and rutabaga add a special depth of flavor. Some people like to add a little vinegar to their carbonnades for an extra tang. Served with collards and brown rice, this is a substantial dish, especially if you are a beer lover.

▶ 1 1/2 pounds seitan, cut into 1-inch cubes (see page 202)

1/2 cup whole wheat flour for dusting

2 tablespoons olive oil

16 small white onions

1 tablespoon sugar

1 cup sliced parsnips

1 1/2 cups rutabaga in 1 1/2-inch chunks

1/2 cup dried cherries

2 cups beer

2 cups strong vegetable broth, plus a tablespoon of powdered broth if needed

6 cloves garlic, sliced

1 bay leaf

2 tablespoons fresh thyme, or 2 teaspoons dried

Pinch of ground red pepper (cayenne)

Salt and ground black pepper to taste

Sugar or molasses to taste

1 to 2 tablespoons fresh lemon or lime juice (optional)

Lightly dust the seitan cubes in whole wheat flour. Heat the oil in a small skillet and brown the cubes lightly on all sides. Remove the seitan to a flameproof casserole. Brown the onions in the leftover oil, adding more oil if necessary. Sprinkle with sugar to help the onions caramelize.

Add the onions, parsnips, rutabaga, and dried cherries to the seitan. Pour in the beer. Cook uncovered to let the alcohol cook off for about 15 minutes. Add the vegetable broth, garlic, bay leaf, thyme, and cayenne. Adjust seasoning to taste with salt, pepper, and sugar. Simmer covered for 1 hour; uncover and continue to cook for another 30 minutes. Add a little lemon juice, if desired.

Serve with collards and brown rice.

SEITAN ROPA VIEJA

▶ 1 (28-ounce) can organic whole peeled tomatoes

2 tablespoons olive oil

3/4 cup diced onion

1 teaspoon sugar

1 1/2 cups red wine

1 to 2 ounces semisweet chocolate, to taste

4 cloves garlic, minced

1 large cinnamon stick, or 1/2 teaspoon ground cinnamon

1/4 teaspoon ground allspice

1 teaspoon fresh marjoram, or 1/3 teaspoon dried

1/2 teaspoon ground cumin

1/2 teaspoon minced jalapeño, or more to taste

2 cups chopped seitan (see page 202)

2 tablespoons currants

1/4 to 1/3 cup chopped good-quality green olives

1 tablespoon capers, rinsed (optional)

2 bay leaves

Salt and ground black pepper to taste

Use ground or chopped pieces of seitan for this version of a Cuban favorite. Serve with rice or in burritos topped with fresh cilantro, grated jalapeño Cheddar cheese, and diced jicama.

Drain the tomatoes. Choose a few of the firmest tomatoes, chop them, and set aside. Purée the rest of the tomatoes in the blender.

Heat the olive oil in a saucepan and sauté the onion for 5 minutes, until softened. Add sugar to help caramelize the onion. Add the wine and boil until reduced by half to cook out the alcohol. Add the chopped and puréed tomatoes. Bring the sauce to a simmer. Add the chocolate, garlic, cinnamon, allspice, marjoram, and cumin. Add jalapeño to taste. Stir in the seitan, currants, olives, capers, and bay leaves. Cook covered for about 45 minutes, or until the sauce browns and thickens slightly. Add salt and pepper to taste. Uncover and cook for another 30 minutes, allowing the sauce to thicken.

Remove the bay leaves and serve with rice or in burritos or corn tacos with grated jalapeño Cheddar cheese, shredded romaine lettuce, and diced jicama.

Serves 6

For this dish, you will need a piece of seitan that is flat and shaped like a rectangular piece of jelly roll spongecake (see page 204). It is spread with a wild mushroom and fig stuffing, then rolled and tied, and finally braised over a bed or mirepoix in a hearty red wine sauce. If you have your own favorite stuffing for, say, a breast of veal, you might also try it here. The technique of stuffing, rolling, wrapping or tying, and then slowly braising over diced vegetables in a wine-flavored sauce is much the same for carnivore and vegetarian alike. If you are new to this kind of dish, enjoy the pleasures of preparing it as well as eating it!

3/4 cup cooked rice or millet

1/2 cup chopped lightly toasted walnuts or pecans

1/2 cup chopped dried figs

2 teaspoons ground sage

Flat piece of seitan (9 × 13 to 16) (see page 204)

▶ THE STUFFING

1 tablespoon olive oil

1/4 cup minced shallots

1/4 cup chopped celery

3 cloves garlic, minced

1/2 pound (2 cups) wild mushrooms, steamed, then chopped fine to about 1 cup cooked

2 tablespoons cognac

1/2 cup medium sherry

1/4 cup vegetable broth plus 2 to 4 tablespoons, if necessary

3/4 cup cooked, squeeze-dried, finely chopped spinach or chard

THE MIREPOIX

3/4 cup diced onion

3/4 cup diced parsnips

3/4 cup diced carrots

3/4 cup diced celery

2 tablespoons olive oil

1/2 cup cognac

1 cup red wine

1 1/2 to 2 cups vegetable broth

2 tablespoons dark miso paste diluted in 1/2 cup boiling water

6 cloves garlic, sliced

Make the stuffing: Heat the oil in a saucepan, add the shallots and celery, and sauté for 5 minutes, until softened. Stir in the garlic and chopped mushrooms. Deglaze the pan with cognac. Add the sherry and vegetable broth and boil until there is almost no liquid in the pan. Add the chopped spinach, rice, walnuts, figs, and sage. Mix the ingredients thoroughly and add more vegetable broth if necessary. The mixture should be moist but not wet and hold together like stuffing. You should be able to spread or pat it onto the flat piece of seitan.

After you have spread the mixture onto the seitan, roll it up like a jelly roll, starting with a short end. Wrap it in a double piece of cheesecloth, tied at either end into handles that can be used to pick up the roast after it has braised. If you prefer, omit the cheesecloth and simply tie the roll in several places with string.

Make the mirepoix: In a deep casserole big enough to hold the roulade, sauté the diced onion, parsnips, carrots, and celery in olive oil. Let them turn a light golden brown. Deglaze the pan with cognac and cook out the alcohol. Add the wine, broth, miso, and garlic and bring to a simmer.

Nestle the stuffed seitan roast into the bed of mirepoix. The liquid should come up to about one-quarter to one-third of the seitan roll. Cook covered in a preheated oven at 350 to 375 degrees for 1 to 1 1/2 hours. You may want to turn the seitan over halfway through.

To serve, gently remove the seitan by the cheesecloth handles and place the roast on a cutting board or serving platter. Cut and peel away the cheesecloth. Slice and serve.

SEITAN SAUERBRATEN

Seitan lends itself well to marinated dishes like sauerbraten. Though it is traditionally served with spaetzle or broad noodles, you might want to serve it with a creamy potato gratin for a richer contrast.

▶ 1/2 cup chopped onion

1/2 cup diced parsnips

1/2 cup diced carrots

1/2 cup diced white turnips

1 tablespoon olive oil

1/3 cup puréed sun-dried tomatoes in oil

1 tablespoon tomato paste

2/3 cup golden raisins

1 tablespoon shoyu

1 cup full-bodied red wine

1/4 cup balsamic vinegar, or to taste

4 juniper berries

2 bay leaves

1/2 teaspoon whole allspice

1 slice fresh ginger

2 tablespoons dark miso, diluted in 2 tablespoons hot water

6 cloves garlic, minced

2 cups vegetable broth

3 cups seitan cut into 2-inch chunks (see page 202)

2/3 to 3/4 cup pulverized gingersnaps, to taste

In a casserole, sauté the onion, parsnips, carrots, celery, and turnips in olive oil until a light golden brown. Add the sun-dried tomatoes, tomato paste, raisins, and shoyu to the mirepoix.

In a saucepan, combine the wine, vinegar, juniper berries, bay leaves, allspice, ginger, miso, garlic, and vegetable broth and bring to a simmer. Add to the mirepoix. Stir in the seitan. Simmer covered for 1 to 1 1/2 hours. Thicken with gingersnap crumbs during the last 30 minutes.

Serve over broad noodles or with a potato gratin.

SEITAN SCALOPPINE STUFFED WITH PÂTÉ

▶ 4 to 8 slices of seitan, cut from a
large roll or a smaller "pull"
(see page 203)

1/2 cup to 1 cup Compass Pâté
(see page 74)

1/2 cup freshly grated Parmesan
cheese

1 cup unflavored bread crumbs

Salt and ground black pepper
to taste

2 to 4 tablespoons mixed canola
and olive oils

*Because seitan is so elastic, it can be hard to form it into thin scaloppine.
You will find it easier to slice individual pieces of seitan from one larger section, which you can then stuff, bread, and sauté.*

Dry each slice, or scallop, of seitan. Spread one side of each with hazelnut pâté. Chill until firm. Put the grated
Parmesan cheese onto a platter. Place the scallops on the platter, pâté side up, so the cheese adheres to the
bottom sides. Sprinkle additional cheese on top; press lightly with your hand.

Gently dip the scaloppine in bread crumbs. Sprinkle crumbs over the top and press lightly with your hand
to make the crumbs adhere. Season with salt and pepper.

Heat the oil in a frying pan and sauté both sides over medium heat until the scaloppine turn golden.

Serve with a romaine and arugula salad.

VEGETABLES

VEGETABLES

You can get tired of eating. My husband, Len, and I were on a trip to France, taking notes for our new fall menu. By this point in our travels we wanted to taste food instead of a cook's ideas about food. We wanted to taste things by themselves — a ripe apricot, warm buttered bread, peas.

We had arrived at a centuries-old château in France. The conscientious but preoccupied chef, who knew my husband and I were in the restaurant business, gave us an obligatory tour of his dining room. The walls were draped with red velvet. His father and his father before him had possessed a love of medieval things, and the crimson served as an imposing backdrop for the family's collection of shields, swords, axes, clubs, and jousting poles. The chef appeared uninterested in armor and eager to move on. I had the queer feeling that we were his only guests and imagined eating a lonely round of foie gras inside this arsenal.

Duty-bound to show us more of his château, the distracted chef led us into a pantry the size of our apartment. I caught him absently staring out the window while we inspected his lace-edged napkins, his collection of silver plate and tureens. I began to wonder if even he felt just a little lost in the midst of all this splendor.

Then he brought us to his kitchen, which was cavernous but full of windows and late-afternoon sunlight. A breeze came through the door that opened onto his garden. The chef relaxed and smiled. He seemed to know where he was again. He pointed to the beautiful landscape and described a lovely walk we could take before dinner.

When we returned, we were seated outside under a large tree whose great limbs spread over many tables. We placed ourselves in his hands, and he served us a great and memorable dish: peas from his garden. I remember a white bowl. I think there was cream. After the meal, he came out to discuss the peas. They were his passion.

213

SAUTÉED

VEGETABLES: SAUTÉED

CONTENTS

Sautéed vegetables are all about simplicity and flavor. More dimensional than steaming, the technique of sautéing allows a vegetable a chance to show its own special qualities, whether enhanced by butter, oil, garlic, herbs, lemon, wine, or another vegetable.

BEETS SAUTÉED WITH CURRANTS

▶ 1/2 cup red Lillet or sweet red
vermouth

1/2 to 2/3 cup dried currants

3/4 cup finely sliced sweet onion,
such as Maui or Vidalia

1 tablespoon olive oil

2 tablespoons unsalted butter

4 medium beets, peeled and thinly
sliced (about 1 1/2 pounds)

Garnish: Fresh tarragon or parsley,
chopped fine

*This inspired combination was created by the legendary Josephine Araldo
and Robert Reynolds for their San Francisco restaurant, Le Trou. Since
fresh currants are hard to get all year-round, try the dried ones.*

In a small saucepan, heat the Lillet and add the currants. Let this steep off the heat for about 1 hour.

Sauté the onion in the olive oil for 8 minutes, until golden. Add the butter and beets. Cover and sweat over low heat for 1 minute, until the beets are almost tender. Add the currants, raise the heat, and sauté until the beets are tender and the sauce has reduced and is slightly sticky. Serve sprinkled with a little chopped fresh tarragon or parsley.

CELERIAC, PARSNIPS, AND TURNIPS
SAUTÉED IN CHAMPAGNE

Serves 4

Here is a root vegetable combination that achieves greatness with the addition of a little leftover bubbly.

▶ 1 cup 3/4-inch celeriac cubes

1 cup 3/4-inch parsnip cubes

1 cup 3/4-inch white turnip cubes

1 tablespoon fruity olive oil

Champagne

Steam the celeriac, parsnips, and turnips until they are half cooked and not quite soft enough to be pierced by a fork. For best results, steam one vegetable at a time. Do not overcook or the roots will become mushy when you sauté them.

Heat the olive oil in a skillet. Add the root vegetable cubes and sauté until lightly browned and tender. Deglaze the pan with champagne, boil until reduced, and serve. Offer low-fat sour cream or kefir at the table.

FRIZZLED BRUSSELS SPROUTS
SAUTÉED WITH GREEN GRAPES

▶ 1 1/4 pounds brussels sprouts, trimmed

1 tablespoon olive oil

1/2 cup finely chopped leeks, white part only

1/2 cup vegetable broth

1/2 teaspoon sugar

2 teaspoons fresh ginger cut into thin matchsticks (optional)

1/2 pound seedless green grapes (see Note)

Pinch of ground sage (optional)

Salt and ground black pepper to taste

You will enjoy the entertaining contrast in both texture and flavor between sprouts and grapes in this dish. The sprouts appear frizzled because they are shredded, just as cabbage would be for coleslaw.

Shred each brussels sprout as you would a cabbage for coleslaw. Use a sharp knife and slice the sprouts very thin down the width, discarding the bitter little bottoms.

Heat the olive oil in a skillet and sauté the leeks until tender but not browned. Add the broth, sugar, and shredded sprouts. Add ginger, if desired. Cook until the sprouts are tender.

Slice the grapes down the middle into coins, about 3 per grape. Add the grapes to the sprouts and heat through completely. Adjust seasoning with sage, if desired, and salt and pepper to taste. Serve immediately.

NOTE: A longer finger variety of grape is easiest to cut, but any ripe but firm green grape will do.

KITFO COLLARDS

Ethiopian yegomen kitfo — spiced collards and curds — is generally served as a side dish. I think it rates a more substantial place at the table. In this recipe, I use a whole-milk feta that is creamy and not too salty in place of the more traditional buttermilk curds.

▶ 3 cups collard greens, stemmed and coarsely chopped

1 1/2 cups finely minced leeks, white and green parts

2 tablespoons olive oil

3 cloves garlic, minced

1 teaspoon freshly grated ginger

1/4 teaspoon very finely minced jalapeño, or more to taste

1/2 teaspoon cardamom

1/2 teaspoon ground coriander

1/2 teaspoon grated nutmeg

1/4 teaspoon ground cinnamon

8 ounces feta cheese

Steam the collards until they are a bright dark green. Do not overcook. Cool. Squeeze the greens slightly in a towel to remove any excess moisture. Chop the greens; set aside.

In a skillet, sauté the leeks in the oil until tender, about 5 minutes. Add the garlic, ginger, and jalapeño. Sauté over low heat until the garlic is soft and the ginger deepens in color. Add the cardamom, coriander, nutmeg, and cinnamon.

Transfer the collard greens to the skillet and mix with the leeks and spices. Crumble the feta cheese into bite-size pieces. Add to the collards, warm through, and serve.

This is delicious over tube pasta or as a side accompaniment to Yassa au Tempeh (see page 187).

HASH BROWNS WITH VEGETARIAN SAUSAGE

▶ 2 tablespoons olive oil

1/2 pound vegetarian sausage or
steamed and crumbled tempeh
mixed with 1 teaspoon poultry
seasoning and a pinch of red
pepper (cayenne), or 1/3 cup soy
bacon bits made from tempeh

2 teaspoons shoyu

1 cup chopped onion

1 teaspoon sugar

1 1/2 to 2 pounds yellow Finn
potatoes cut into small cubes and
placed in water to keep from
browning

2 tablespoons canola oil

Salt and ground black pepper
to taste

Garnish: Yogurt Cheese (see page
375), kefir, or low-fat sour cream

*If you don't want to make your own sausage, try using one of the many
very acceptable and tasty vegetarian products that are widely available.
Or use a crumbled tempeh seasoned with either sage and garlic or, for a
quick flavoring, powdered poultry seasoning.*

Heat 1 tablespoon of the olive oil in a small skillet. Crumble the sausage into the pan and add the shoyu to darken the color. Cook over medium heat while stirring until golden brown and crisp. Set aside.

Sauté the onion in the remaining tablespoon of olive oil until it begins to brown. Add the sugar and stir until caramelized. Set aside.

Drain the potatoes and pat them dry. Heat the canola oil in a large skillet and sauté the potatoes over medium-low heat, turning with a spatula until golden brown on all sides. When the potatoes are done, add the onions and crispy bits of sausage. Season with salt and pepper. Heat through and serve. Garnish with Yogurt Cheese.

SAUTÉED ROOT VEGETABLE STICKS

Serves 4

The beauty and charm of this dish depend on making all the sticks a uniform size. I prefer a short 2-inch stick. This version is sautéed in sesame and canola oil, but olive oil will work, too. If you find you want to deglaze with a little liquid, try 1 tablespoon of dark rum mixed with 1 tablespoon of water, or, if you are a beer fan, add 1/4 cup of dark beer.

▶ 1 cup parsnip sticks
(2 inches long, 1/2 inch thick)

1 cup carrot sticks
(2 inches long, 1/2 inch thick)

1 cup rutabaga sticks
(2 inches long, 1/2 inch thick)

1 tablespoon canola oil

2 teaspoons toasted sesame oil

1 or 2 cloves garlic, minced

1/4 teaspoon freshly grated
nutmeg

Salt and ground black pepper
to taste

Garnish: 2 tablespoons chopped
chives

Steam the parsnips, carrots, and rutabaga until they are half cooked and not quite soft enough to be pierced by a fork. For best results, steam one vegetable at a time. Do not overcook or the roots will become mushy when you sauté them.

Heat the canola and sesame oils in a nonstick skillet. Add the vegetable sticks and toss over medium heat to combine. Add the garlic and nutmeg and season with salt and pepper. Sauté until tender. Serve sprinkled with chopped chives.

ZUCCHINI RIBBONS SAUTÉED
WITH HONEY AND SUNFLOWER SEEDS

▶ 1 tablespoon olive oil

2/3 cup chopped onion

2 medium yellow zucchini, sliced into thin ribbons

2 medium green zucchini, sliced into thin ribbons

1 clove garlic, minced

1/2 teaspoon dried oregano

1 1/2 tablespoons honey

1 tablespoon amaranth flour (optional)

1/4 to 1/2 cup lightly toasted sunflower seeds

Garnish: Lemon wedges

There are several ways of slicing zucchini into long pappardelle-like ribbons. You can use a regular vegetable peeler or a mandoline, but I find a cheese plane the easiest method. Simply pull the plane down along the length of the zucchini. Each slicing stroke will create a thin, noodle-like strand.

This dish is based on one of my earliest favorite vegetarian dishes from The New York Times Natural Foods Cookbook. *The amaranth flour adds a nutty flavor and an unusual coarse texture.*

Heat the olive oil in a large nonstick skillet and add the onion. Sauté for about 8 minutes or until golden. Add the yellow and green zucchini ribbons. Sauté until golden and tender, about 7 minutes.

Stir in the garlic and oregano and drizzle the honey in a long thin stream, covering the ribbons evenly. Sprinkle on the flour and the sunflower seeds. Toss gently. The sauce will thicken slightly. Serve with lemon wedges.

BRAISED

VEGETABLES: BRAISED

CONTENTS

RAGOUT OF SWISS CHARD
IN GINGERED MISO

Serves 4 to 6

In this richly flavored ragout, Swiss chard braises in liquid with butter or oil, which is then reduced until it emulsifies. The chard is transformed during the braising process from a delicate green into one with a rich meaty flavor. Though red or green chard can be used, this flavor comes through particularly well with red.

If you want to add a protein to the ragout and serve it as a main course, try slicing some aburage into it.

▶ 1/4 cup white wine

1 1/2 tablespoons mellow white miso

1/2 cup currants or golden raisins

1/4 cup garlic cloves, peeled and sliced into rounds

1 tablespoon fresh ginger cut into thin matchsticks

3 tablespoons fruity olive oil

4 to 6 cups chopped Swiss chard leaves

Bring the wine and 1 1/4 cups of water to a boil in a large saucepan. Whisk in and dissolve the miso. Add the currants, garlic, ginger, and oil. Bring to a simmer. Add the chard. Cover and cook until the greens have wilted, about 2 minutes. Uncover and stir the chard and broth. Raise the heat and cook uncovered for 5 minutes or until the sauce reduces and emulsifies. Coat the chard with the sauce before you serve it.

RAGOUT OF CABBAGE
IN BUTTER WITH STAR ANISE

▶ 2 tablespoons olive oil

2 tablespoons unsalted butter

1/2 cup vegetable broth

1 teaspoon white miso, dissolved in 1 tablespoon water

1 star anise, or pinch of ground anise, to taste

1 cinnamon stick (optional)

4 cups coarsely chopped cabbage

Ground black pepper to taste

This is a simple but delicious ragout. Be sure to remove some of the darker leaves from the cabbage and do not use the bitter core. Star anise is very aromatic. Either grind it and use a judicious pinch of its powder, or place a star in with your broth, wait until you smell it, then taste the broth and remove the star when you feel it has done its job.

In a saucepan, combine the oil, butter, broth, dissolved miso, anise, and cinnamon stick if desired. Bring to a simmer. Add the cabbage. Cook covered for about 10 minutes, then uncover and cook for another 5 minutes or until the broth reduces and the sauce remains. Season with pepper. Stir to coat the cabbage with the sauce. Serve with Tempeh in Coconut Mango Rice (see page 184).

COLLARDS BRAISED WITH
TOMATOES AND THYME

Serves 4

The longer you cook these, the tastier they are. They are also great served over noodles.

- ▶ **4 cups chopped greens: kale or collards**

  1 1/2 cups peeled, seeded, chopped tomatoes

  1/2 cup red wine

  1 teaspoon sugar

  1 tablespoon vegetable bouillon powder

  3 cloves garlic, minced

  1 or 2 sprigs fresh thyme

  1 cinnamon stick

  2 tablespoons fruity olive oil

Combine all ingredients in a nonreactive saucepan and simmer covered for 1 hour. Uncover and cook another 15 minutes, or longer to reduce slightly if you prefer a thicker sauce.

Serve as a side dish or over noodles.

APPLES AND SAUERKRAUT

- 1/2 cup chopped leeks, white part only

2 tablespoons fruity olive oil

1 pound sauerkraut, preferably from a jar, squeezed dry of juice

2 pounds apples, peeled, cored, and cut into chunks

1 tablespoon sugar

1/4 cup dark rum

1/4 cup apple cider

1 whole clove

Good with vegetable sausages.

In a nonreactive saucepan, sauté the leeks in the olive oil for 8 minutes or until golden. Add the sauerkraut, apples, and sugar. Stir in the rum and reduce over high heat until the alcohol cooks out. Add the cider and clove. Simmer uncovered until the apples soften and cook through. Serve hot.

Serves 4 to 6

Where greens are concerned, youth isn't everything. This dish tastes light and flavorful in the spring when greens are young and small, and it has an altogether different depth of character when older greens are used, later in the season. I like to cook the young leaves only briefly; older greens become less tough and more interesting the longer they braise. Either way, this is a dramatic dish for company, because so few people ever see a big bowl full of greens arrive at the table. Sometimes I like to include a chile pepper to braise along with darker, more mature greens.

▶ 2 tablespoons fruity olive oil

2 cups chopped leeks, both white and light green parts

1 cup pitted kalamata or Gaeta olives or spicy green olives (see recipe page 109)

3 cloves garlic, minced

1 1/4 cups vegetable broth

1 cup bok choy greens, rinsed and coarsely chopped

1 cup green or red kale, rinsed, stemmed, and sliced into ribbons

1 cup collard greens, rinsed and stemmed

1 cup beet greens or mustard greens, rinsed and stemmed

1 cup chard leaves, rinsed and coarsely chopped

Ground black pepper to taste (optional)

1 small fresh chile, or Chipotle Purée to taste (see page 370), for older greens (optional)

2 or 3 fresh bay leaves, or 1 dried (optional)

1/2 teaspoon ground allspice (optional)

In a large saucepan, heat the olive oil and sauté the leeks for 8 minutes or until golden. Add the olives, garlic, and broth and bring to a simmer. Stir in the greens and simmer covered until the leaves turn color. If the greens are young, or you want to cook them only briefly, cook uncovered until the liquid evaporates and olive oil coats all the greens and serve. Do not add salt, but add fresh pepper if you are so inclined. If it is later in the season and the greens are older and tougher, let them simmer gently, covered, with a chile, fresh bay leaves, and allspice for as much as an hour, then serve them with their sauce. Or cook them uncovered and let the liquid reduce and the oil coat the leaves of the greens.

RED CHARD RAGOUT
WITH BLACK MUSHROOMS

▶ 6 to 8 dried Chinese black mushrooms

1 tablespoon miso

2 tablespoons olive oil

1 bunch red chard (8 to 10 leaves, or about 3 cups), stemmed and rinsed

1 large potato, peeled and cut into small chunks (about 1 cup)

1 large tomato, peeled, seeded, chopped

4 cloves garlic, sliced

1 cup watercress, leaves only

2 tablespoons kefir, Yogurt Cheese (see page 375), or low-fat sour cream

The color and variety of vegetables involved here make it an elegant choice to serve to company: Red chard gives this dish robust flavor, the kefir adds a Stroganoff-like richness, and the watercress contributes a peppery bite. It is fine as an entree or side dish.

Soak the mushrooms in hot water to cover until soft, 15 to 30 minutes. Drain, remove and discard the stems, and slice the mushrooms.

Combine the miso with 1 cup of water and the olive oil in a saucepan. Bring to a simmer. Add the mushrooms, chard, potato, tomato, and garlic. Cover and simmer gently at least 10 minutes or until the potatoes are soft.

Add the watercress and kefir and simmer another 5 minutes.

As an entrée, serve with rice or grains. As a side dish, serve with a simple bean dish, rice, or grains.

VARIATION: I have at times used only 1/2 cup white potatoes and added 1/3 cup diced beets, and 1/2 cup diced sweet potato.

CHINESE LONG BEANS AND ELEPHANT GARLIC OVER PARSNIP MIREPOIX

Serves 2 to 4

You've seen them in the market in Chinatown and wondered if they'd fit in your pot — or any pot, for that matter — and if they taste the same as green beans as you know them. Dau gok, or long beans, are available in light and dark shades of green, the dark being firmer, less bland, and, to my taste, more desirable. These beans are slightly bitter (think of them as the broccoli raab of green beans), with a crisper yet denser texture than the green beans most of us are used to snapping and stripping the strings off. There is something very entertaining about slicing one's way through a long green bean, as though it were a steak. Usually dau gok are sliced into pieces, but here I use them whole for a dramatic presentation when braised over mild-flavored elephant garlic and a contrasting sweet parsnip mirepoix.

▶ **THE MIREPOIX**

3 tablespoons olive oil

2 cups diced parsnips

1/2 cup diced celery

1/2 cup diced turnips

1 head elephant garlic, or 2 heads large-cloved garlic, peeled

1 cup white wine

1/2 cup vegetable broth

1/2 teaspoon white miso

2 tablespoons fresh savory, or 1 tablespoon dried

1 pound Chinese long beans, rinsed

Fresh lemon juice (optional)

Make the mirepoix: Using a casserole or wide pot with a cover, heat the olive oil and sauté the parsnips, celery, and turnips until golden, about 5 to 8 minutes over medium-low heat. Stir in the garlic. Add the white wine and boil to reduce the liquid by half.

Add the broth, miso, and savory and simmer slowly, covered, for 15 to 20 minutes or until the garlic is very tender and sweet. Uncover, raise the heat slightly, add the long beans, and boil until the liquid is reduced and the beans are tender. The cooking liquid should be on its way to emulsifying.

Serve the beans, garlic, and parsnip mirepoix over brown rice and pour sauce over all. A squeeze of fresh lemon juice is optional.

STEAMED AND MASHED

VEGETABLES: STEAMED AND MASHED

CONTENTS

There are several good reasons to steam vegetables. Steaming is easy and adds no calories or unnecessary oils and fats, and the simplicity of preparation really lets you taste the flavor and texture of the food you are preparing. Steaming can be an end in itself, or a point of departure for a dish, as in the technique of steaming mushrooms before you sauté them so that they soak up less oil. Other, more complicated preparations such as puddings and custards may be steamed as well.

To mash, or purée, is another matter entirely. It removes all texture beyond that of *smooth* and lets you savor the essence of a vegetable. A purée lets the cook marry flavors in a simple but concentrated way, like mashed potatoes and turnips or rutabaga and pears.

POTATO CAKES
WITH ROASTED GARLIC AND TARRAGON

▶ 1 1/2 pounds boiled potatoes, peeled (2 1/2 cups mashed)

1 egg yolk plus 3 egg whites

2 tablespoons clarified butter

1 tablespoon Roasted Garlic purée (see page 373), or 2 fresh cloves garlic, minced

2 tablespoons olive oil

2 teaspoons fresh tarragon, or 1 teaspoon dried

2 teaspoons fresh chervil, or 1 teaspoon dried

2 teaspoons chopped fresh parsley, or 1 teaspoon dried

1 teaspoon freshly grated nutmeg, or to taste

Salt and ground white pepper to taste

1/2 to 2/3 cup all-purpose flour

2 tablespoons kefir or Yogurt Cheese (see page 375)

These are based on a recipe for pommes de terre en lichettes by Simone Beck. I have lightened the recipe, cutting back on both butter and egg yolks. Use Idaho baking potatoes; the drier the potato, the better the dough for these easy-to-make festive little cakes.

Preheat the oven to 375 degrees.

If the potatoes are wet, place them in a preheated oven for about 5 minutes to dry out. Mash them by hand, or pulse them quickly in a food processor with the egg yolk, egg whites, butter, and roasted garlic purée. (Too much time in the processor will give the potatoes a gluey texture.) Add enough kefir to smooth the potato purée without making it too wet. Add half the herbs and 1 teaspoon of nutmeg. Season with salt and pepper to taste.

Turn out onto a floured board. Knead the potato purée into the flour, trying to shape into a cohesive dough. Break off little pieces of dough. Flatten each piece by hand or with a rolling pin to 1/2-inch-thick cakes. Arrange on baking sheets.

Heat the olive oil and combine with the remaining half of the herbs. Brush the tops of the potato cakes with the seasoned oil and add more grated nutmeg, to taste. Bake for 20 to 30 minutes, or until nicely browned.

MASHED CELERY ROOT WITH FENNEL, SHALLOTS, ROSEMARY, AND PERNOD

Serves 4

I prefer to steam rather than boil vegetables in order to keep them as dry as possible so that they have a firm body and texture when they are mashed. If you want a firmer combination, try adding more potato. Steam the vegetables a little longer than you would if you were serving them sliced, especially the fennel. Mash by hand.

- ▶ 1/2 cup coarsely chopped fennel
- 1 cup cubed celery root (celeriac, or knob celery)
- 3/4 cup cubed potatoes
- 2 tablespoons olive oil
- 1 cup chopped shallots
- 1 teaspoon sugar
- 1 teaspoon Pernod
- 1 tablespoon finely chopped fresh rosemary, or 1 teaspoon dried
- Salt and ground black pepper to taste
- Garnish: 1 tablespoon chopped chives, fruity olive oil

Put the fennel in a single layer in a steamer basket over 2 inches of boiling water. Cover and steam until very tender when tested with the tip of a sharp knife. Transfer to the workbowl of a food processor.

Put the celery root cubes and potatoes in a single layer in the steamer basket; steam until soft. Remove from the heat and set aside.

In a small skillet, heat the oil and sauté the shallots over medium-low heat until softened but not brown. Add the sugar, cover, and sweat the shallots for a few minutes. Add the Pernod and cook uncovered until the liquid evaporates. Transfer to the food processor.

Process the fennel and shallots to a smooth purée. Mash the celery root and potatoes by hand in a saucepan and add the fennel mixture and rosemary. Mix well, season with salt and pepper, and heat until hot. Serve topped with chives and a drizzle of fruity olive oil.

MASHED PARSNIPS AND
CAULIFLOWER WITH MILLET

Serves 6 to 8

▶ 2/3 cup finely chopped onion

1/4 cup olive oil plus 1 tablespoon
olive oil or toasted sesame oil

1 teaspoon sugar

1 cup millet

6 cloves garlic, whole

2 cups vegetable broth, heated

2 teaspoons minced fresh winter
savory or thyme, or 1 teaspoon
dried

2 cups sliced parsnips
(1/4 inch thick)

1 cup cauliflower florets

Salt and ground black pepper
to taste

Lightly mashed vegetables folded into grains can be wonderful. Especially good are kasha and millet. Here, sweet parsnips and earthy cauliflower are lightly mashed, then added to the grain. This great combination brings out the sweet and substantial qualities of millet.

It is important to cook the millet slowly and let it steam through at the end, which really opens up its flavor. Do not let the millet stand too long; prepare it so that it rests no more than 30 minutes before you fold the other vegetables into it. Millet tends to harden as it stands, and the success of this dish depends on the texture of a fluffy grain.

In a heavy saucepan, sauté the onion in 1 tablespoon of olive or sesame oil until softened. Add the sugar, cover, and sweat the onions for a few minutes. Stir in the millet, whole garlic cloves, and hot vegetable broth. Cover and simmer over low heat for 35 to 45 minutes, until the liquid is absorbed. Turn off the heat and let stand for 15 minutes to steam through.

Heat the 1/4 cup of olive oil and add the minced herbs. Set aside.

Put the parsnips and cauliflower in a single layer in a steamer basket. Cover and steam over 2 inches of boiling water until tender when pierced with the tip of a knife. Transfer to a bowl and mash by hand. Season with salt and pepper.

Spill the millet into a large serving bowl. Gently fold in the mashed vegetables. Serve while still hot. Offer a light drizzle of the warm olive oil and herbs over the millet.

WILD MUSHROOM AND RADISH PUDDING

Serves 2 to 4

Here is an interpretation of another Huberts favorite, but made without Chinese sausage. This radish pudding can be steamed in individual ramekins in about 20 minutes, or in one baking dish, as it is presented here. The pudding can be served as is or, more traditionally, cut into squares and then sautéed until crisp and golden on both sides.

▶ 1 tablespoon toasted sesame oil

3/4 cup finely chopped shiitake mushrooms

2 1/2 cups freshly grated daikon radish (about 2 pounds)

1/2 cup chopped scallions, both white and green parts

4 ounces (about 1 cup) rice flour

3 tablespoons chopped fresh cilantro leaves

2 teaspoons shoyu

1 tablespoon minced fresh ginger

1 tablespoon sugar

1/2 teaspoon ground star anise

1/2 teaspoon grated nutmeg

1/4 teaspoon ground cinnamon

Have ready an oiled or buttered shallow 4-cup Pyrex baking dish that will fit into a bamboo steamer.

Heat the sesame oil in a skillet, add the mushrooms, and sauté over high heat, stirring often, until they begin to color, 5 to 7 minutes. Remove from the heat, cool slightly, and combine the daikon and any of its juices with the mushrooms.

Stir in the scallions, flour, cilantro, and the rest of the ingredients. Mix well. Transfer to the prepared dish, cover, and steam over 2 inches of boiling water for about 1 hour or longer, depending on the width of the pudding. Replenish the boiling water as needed. The pudding is done when firm to the touch.

STEAMED RATATOUILLE
IN TOMATO AND RED PEPPER COULIS

▶ 2 scant cups mushroom caps

1 cup sliced or chunked long, thin, seedless Japanese eggplant

1 cup sliced or chunked yellow crookneck squash

1 cup sliced or chunked zucchini

1 1/2 cups sliced asparagus

1 cup chopped onion

3 tablespoons olive oil

1 tablespoon sugar, or more to taste

4 cups peeled, seeded, and chopped tomatoes

4 cloves garlic, minced

1/4 cup chopped fresh basil

1 3/4 cups roasted red bell pepper strips

1 tablespoon fresh thyme leaves, or 1 teaspoon dried

1 tablespoon fresh marjoram, or 1 teaspoon dried

Salt and ground black pepper to taste

Ratatouille is usually made of sautéed vegetables that soak up oil like sponges, but the vegetables in this version are steamed first, then simmered in a light red pepper and fresh tomato coulis. The result is a different ratatouille, to be sure, but a fine alternative to the familiar classic.

Steam the mushrooms until tender. Cool and slice; set aside.

Steam the vegetables one variety at a time until tender: eggplant, yellow squash, zucchini, and asparagus. Set aside.

Sauté the onion in 1 tablespoon of the olive oil with the sugar until golden, about 7 minutes. Add the tomatoes, garlic, and basil. Simmer uncovered for 10 to 15 minutes or until the tomatoes have melted down and darkened. Using a blender or food processor, purée the onions, tomatoes, and 3/4 cup of the roasted red peppers.

In a large saucepan, heat the remaining 2 tablespoons of olive oil. Sauté the eggplant, squash, and zucchini until golden. Add the tomato and pepper sauce, thyme, and marjoram and simmer, covered, for 15 minutes. Add the asparagus and remaining roasted red pepper. Season with salt and pepper to taste. Simmer for another 5 to 10 minutes uncovered or until the sauce has been reduced and absorbed by the vegetables.

STEAMED RED KALE
WITH WHITE MISO DRESSING

Serves 4 to 6

Hearty kale stands up to the sweet and salty quality of this thick, rich-tasting dressing. Red Russian kale with its red stems and almost oak-shaped leaves has become a familiar sight at farmers' markets around the country. It has a robust, meaty flavor we associate with kale or collards, and its stems are more tender than those of some other of its brassica cousins.

▶ 2 bunches red kale, rinsed and stemmed

3 tablespoons white miso

2 tablespoons cider vinegar

1 tablespoon honey

1 1/2 teaspoons Dijon mustard

1 1/2 teaspoons sesame paste

1 tablespoon white wine or sake

Tear or chop the kale into bite-size pieces. Steam for 3 minutes or until it changes color. You may steam longer if you like your kale well done.

In a serving bowl, combine the miso, vinegar, honey, mustard, sesame paste, and wine. Blend well. Toss the kale in the dressing and serve immediately.

STEAMED ROOT VEGETABLES
WITH BLUE CHEESE RÉMOULADE

Serves 6 to 8

▸ 1 cup raw parsnips cut into 2-inch sticks

1 cup turnips cut into 2-inch sticks

1 cup rutabaga cut into 2-inch sticks

1 cup celeriac cut into 2-inch sticks

1 cup beets cut into 2-inch sticks

1 to 2 cups lotus root (available in Asian markets) cut into thin, crisp rounds

1 whole egg plus 1 egg white (see Note)

4 teaspoons fresh lemon juice, or more to taste

1 teaspoon Dijon mustard

2 cloves garlic, minced

Here is an amusing variation on celeriac rémoulade. Cut all the vegetables into the same length sticks for the best visual presentation. The lotus root offers a lovely contrast of shape.

1 cup olive or canola oil or a combination of both

Salt and ground black pepper to taste

2/3 to 1 cup crumbled blue cheese or Gorgonzola

1/2 cup minced sweet onion, such as Maui or Vidalia

1/4 cup chopped cornichons, gherkins, or for a sweeter flavor use sweet pickles

1 tablespoon capers, rinsed of salt or brine

Put the parsnip sticks in one layer in a steamer basket, cover, and steam over 2 inches of boiling water just long enough to serve al dente. Repeat this process with the turnips, rutabaga, celeriac, beets, and lotus root. As the vegetables are cooked, transfer them to a large bowl.

Place the egg, egg white, lemon juice, mustard, and garlic in a blender. Process and slowly add the oil in a thin stream to make a thick mayonnaise. Season with salt, pepper, and more lemon juice, if desired. Fold in the blue cheese or Gorgonzola, onion, cornichons, and capers.

Pour the rémoulade sauce over the steamed vegetables and gently toss until well combined. Or serve the sauce on the side.

NOTE: If the possibility of salmonella from raw eggs is a concern, you may use 1 cup of store-bought mayonnaise in place of the egg, lemon juice, and oil. Omit the processing in a blender and simply stir the mustard, garlic, and seasonings into the mayonnaise. Fold in the blue cheese, onion, cornichons, and capers as directed.

244

MASHED ROOT VEGETABLES
WITH CARDAMOM AND CRISPY LEEKS

Serves 4

Roasting the root vegetables used for this dish gives it a rich, deep flavor. If you can find them, use small turnips, which are mellower than big ones.

▶ **2 cups peeled and chunked parsnips**

1 cup peeled and chunked white turnips

1 tablespoon plus 1 teaspoon olive oil

1 medium potato, baked in jacket or steamed

1 teaspoon ground cardamom, or more to taste

Salt and ground black pepper to taste

2 teaspoons clarified butter

1 cup leeks cut into thin rounds (white and pale green parts)

Preheat the oven to 350 degrees.

Rub the parsnips and turnips with 1 tablespoon of olive oil. Place them in a single layer in a baking pan and bake uncovered for about 1 hour or until tender. If you have baked the potato, scoop out the flesh (you should have about 1 cup). Cut away any portion of the turnips or parsnips that may have turned tough or too dark while roasting. Mash the vegetables together by hand or quickly pulse in a food processor. Season with cardamom, salt, and pepper.

Combine the clarified butter with the remaining teaspoon of olive oil in a skillet and sauté the leeks over medium-high heat until crisp and golden brown.

Serve the mashed vegetables with the leeks on top.

RUTABAGA AND WINTER SQUASH WITH NUTMEG

▶ 2 cups peeled rutabaga chunks

2 cups peeled kobocha or acorn squash chunks

1/2 teaspoon ground cinnamon

1/2 teaspoon grated nutmeg

1 tablespoon honey, or to taste

1/2 cup grated sharp white Cheddar (optional)

Garnish: 1/4 cup chopped fresh cilantro

I prefer a rich, meaty squash, such as hokkaido or kobocha, for this recipe. You may wish to add more honey to suit your own taste. I mash the vegetables by hand since I prefer this dish with some texture. I like grating a little Cheddar into it, or topping it with a dollop of kefir.

Put the rutabaga chunks in one layer in a steamer basket, cover, and steam over boiling water until tender. Transfer to a saucepan. Steam the squash until tender and add to the rutabaga. Mash the vegetables coarsely, leaving some texture. Add the cinnamon, nutmeg, and honey to taste. Heat through and serve hot as is, or mixed with a little Cheddar. Sprinkle cilantro on top just before serving.

BAKED SWEET POTATOES SMOTHERED
WITH LONG-COOKED SPICY GREENS

Serves 4

I love this dish. It's a great meal with a variety of contrasting flavors. The combination of bitter and spicy greens with collards works nicely, but if you are not a fan of such heat, substitute collards, kale, or any other long-cooking mild greens. Although I am always a great fan of collard stalks, in this dish, only the leaves are used.

If you can spare the calories and fat, you may wish to scoop out the sweet potato flesh and add butter and cream to it, as you would a stuffed potato, though I think it is delicious without such additions, and the collards napped in light sauce add enough of a luxuriant touch.

▶ 4 medium to medium-large sweet potatoes or yams

1 teaspoon canola oil

1 pound collard greens, or 8 cups loosely packed collards, leaves only

1/4 pound mustard or turnip greens

1 1/2 cups vegetable broth

1/2 cup white wine

3 tablespoons fruity olive oil

4 cloves garlic, sliced

1 jalapeño, or 1/4 teaspoon red pepper flakes (optional)

Preheat the oven to 400 degrees. Scrub the potatoes, pat dry, and rub with canola oil. Pierce the skin in 2 or 3 places. Place on a baking sheet and bake for 1 hour or until the potatoes are soft.

While the potatoes are baking, bring a large pot of water to a boil and plunge in the greens to rid them of bitterness. Boil just until their color turns, then drain and refresh them under cold water. Chop the greens into bite-size pieces.

Combine the broth, wine, olive oil, and garlic in a saucepan and bring to a boil. Lower the heat to a simmer, put in the greens, and cover the pot. Every few minutes, move the greens around. When the greens have wilted sufficiently, add the jalapeño, if desired. Taste your broth every 10 minutes to see if the jalapeño has imparted enough heat for your taste and remove the chile as soon as you like the flavor. Cook the greens for 45 minutes to 1 hour. When they are done, remove the cover and cook over high heat until the liquid evaporates and oil coats the leaves.

Serve the sweet potato in the center of a plate. Open the potato and push the baked flesh up and out over the skin by pinching the sides of the potato with your fingers. Using a slotted spoon, place a generous amount of collards over the potato and serve.

FIGS AND FENNEL EN PAPILLOTE

2 bulbs fennel

1 tablespoon olive oil, or as needed

Salt and ground black pepper
to taste

4 to 6 figs, green or black

4 thin slices chèvre cheese

6 pitted, chopped kalamata olives
(optional)

It is my dream to one day live in a stone house surrounded by fig trees. Although this dream has yet to come true, happily, the figs are real enough whenever I prepare this lovely and simple steamed dish baked in paper, or en papillote.

Have ready 2 to 4 pieces of parchment paper, 10 by 12 inches. Preheat the oven to 375 degrees.

Cut off the feathery tops and stalks from the fennel and remove any tough outer layers. Trim the base. Shred the bulbs, cutting across the width; you should have 1 1/2 to 2 cups of shredded fennel.

Heat 1 tablespoon of olive oil in a skillet and sauté the fennel over medium-high heat until softened, 5 to 7 minutes. Season with salt and pepper.

Slice the figs across the width into circles or coins.

Fold each piece of parchment paper in half lengthwise and cut its edges to form a heart shape. Open each sheet. Divide the sautéed fennel equally into 2 or 4 portions and place the fennel on one half of the paper heart.

Arrange the sliced figs and chèvre on top of the fennel. Sprinkle with chopped olives, only if desired, and drizzle a little olive oil over the figs and goat cheese.

To close the paper heart and seal it for baking, start at the inside curve of the heart and begin making small folds that follow along the curve of the heart. At the very bottom, the pointy end of the heart, make your final fold and either fold your last pleat under the paper package or just twist it to seal.

Place on a baking sheet and bake for about 10 minutes. Steam will puff up the paper from inside, so open with care; use a sharp knife or scissors and keep your fingers safe from the gust of hot steam as it escapes after the first cut is made.

SOUFFLÉS

VEGETABLES: SOUFFLÉS

CONTENTS

To bouilli or not to bouilli, that is the question.

A bouilli is a floury roux enriched with egg yolks into which a soufflé's main ingredient, or flavor, is incorporated before being folded into whipped egg whites and baked. Defenders of the classic soufflé stand on one side of the bouilli issue while those trying to rid soufflés of extra empty calories stand on the other. In fact, the argument over whether or not to turn a culinary prima donna into a healthier gal seems a mere distraction from the more obvious question of whether or not to indulge in the egg in the first place.

I will leave the question of cholesterol up to your own conscience, but I assure you that soufflés *can* be made without a bouilli. They may be a little heartier and richer than those without, but, in compensation, they will perhaps be a touch more stable.

Owing to the miraculous leavening power of the egg, soufflés are more reliable creatures than any of us have been led to believe. Swiss chef Frédy Giradet is credited with discovering that soufflés can be successfully made without use of a bouilli, although American authors — all women — reported this same culinary phenomenon as early as the 1940s. One food writer categorized these lighter soufflés as "puffs." All of which goes to prove that what is culinary discovery to one generation is mere curiosity to another.

Soufflés can actually be made by several different methods, depending on your taste for butter, flour, and egg yolks. The classic soufflé uses a butter and flour roux and an equal amount of egg yolks and whites. A lighter soufflé can be prepared by forgoing roux. The basic recipe can be made lighter still by using fewer egg yolks than whites, say two yolks to five or six whites.

Parmesan cheese plays a noticeably important part in many soufflé recipes, and not just in this book, because it is a simple solution to the need for a strong, sharp, and distinct flavor. Ways of ensuring richer flavor without resorting to cheese include: using 1 or 2 teaspoons of a good vegetable bouillon powder, garlic, concentrated dry soup mixes, ground dried herbs, such prepared vegetarian seasonings as Spike brand or others available in your natural food store, Dijon mustard, shrimp paste or sauce, nuoc nam, chilies, sambal oelek, Thai curry spices, Szechuan hot bean paste, or other ethnic flavorings. If you use a powdered broth, do not season your mixture with salt, or else use salt sparingly.

COMPASS PÂTÉ SOUFFLÉ

Serves 2 to 4

In order to make this delicious and surprisingly textured soufflé, you first have to make the Compass pâté, a lovely and rich-flavored pâté that features minced mushrooms, onions, crumbled tofu, and walnuts. It is easy enough to assemble, and if you are preparing some for company, mix up an extra batch.

▶ 1/4 cup grated Parmesan cheese (optional)

1 cup Compass Pâté (see page 74), at room temperature

Salt and ground black pepper to taste

1 teaspoon vegetable bouillon powder (optional)

2 egg yolks plus 5 egg whites

Pinch of cream of tartar (optional)

Preheat the oven to 375 degrees. Butter a 1 1/2-quart soufflé dish and place it in the freezer to chill.

Add Parmesan cheese to the Compass pâté. Season with salt, pepper, and 1 teaspoon of vegetable bouillon powder if a stronger flavor is desired. Stir to combine thoroughly.

Using an electric beater or a balloon whisk, beat the egg yolks until they thicken and turn a pale yellow. Fold the yolks into the pâté mixture.

Whip the egg whites with the cream of tartar until smooth creamy peaks are formed. Stir one-third of the whites into the pâté mixture. When well blended, gently fold in the rest of the whites.

Pour the mixture into the prepared soufflé dish and bake for 20 to 25 minutes or until the soufflé has risen and the center seems firm and not excessively jiggly. Serve at once.

MIREPOIX SOUFFLÉ

▶ 1 tablespoon olive oil

1/3 cup diced carrots

1/3 cup diced parsnips

1/3 cup diced rutabaga

1/3 cup diced yellow or green zucchini skin, seeds removed (skin and a little pith used for color)

1/3 cup diced celery

1 teaspoon sugar

1/4 cup white wine

2 cloves garlic, minced

2 tablespoons chopped fresh dill

1/3 cup grated Parmesan cheese

1 teaspoon vegetable bouillon powder

Salt and ground black pepper to taste

2 or 3 egg yolks plus 5 egg whites

Pinch of cream of tartar (optional)

A mélange of diced vegetables, the sort usually hidden under pot roasts, makes an especially pretty soufflé. Dill is a perfect complement. Any combination of diced vegetables is good, keeping in mind that after you sauté them, you want to end up with 1 1/3 cups of cooked veggies. The smaller the dice, the better.

Preheat the oven to 375 degrees.

Butter a 1 1/2-quart soufflé dish and place it in the freezer to chill.

Heat the olive oil in a skillet and sauté the diced vegetables over moderate heat for about 8 minutes or until softened. Add the sugar, white wine, and garlic and boil until all the liquid evaporates. Transfer to a mixing bowl. Add the dill, Parmesan, and bouillon powder. Season with salt and pepper. Set aside to cool.

Using an electric beater or a balloon whisk, beat the egg yolks until they thicken and turn a pale yellow. Fold the vegetable mixture into the egg yolks.

Whip the egg whites and cream of tartar until they form smooth creamy peaks. Stir one-third of the egg whites into the egg yolk and vegetable mixture. When well blended, gently fold in the rest of the egg whites.

Pour into the prepared soufflé dish and bake for 20 to 25 minutes or until the soufflé has risen and the center seems firm and not excessively jiggly. Serve at once.

HOISIN TOFU SOUFFLÉ

I like to make this with baked tofu, because it is drier and tastier, but regular tofu will work fine, as long as you squeeze any extra liquid out of it. Place the tofu in a clean dish towel, or just squeeze it in your hands. Hoisin sauce gives this soufflé a deep and unusual flavor. If you wish to include grated cheese in this recipe, add it to the egg yolks. A smoked cheese, such as smoked Gouda, is especially good; use about 1/2 cup finely grated.

▶ 8 ounces baked tofu

1/3 cup hoisin sauce

2 teaspoons vegetable bouillon powder

1/3 cup Chinese dried black mushrooms, presoaked, squeezed dry, and chopped

2 cloves garlic, minced

1 tablespoon fresh ginger cut into fine matchsticks

1/3 cup chopped chives

1/2 cup grated smoked Gouda cheese, about 2 ounces (optional)

Salt and ground black pepper to taste

Chile oil to taste (optional)

2 egg yolks plus 4 or 5 egg whites

Pinch of cream of tartar (optional)

Preheat the oven to 375 degrees. Butter a 1 1/2-quart soufflé dish and place it in the freezer to chill.

In a food processor, purée the tofu, hoisin sauce, and bouillon powder. Remove the purée to a mixing bowl. Fold in the mushrooms, garlic, ginger, and chives. Add the smoked cheese, if desired. Season with salt, pepper, and chile oil. The flavor should have some intensity.

Using an electric beater or a balloon whisk, beat the egg yolks until they thicken and turn a pale yellow. Fold the egg yolks into the tofu mixture.

Whip the egg whites and cream of tartar until they form smooth creamy peaks. Stir one-third of the egg whites into the tofu mixture. When well blended, gently fold in the rest of the egg whites.

Pour into the prepared soufflé dish and bake for 20 to 25 minutes or until the soufflé has risen and the center seems firm and not excessively jiggly. Serve at once.

MEXICAN SOUFFLÉ

▸ 1 cup cooked squash or pumpkin purée

2 teaspoons ancho or poblano purée, or Chipotle Purée (see page 370) or 1/2 teaspoon chipotle powder

1 teaspoon vegetable bouillon powder

1/3 cup diced firm avocado

1/3 cup adzuki beans or chopped black or pink beans

1/4 cup fresh corn kernels

3 ounces sharp Cheddar cheese or jalapeño cheese, grated (about 1 cup)

Salt and ground black pepper to taste

2 or 3 egg yolks plus 5 egg whites

Pinch of cream of tartar (optional)

Tomatillo Salsa I (see page 369)

The avocado in this colorful Mexican-inspired soufflé adds a buttery texture and taste. Choose acorn or butternut squash for a light soufflé, or kabocha for deeper flavor and denser texture. This soufflé also works well using a combination of sweet potato and squash or pumpkin.

If you use jalapeño-studded cheese, adjust the amount of chipotle chile powder to taste.

Preheat the oven to 375 degrees. Butter a 1 1/2-quart soufflé dish and place it in the freezer to chill.

Combine the squash, chile, and bouillon powder in a bowl and mix well. Add the avocado, beans, and corn. Fold in the grated cheese. Season with salt and pepper to taste.

Using an electric beater or a balloon whisk, beat the egg yolks until they thicken and turn a pale yellow. Fold the egg yolks into the squash and vegetable mixture.

Whip the egg whites and cream of tartar until they form smooth creamy peaks. Stir one-third of the egg whites into the egg yolk and vegetable mixture. When well blended, gently fold in the rest of the egg whites.

Pour into the prepared soufflé dish and bake for 20 to 25 minutes or until the soufflé has risen and the center seems firm and not excessively jiggly.

Serve at once with tomatillo salsa.

PARSNIP POBLANO SOUFFLÉ

Serves 2 to 4

This soufflé contrasts the sweet flavor of parsnips, the smoky poblanos, and the spicy tang of jalapeño-studded cheese; ricotta lightens the soufflé and the rise. Steam — do not boil — your parsnips in order to make sure your mixture stays dry. Jalapeño Jack or Cheddar cheese is available in the dairy case of many supermarkets and most natural food stores.

▶ 1 1/2 cups peeled and sliced parsnips (about 1/2 pound), to make 1 cup mashed or puréed

1/2 cup ricotta cheese

1/2 cup grated jalapeño Jack or Cheddar cheese (optional), or 1/4 jalapeño, or more to taste, minced

2 tablespoons poblano pureé or Chipotle Purée (see page 370), or 1/2 teaspoon chipotle powder

1 teaspoon vegetable bouillon powder

1/4 teaspoon freshly grated nutmeg

Salt and ground black pepper to taste

2 egg yolks plus 5 egg whites

Pinch of cream of tartar (optional)

Preheat the oven to 375 degrees. Butter a 1 1/2-quart soufflé dish and place it in the freezer to chill.

Put the parsnips in a steamer basket over boiling water; cover and steam until tender. Remove from the heat and let cool. Transfer to a bowl and purée or mash the parsnips, using a food mill, food processor, or hand masher. Try to avoid lumps. You should have 1 cup of mashed or puréed parsnips.

Fold the ricotta cheese into the purée. Add the jalapeño Jack to taste, the chipotle purée, bouillon powder, and nutmeg. Season with salt and pepper.

Using an electric beater or a balloon whisk, beat the egg yolks until they thicken and turn a pale yellow. Fold the egg yolks into the parsnip mixture.

Whip the egg whites and cream of tartar until they form smooth creamy peaks. Stir one-third of the egg whites into the parsnip mixture. When well blended, gently fold in the rest of the egg whites.

Pour into the prepared soufflé dish and bake for 20 to 25 minutes or until the soufflé has risen and the center seems firm and not excessively jiggly. Serve at once.

QUINOA AND GJETOST SOUFFLÉ

Serves 2 to 4

▶ 1 1/2 cups cooked quinoa, loosely packed

1 teaspoon ground cardamom

1/2 teaspoon freshly grated nutmeg

1/4 teaspoon ground cinnamon, or more to taste

1/2 teaspoon chopped dried rosemary

1/3 cup chopped cooked collards, patted or squeezed dry if necessary

3 ounces grated gjetost cheese, or about 1 to 1 1/4 cups loosely packed

2 tablespoons Parmesan cheese, or 1 to 2 teaspoons vegetable bouillon powder (optional)

Salt and ground black pepper to taste

2 or 3 egg yolks plus 5 or 6 egg whites

Pinch of cream of tartar (optional)

Because quinoa is light and has a pretty curlicue shape it seems a perfect grain for using in soufflés. Gjetost (pronounced YEHT-ost) is a caramel-flavored goat cheese that adds distinctive, sweet flavor to this unusual recipe.

Keep your gjetost cold before you grate it. Gjetost softens quickly, and the grated strips will immediately start to stick together. One way to deal with this is to cut off a cold 3-ounce chunk and grate it as you fold it into the quinoa so that it distributes evenly through the grain and doesn't clump up.

I love this soufflé's delicacy, but should you want additional flavor, add Parmesan cheese or vegetable bouillon powder.

Preheat the oven to 375 degrees. Butter a 1 1/2-quart soufflé dish and place it in the freezer to chill.

Flavor the quinoa with cardamom, nutmeg, cinnamon, and rosemary. Add the collards and toss with a fork to keep the quinoa grains fluffy. Sprinkle in the grated gjetost and the optional Parmesan and toss lightly with a fork so that cheese and grain are well blended. Season to taste with salt and pepper.

Using an electric beater or a balloon whisk, beat the egg yolks until they thicken and turn a pale yellow. Fold the yolks into the quinoa mixture.

Whip the egg whites and cream of tartar until they form smooth creamy peaks. Stir one-third of the egg whites into the egg yolk and quinoa mixture. When well blended, gently fold in the rest of the egg whites.

Pour into the prepared soufflé dish and bake for 20 to 25 minutes or until the soufflé has risen and the center seems firm and not excessively jiggly. Serve at once.

RICOTTA AND ORZO SOUFFLÉ WITH CARAMELIZED RED PEPPERS, OLIVES, AND SUN-DRIED TOMATOES

Serves 2 to 4

This soufflé is made by placing vegetables on the bottom of a buttered soufflé dish before the soufflé mixture is poured on top and baked. It is a beautiful dish to unmold, especially impressive for company. You can try the same technique with other vegetables, such as chopped cooked spinach or chard, julienned carrots, Chinese long beans, or even asparagus, tossed in a little garlic and olive oil. Remember to butter your soufflé dish generously, and to chill it well.

Oil from the pepper and tomatoes gives the inverted soufflé a rosy caramelization, while the orzo suspended in the delicate ricotta cheese base makes this an ideal entree soufflé.

▶ 1 roasted red bell pepper

1 tablespoon olive oil

2 cloves garlic, minced

Pinch of salt

Pinch of sugar

12 to 16 black kalamata olives, pitted and coarsely chopped

1/3 cup reconstituted sun-dried tomatoes, preferably packed in oil

1 cup cooked orzo, cooled

3/4 cup low-fat ricotta cheese

1/3 cup grated Parmesan cheese

1 teaspoon vegetable bouillon powder

Salt and ground black pepper to taste

Grated nutmeg to taste

3 egg yolks plus 6 egg whites

Pinch of cream of tartar (optional)

Preheat the oven to 375 degrees. Butter a 1 1/2-quart soufflé dish and place it in the freezer to chill.

Tear the roasted red pepper into thin strips and place in a small bowl. Add the olive oil and garlic, salt and sugar, and toss. Add the olives. Chop the sun-dried tomatoes and add to the bowl. Toss together. You should have about a cup of vegetable mixture plus any oils. Let the vegetables marinate briefly.

Remove the soufflé dish from the freezer. Using a slotted spoon or your fingers, arrange the pepper, olive, and tomato mixture at the bottom of the soufflé dish, being careful not to add any more oil to the soufflé bottom than naturally comes as you lift and place the vegetables. Return the soufflé dish to the freezer to let the oils from the pepper and tomatoes chill and harden a little.

Combine the orzo, ricotta, Parmesan, and bouillon powder in a mixing bowl. Season with salt, pepper, and nutmeg.

Using an electric beater or a balloon whisk, beat the egg yolks until they thicken and turn a pale yellow. Fold the orzo and ricotta mixture into the egg yolks.

Whip the egg whites with the cream of tartar until they form smooth creamy peaks. Stir one-third of the egg whites into the egg yolk and orzo mixture. When well blended, gently fold in the rest of the egg whites.

Remove the soufflé dish from the freezer. Pour the mixture into the prepared dish and bake for 20 to 25 minutes or until the soufflé has risen and the center seems firm and not excessively jiggly. Remove from the oven, place a large plate over the top of the soufflé dish, and invert the soufflé so that the bottom becomes the top. Serve immediately.

ROQUEFORT CHEESE SOUFFLÉ

Here is a rich but wonderful soufflé that was a favorite in Huberts restaurant, where it was served in individual ramekins that could be prepared ahead of time, then reheated as they were ordered. This particular soufflé uses a bouilli (see page 251).

▶ 1 tablespoon cornmeal

1 1/2 cups milk

3 tablespoons unsalted butter

2 tablespoons flour

1 tablespoon cornstarch

1 1/4 cups crumbled Roquefort cheese, lightly packed, about 9 ounces

3 egg yolks plus 5 egg whites

2 tablespoons cognac or good brandy

2 teaspoons Worcestershire sauce

2 to 5 drops Tabasco

Freshly grated nutmeg to taste

Salt and ground black pepper to taste

Preheat the oven to 350 degrees. Butter six 4-ounce ramekins, or a 1 1/2-quart soufflé dish, then dust with cornmeal. Set this in the freezer to chill.

Heat the milk in a small pan or the microwave but do not boil.

Melt the butter in a saucepan. Add the flour and cornstarch, and stir to make a roux. Slowly stir the hot milk into the roux and continue stirring until it thickens. Remove from the heat and mix in the crumbled cheese. Let this mixture cool to a warm but not hot temperature.

In a bowl, beat the egg yolks until thick and light in color. Slowly add the warm cheese mixture to the yolks and stir until completely blended. Add the cognac, Worcestershire, and Tabasco. Season to taste with nutmeg, salt, and pepper.

Whip the egg whites until they form soft peaks. Stir one-third of the whites into the cheese mixture. When well blended, fold in the rest of the whites.

Turn into the prepared baking dish or dishes. For the 4-ounce ramekins, bake 20 minutes. For the 6-cup mold, bake 30 to 35 minutes.

Serve at once. Red cabbage pickled with juniper berries is a nice accompaniment.

GRATINS

VEGETABLES: GRATINS

CONTENTS

In a world of constantly changing food style, gratins never fail to satisfy. Ingredients and flavors slowly meld together, then turn brown and crispy on top; how can they miss?

I suggest trying a variety of liquids for the base of your gratin, from vegetable or mushroom broth to rice milk or cream, or combinations of them. The choice of liquid is up to your sense of taste and your need to keep fat in or out of your life.

RUTABAGA AND GJETOST GRATIN

Serves 4 to 6

1 cup chopped red onion

1 tablespoon olive oil

1 teaspoon honey

1 1/2 cups thinly sliced rutabaga, about 3/4 to 1 pound (use 3 cups if you are using only rutabaga)

1 1/2 cups thinly sliced butternut squash or buttercup or pumpkin

1 1/2 cups grated gjetost, loosely packed, about 4 ounces

1 1/2 cups hot vegetable broth, or 1 1/4 cups broth and 1/4 cup cream

Olive oil

Gjetost is a caramel-flavored Norwegian goat cheese that is sweet and melts evenly. It is delicious in gratins with white and sweet potatoes, orange-colored root vegetables, and winter squashes and pumpkins. The gratin in this recipe works well with just rutabaga, but the addition of squash or sweet potato will sweeten it.

Depending on the size and depth of your baking dish, you can make either two or three layers of rutabaga and squash, placing the onions on the bottom and in the middle of the gratin and the gjetost in the middle. If desired, gjetost may also be added to the top of the gratin at the end of baking.

Preheat the oven to 375 degrees. Have ready a medium-size gratin dish or a shallow 2-quart ovenproof casserole.

Sauté the red onions in the olive oil for 5 to 7 minutes, until softened. Add the honey and cook over medium heat to caramelize slightly. Place half the onions on the bottom of the gratin dish.

Depending on the size of your baking dish, make 2 or 3 layers alternating the onions, rutabaga, squash, and gjetost. The top layer should be vegetables, not cheese. Pour in enough hot vegetable broth to come a little more than halfway up the layers.

Cover the dish and bake for 35 minutes. Remove the cover; the broth should be bubbling and the vegetables al dente. Raise the temperature to 400 degrees and continue baking until lightly browned, 10 to 20 minutes longer. If a cheese topping is desired, add more grated gjetost for the final 2 minutes of baking.

266

GRATIN OF SAVOY CABBAGE
IN BEER AND CREAM

Serves 4

Use your favorite beer here, though I do think a sweet beer works best. If you are not a beer drinker, try hard cider or an authentic ginger beer. In this recipe, butter is better.

▸ **4 cups shredded savoy cabbage**

2 tablespoons clarified butter (ghee) or canola oil

2 cloves garlic, minced

1 tablespoon fresh ginger cut into thin matchsticks (use less if you cook with ginger beer)

1/2 cup beer

2 tablespoons cream

Salt and ground black pepper to taste

3 tablespoons bread crumbs

2 tablespoons grated Parmesan or Gruyère, Cheddar, or gjetost cheese

Preheat the oven to 400 degrees. Have ready a medium-size gratin dish or a shallow 2-quart ovenproof casserole.

Steam the cabbage briefly, or blanch it in a large pot of boiling water for a few seconds, just long enough for it to wilt and turn color. This helps it fit into a gratin dish. Drain well.

Heat the butter in a skillet, add the cabbage, and toss over moderate heat until limp. Add the garlic, ginger, beer, and cream. Season with salt and pepper. Pour into the gratin dish. Cover with foil and bake for 10 to 15 minutes. The liquid should be bubbling. Remove the foil and sprinkle the gratin with bread crumbs and cheese. Bake another 10 minutes or until the top is lightly browned and the liquid has thickened slightly.

YOUNG TURNIP AND CHÈVRE GRATIN

▶ 4 golden Finn potatoes, sliced thin, a scant pound

4 white turnips, sliced thin, a scant pound

4 ounces fresh chèvre cheese

1 cup vegetable broth or a combination of rice milk and broth, or 3/4 cup broth and 1/4 cup cream

1 1/2 teaspoons ground cardamom

Salt and ground black pepper to taste

White turnips, especially young ones, have an earthy sweetness that is ideally paired with fresh goat cheese. Try this with just turnips, too, omitting the potatoes.

Until you are ready to use the potatoes, place them in cold water mixed with a few drops of vinegar or lemon juice so they don't turn brown.

Preheat the oven to 375 degrees. Lightly oil a medium-size gratin dish or a shallow 2-quart ovenproof casserole.

Layer the drained sliced potatoes, turnips, and thin slices of chèvre in the prepared gratin dish. Save some slices of chèvre for the top.

Heat the broth and add the cardamom, salt, and pepper. Pour the liquid over the gratin. Cover with foil and bake for 35 to 45 minutes. Remove the foil. The liquid should be bubbling and the potatoes and turnips should be al dente. Raise the heat to 400 degrees and bake for another 10 to 15 minutes until the gratin turns golden brown on top.

RHUBARB AND CHARD GRATIN

Rhubarb offers a piquant foil to earthy chard stems in this dish inspired by Josephine Araldo, whose instinctive understanding of flavor was her greatest legacy.

▶ 1/4 to 1/3 cup Gewürztraminer

1/3 cup golden raisins

1 tablespoon honey, or more to taste

1 cup sliced rhubarb

3 cups sliced chard stems
(use leaves for another dish)

1/4 cup strong vegetable broth

1/4 cup cream

2 cloves garlic, minced

1/3 cup bread crumbs

1 tablespoon grated Parmesan cheese

Freshly grated nutmeg

Preheat the oven to 375 degrees. Have ready a medium-size gratin dish or a shallow 2-quart ovenproof casserole.

Heat the wine in a saucepan. Add the raisins, honey, and rhubarb. Cover and simmer for about 7 minutes or until the rhubarb softens and melts. The rhubarb should be sweet but not cloying. Add more honey to taste if necessary. Pour the mixture into the bottom of the gratin dish.

Put the chard in a steamer basket, cover, and steam over boiling water just long enough to heat through and soften slightly. Place the chard on top of the rhubarb.

Heat the broth and cream together; add the garlic and pour over the chard. Bake, covered, for 10 to 12 minutes.

Combine the bread crumbs and Parmesan cheese.

Uncover the gratin, sprinkle the crumbs on top of the chard, and grate a little fresh nutmeg over all. Raise the heat to 400 degrees and bake uncovered for another 10 to 15 minutes or until the liquid has thickened and the top has turned golden. Keep your eye on the gratin, and if you think you need to add more liquid, do so sparingly.

POTATO GRATIN
STUFFED WITH COLLARDS

Serves 6

▶ 1 bunch collard greens (to yield
1 cup steamed and finely chopped
collard leaves)

1 tablespoon olive oil

3/4 cup chopped leeks, white and
pale green parts

2 cloves garlic, minced

2 tablespoons grated Parmesan
cheese, plus additional as needed

1/4 teaspoon grated nutmeg

Salt and ground black pepper
to taste

*A handy side dish or entrée, this simple gratin holds a surprise inside:
chopped collards and leeks. Top with cheese if you wish.*

2 1/2 pounds potatoes, sliced
(about 3 cups)

1/2 to 2/3 cup vegetable broth

2 to 4 tablespoons cream, milk,
or rice milk

1/3 cup loosely packed grated
Gruyère or Cheddar cheese
(optional)

Rinse the greens and strip the leaves from the stalks. Put the leaves in a steamer basket, cover, and steam over boiling water for 10 minutes or until tender but not mushy. Cool, chop fine, and measure out 1 cup for the gratin.

Preheat the oven to 400 degrees. Butter or oil a medium-size gratin dish or a 2-quart ovenproof casserole.

Heat the olive oil in a saucepan and sauté the leeks until translucent. Add the garlic, collards, 2 tablespoons of Parmesan, and the nutmeg and mix well. Cool. Season with salt and pepper. Set aside.

Arrange a layer of potatoes on the bottom of the baking dish. Add the collard and leek mixture. Top with the remaining potatoes. Combine the liquids and heat in a small saucepan. Pour enough liquid over the gratin to come about halfway up the dish. Cover with foil and bake for 25 minutes or until the liquid is bubbling and the potatoes are al dente. Uncover the dish, drizzle the top with a little olive oil, and sprinkle with 2 tablespoons of Parmesan or the Gruyère if desired. Bake another 15 minutes or until the top has turned golden brown.

VARIATION: I have also made this by adding to the collard mix 1/3 cup of finely chopped sun-dried tomatoes in olive oil.

Serves 4

I like this custard base best with beets, though other root vegetables can be used as well.

▶ 1 tablespoon olive oil

1 cup chopped onion

1 teaspoon sugar

2 1/2 to 3 cups peeled and thinly sliced beets

2 tablespoons chopped dill weed

1 tablespoon clarified butter

2 tablespoons flour

2/3 cup milk or rice milk

1 whole egg plus 2 whites, or 4 egg whites

1/2 cup ricotta cheese

1/2 cup cubed tofu

1/2 teaspoon freshly grated nutmeg, or to taste

Salt and ground black pepper to taste

Preheat the oven to 375 degrees. Butter a medium-size gratin dish or a shallow 2-quart ovenproof casserole.

Heat the olive oil in a small skillet, add the onion, and sauté until softened, about 5 minutes. Add the sugar and stir briefly over medium-high heat to caramelize.

Spread half the onion on the bottom of the gratin dish. Arrange half the beets in a layer on top of the onion. Sprinkle on half the dill. Spread with the rest of the onion. Top with the remaining beets and sprinkle with the rest of the dill. Set the gratin aside.

Heat the butter in a saucepan, add the flour, and cook slowly for a few minutes to make a roux. Stir in the milk and cook until smooth. Cool. Beat in the egg and egg whites.

Using a food processor or hand mill, purée the ricotta and tofu. Add this mixture to the egg mixture and combine well. Add the nutmeg and salt and pepper to taste. Pour this custard on top of the beets.

Bake uncovered for 35 to 45 minutes or until the custard is golden brown, the beets are tender, and a knife comes out clean after piercing the center of the custard.

VEGETABLE COBBLER

The crisp, buttery topping for this cobbler is based on the biscuits we served at Huberts. Your favorite combination of herbs may be used, but the dill adds something special.

▶ 1/4 pound chanterelles (about 1 cup)

1/2 cup sliced carrots

1/2 cup shelled fresh fava beans or canned white beans (cannellini)

1/2 cup sliced parsnips

3/4 cup chopped kale

1 medium potato, peeled and diced (to yield 1/2 to 2/3 cup mashed)

2 tablespoons olive oil

3/4 cup chopped leeks, both white and green parts

1/3 cup white wine

2 to 3 tablespoons chopped dill

1/2 cup diced tofu or creamy feta cheese (optional)

Salt and ground black pepper to taste

SAUCE

2/3 to 3/4 cup vegetable broth

2 tablespoons cream (optional)

2 cloves garlic, minced

BISCUIT TOPPING

1 cup unbleached flour

1 1/2 teaspoons baking powder

1/2 teaspoon salt

Ground black pepper to taste

1 1/2 tablespoons sugar

4 tablespoons whipped unsalted butter, at room temperature

1/3 cup milk or rice milk

1 tablespoon chopped dill weed

1 tablespoon chopped chives

Put the chanterelles in a steamer basket, cover, and steam over boiling water until soft. Remove to a bowl and set aside.

Steam the carrots, fava beans, and parsnips in separate batches until tender; add to the mushrooms.

Steam the kale until tender but not mushy. Add to the other steamed vegetables.

Put the diced potato in a medium saucepan with cold water to cover. Bring to a boil and cook until tender. Drain and mash.

Preheat the oven to 350 degrees. Lightly oil a 2-quart ovenproof casserole.

In a heavy saucepan, heat the olive oil and add the leeks. Sauté over moderate heat until softened, about 5 minutes. Add the wine and boil until reduced completely. Add the steamed chanterelles, carrots, beans, parsnips, and kale; stir gently until heated through. Stir in the dill and the tofu if using. Season with salt and pepper and transfer to the prepared baking dish.

Make the sauce: Heat 2/3 cup of broth in a heavy saucepan; add the cream and the garlic. Slowly add mashed potatoes to thicken the sauce according to your taste; add more broth if needed. Pour over the vegetables.

Make the biscuit topping: Whisk together the flour, baking powder, salt, pepper, and sugar in a mixing bowl. Using your fingers, lightly mix the whipped butter into the flour until it has a coarse, mealy texture. Stir in the milk and herbs. Place the dough on a floured surface and gently knead 4 or 5 times, just until the dough holds together.

To assemble the vegetable cobbler, pinch off pieces of biscuit dough and place on top of the vegetables. Bake uncovered for 20 to 25 minutes, until the biscuits are golden and crisp.

ROLLED OR STUFFED

VEGETABLES: ROLLED OR STUFFED

CONTENTS

CHARD LEAVES
STUFFED WITH PORTOBELLO PÂTÉ

Makes 16 to 24 rolls

No chapter on rolled and stuffed vegetables would be complete without the ubiquitous stuffed chard leaf. Swiss chard has many virtues that make it the perfect wrap: it's big and soft and adds a robust quality that is further enhanced by braising. Though it can be stuffed with anything — pasta, grains, or minced vegetables — a great leaf deserves a great filling, such as portobello pâté.

▶ 8 to 12 chard leaves

2 to 3 cups portobello pâté

2 tablespoons olive oil

3 cloves garlic, minced

1/3 cup diced onion

1/3 cup diced parsnips

1/3 cup diced carrots

1/3 cup diced celery

1/2 cup white wine

1/2 cup vegetable broth

Soften the chard leaves by placing them in a pan and pouring boiling water over them. Refresh in cold or ice water. Pat the leaves dry on clean kitchen towels. Remove the stalks, or ribs, of the chard and reserve.

Flatten out the leaves on a work surface. Place 1 to 2 tablespoons of pâté in the middle of each chard leaf. Roll up and tuck in the ends as you would for a blintz or an egg roll.

Make a mirepoix: Heat the olive oil in a skillet, add the garlic, onion, parsnips, carrots, and celery. Dice the reserved chard ribs and add. Cover and sweat over low heat until softened.

Bring the wine and broth to a boil in a separate pan and cook uncovered until slightly reduced. Pour over the mirepoix.

Spread the mirepoix over the bottom of a rectangular Pyrex baking dish or shallow pan. Arrange the stuffed chard leaves seam side down on top. Cover with foil and bake for 10 to 15 minutes or until heated through.

Serve with pappardelle or broad egg noodles.

MUSHROOM-FILLED SESAME CRÊPES

Makes 6 to 8 crêpes

▸ **SESAME CRÊPES**

1/2 cup unbleached flour

4 egg whites

1/2 cup rice milk

1/2 teaspoon salt

2 tablespoons sesame seeds

1 teaspoon brown sugar

1 tablespoon toasted sesame oil or fruity olive oil

1 pound fresh wild mushrooms: chanterelles, morels, cepes, shiitake, porcini

2 tablespoons olive oil

3/4 cup minced shallots

2 tablespoons cognac

1/2 cup vegetable broth

Crêpes made with rice milk are soft, buttery, and easy to fill and fold, and the addition of sesame seeds makes for a nice flavor and slight crunch. The filling is wild mushrooms that are first steamed, then thinly sliced, and then sautéed with shallots, cognac, and a modest addition of cream.

3 tablespoons cream

1 teaspoon freshly grated nutmeg

Pinch of ground red pepper (cayenne)

Salt and ground black pepper to taste

1 teaspoon fresh tarragon (do not use dried) (optional)

2 tablespoons chopped chives

Make the crêpes: Mix the flour, egg whites, rice milk, salt, sesame seeds, sugar, and oil in a blender or food processor and blend until smooth. If you want a very thin crêpe, add 1/4 cup of water. Lightly brush a pre-heated griddle or crêpe pan (Teflon or cast iron is fine) with sesame oil. Use 2 or 3 tablespoons of batter for each crêpe. Pour the batter into the pan, tilting and rotating the pan to spread the batter into a thin even layer. Cook until the top is set, 30 to 60 seconds. Lift with your fingers and cook on the other side for a few seconds, until lightly browned. Brush the pan with oil as needed. Stack the crêpes and cover with plastic wrap until you are ready to fill them.

Remove the stems from the mushrooms and reserve for another purpose. Put the whole mushroom caps in one layer in a steamer basket; cover and steam over boiling water for about 1 minute or until they are soft and tender. When the mushrooms are cool to the touch, slice them very thin, into julienned strips.

Heat the olive oil in a saucepan and sauté the shallots for 5 minutes or until soft. Deglaze the pan with cognac. Add the mushrooms and sauté briefly. Add the broth and cream and boil until the sauce thickens slightly. Season the filling with nutmeg, cayenne, salt, and pepper and stir in the tarragon and chives.

Spoon some of the filling down the center of each crêpe and roll up. Arrange seam side down in a single layer in a serving dish. Serve warm.

PUMPKIN CHILE ROULADE
FILLED WITH TOMATILLO SALSA

▶ 2 cups pumpkin purée

2 tablespoons flour

2 whole eggs plus 6 egg whites,
at room temperature

1/2 cup ricotta cheese

1/2 cup grated Cheddar cheese, or
1/3 cup grated gjetost

1/2 to 1 teaspoon Chipotle Purée
(see page 370) or ancho purée to
taste, or 1/4 teaspoon chipotle
powder

2 cloves garlic, minced

Pinch of cream of tartar

2/3 cup Tomatillo Salsa I, drained
of liquid (see page 369)

1 1/2 cups kefir or low-fat sour
cream

For this delicious and colorful roulade use a pumpkin or squash that has rich, dense meat, like hokkaido. Avoid butternut or acorn squash, which would be too watery. If you can find chipotles or smoked chilies, they will provide a wonderful depth of flavor. If not, use any dry chile, such as ancho or mulato, or a good freshly ground dry chipotle.

For the filling, fresh tomatillo salsa cruda is best, but you can substitute a mild prepared green salsa with the same results. Several good varieties can be found in natural food stores; the best are organic. Just be sure to drain the salsa of its liquid before you add it to the kefir so that the filling stays firm.

For a very interesting variation to Cheddar cheese, try adding gjetost, the caramel-flavored Norwegian goat cheese.

Preheat the oven to 375 degrees. Line an 11 × 17-inch jelly-roll pan with parchment or waxed paper. Butter and flour the paper and the sides of the pan; tap out any excess flour.

In a mixing bowl, combine the pumpkin purée, flour, whole eggs, ricotta, grated Cheddar, chile, and garlic. Beat until smooth.

Whip the egg whites until they stand in soft peaks. Stir one-third into the pumpkin mixture. Gently fold in the rest of the egg whites. Spread evenly over the prepared jelly-roll pan.

Bake for approximately 20 minutes or until the top of the soufflé roll springs back when lightly pressed and a toothpick inserted near the center comes out clean.

When the roll is done, loosen the sides with a knife and invert the tray onto a towel. Carefully peel off the parchment or waxed paper; let cool to room temperature.

Drain the tomatillo salsa of any extra liquid. Fold the salsa into the kefir. Spread the filling over the cooled pumpkin roulade. Starting with a long end, roll up the cake jelly-roll fashion, using the towel to guide you. Transfer to a platter and use a serrated knife to cut into serving portions.

EGGPLANT BANH TRANG

Who can resist an unctuous eggplant filling wrapped in light, fresh-tasting rice paper, or banh trang, the Vietnamese spring roll wrappers. Banh trang can be bought at any good Asian grocery. Try to find the long, thin purple eggplant, sometimes known as pickling eggplant or Asian egg-plant; it is sweeter and practically seedless.

▶ 1 pound eggplant, preferably Asian

2 tablespoons toasted sesame oil

1/2 cup medium sherry

1 teaspoon sugar

1/4 cup vegetable broth

3 cloves garlic, minced

1 tablespoon ginger cut into thin matchsticks

2 to 4 tablespoons hoisin sauce, or to taste

1/2 cup chopped scallions

8 to 12 round sheets of rice paper

8 to 12 Bibb lettuce leaves

Cut the eggplant into 1-inch cubes and place in one layer in a steamer basket. Cover and steam over boiling water until tender. Remove from the heat.

Heat the sesame oil in a saucepan, add the eggplant, and cook over high heat, stirring, until the eggplant starts to brown. Add the sherry and boil until the liquid is reduced completely. Stir in the sugar and cook until caramelized and browned. Add the broth, garlic, and ginger and reduce again until the eggplant is coated with a light sauce. Stir in the hoisin sauce and scallions. Remove from the heat.

Soak the rice paper wrappers one at a time in hot water. As soon as they soften, remove and place them between the folds of a damp towel. Work with only a few wrappers at a time, as they must stay moist.

Lay a rice paper wrapper out on a work surface. Place a lettuce leaf on top and on top of this spoon 2 to 3 tablespoons of the warm eggplant mixture. Roll up, tucking the ends in halfway as you would a blintz or an egg roll. Serve while the filling is still warm.

SPRING ROLLS WITH BAKED TOFU

▶ 2 ounces cellophane noodles

1 tablespoon shoyu

2 tablespoons toasted sesame oil

1 cup bean sprouts

1/2 cup julienned leeks

1/2 cup seeded and julienned cucumber

1/2 cup julienned red bell pepper

2/3 cup peeled, seeded, chopped tomatoes

2 cloves garlic, crushed

1 teaspoon sugar

1 teaspoon nam pla (fermented fish sauce)

1/4 cup Thin Coconut Milk (see page 376)

1/4 cup chopped cilantro

1 teaspoon fresh lime juice, or to taste

1/2 cup julienned baked tofu

Here rice wrappers are stuffed with cellophane noodles and julienned vegetables for a light dish that is heartier than the traditional Vietnamese spring roll, but still just right for dipping into an accompanying lime vinaigrette.

8 to 12 round sheets of rice paper, or banh trang

Bibb lettuce leaves

LIME DIPPING SAUCE

1/3 cup fresh lime juice

1/3 cup toasted sesame oil

1 tablespoon rice vinegar or balsamic vinegar

1 teaspoon nam pla

1 to 2 tablespoons sugar, to taste

2 cloves garlic, minced

1/2 teaspoon grated fresh ginger

1/4 cup chopped scallions

1/4 cup chopped cilantro leaves

1/4 teaspoon minced jalapeño, or to taste

Soak the noodles in hot water and shoyu for at least 15 minutes or until soft.

Heat the sesame oil in a saucepan. Add the bean sprouts, leeks, cucumber, and bell pepper and sauté over high heat until softened. Add the tomatoes and cook until the liquid is reduced. Stir in the garlic, sugar, nam pla, and coconut milk; cook briefly until thickened. Drain the noodles and add to the vegetables; stir in the cilantro and lime juice to taste. Fold in the tofu and heat the filling through. Set aside.

Dip a rice paper wrapper into a bowl of hot water until it is soft and pliable. Remove immediately and place on a damp kitchen towel. Work with one wrapper at a time, as they must stay moist.

Arrange a lettuce leaf on the wrapper and top with a portion of the filling. Roll the wrapper closed, tucking in the edges midway through the roll. Place seam side down on a serving platter and cover with a damp towel. Repeat with the remaining wrappers and filling.

Prepare the dipping sauce: Combine all the ingredients and 2 tablespoons of water in a bowl and mix well.

Cut each spring roll crosswise into 4 pieces, or serve whole if desired. Serve with the dipping sauce.

RUTABAGA CANNELLONI

▶ 1 large rutabaga

RICE

3/4 cup sticky or "sweet" glutinous rice

3/4 cup brown rice

2 small bulbs lemongrass, split, or 4 inches of lemongrass, split (optional)

1 cup milk

1 teaspoon raw sugar

1 teaspoon fresh ginger cut into thin matchsticks

2/3 cup vegetable broth

2 cloves garlic, minced

1 teaspoon fresh ginger cut into thin matchsticks

1 1/2 tablespoons fruity olive oil

1/2 cup dried cranberries

1 cup cooked lima beans

2 tablespoons cream

1 teaspoon dried thyme

1/2 teaspoon freshly grated nutmeg, or to taste

Salt and ground black pepper to taste

Cooking as artful meditation has its appeal. Every so often you just want to sit in your kitchen and carve a rutabaga into paper-thin strips you can poach, cool, and stuff like little cannelloni. Why use pasta sheets when you can spend an hour or two practicing such an exotic technique? This is a great Saturday-night-company's-coming-to-dinner dish, one that is guaranteed to help fight depression and the universal feeling that your life isn't under control. On the other hand, the procedure does take practice, and if at first you find that not only are you not succeeding, but that you're not even remotely interested in succeeding at this, then try the second presentation of this dish, which is only slightly less spectacular. Instead of making these vegetables cannelloni or paupiette style, cut thin slices and turn the dish into rutabaga lasagne. You will love the flavors just as much and the effect is still entertaining, though much easier.

The technique of cutting a thin, continuous strip of large root vegetable — most often turnips such as rutabaga, or daikon — is Japanese, and generally a cleaver-type knife is best for it, such as the Japanese nakiri bōchō or usuba bōchō, which are also great for chopping and slicing. For cannelloni, begin by cutting the rutabaga into a four-sided rectangle or square. Now soften the corners with your knife until you have carved out an oblong log shape.

Don't work on a table, but midair, out from your chest. Hold the knife with your thumb close to the blade so that it can guide the cutting. Move the knife backward and forward in a swiveling motion that seesaws the blade along the outside of the vegetable. Move the rutabaga along the knife's blade as opposed to pushing or forcing the blade through the rutabaga. Remember you are trying for length and a uniform thin cut. Think about peeling the skin off an apple. Meditate.

If you prefer an easier presentation, make lasagne noodles: cut the rutabaga into a square or rectangle. Cut thin, sheer slices of rutabaga by hand, preferably. This can also be achieved by using the food processor, though the slices may not be uniform in shape.

Peel the rutabaga, carve into a log shape as described, and cut into eight 6-inch-long strips for cannelloni *or* 48 thin sheets for lasagne. Dice the remaining rutabaga, measure out 1 1/2 cups, and set aside.

Make the rice: Combine the glutinous and brown rice, lemongrass, 2 cups of water, milk, sugar, and 1 teaspoon of ginger in a saucepan. Bring to a simmer. Cover and cook for 45 minutes. Let stand for 10 to 15 minutes to steam through and finish cooking. Remove and discard the lemongrass.

Put the rutabaga strips in a steamer basket, cover, and steam over boiling water until they are soft and pliable. Let cool.

Bring the vegetable broth to a simmer in a saucepan with the garlic, teaspoon of ginger, and olive oil. Braise the dried cranberries in the broth for 15 minutes, then add the diced rutabaga. Simmer together uncovered until the rutabaga is tender. Add the cooked lima beans and heat through. Remove the vegetables with a slotted spoon and let the liquid cook down until it emulsifies and becomes a sauce. Add the cream and reduce a few seconds more. Add the cooked rutabaga, cranberries, and lima beans, the thyme and nutmeg. Season the sauce with salt and pepper. Set aside.

To make cannelloni: Lay the rutabaga strips out on a work surface and place 2 or 3 tablespoons of rice on the lower third of each strip. Roll up, starting with a short end, and place the rolls seam side down in a steamer basket. Cover and steam over hot water just long enough to heat through. Meanwhile, reheat the sauce. Spoon the sauce over the cannelloni and serve immediately, allowing 2 per person.

To make lasagne, lay 4 warm rutabaga squares on a warm plate and alternate layers of creamy braised vegetables with the squares. Build up to a height of 3 layers, with braised vegetables on top. Serve lemongrass-flavored rice on the side.

HUBERTS VEGETABLE STRUDEL

▶ 2 tablespoons olive oil

1 cup finely shredded savoy cabbage

1 cup julienned carrots

1 cup julienned leeks (white and green parts)

1 cup julienned celery root or parsnips

1 tablespoon fresh ginger cut into fine matchsticks

2 cloves garlic, minced

1 tablespoon fresh thyme, or 1 teaspoon dried

This unusual setting for vegetables was a great favorite at Huberts.

Salt and ground black pepper to taste

3 sheets phyllo

Melted unsalted butter

1/2 cup toasted, skinned, and crushed hazelnuts

1 tablespoon chopped parsley

Preheat the oven to 375 degrees.

Heat the oil in a skillet and add the cabbage, carrots, leeks, and celery root. Sauté over moderate heat until softened. Add the ginger, garlic, thyme, and salt and pepper to taste. Toss frequently and let any liquid from the vegetables evaporate. Remove from the heat and let cool.

Lay out a single sheet of phyllo on a work surface. (Cover the remaining 2 sheets with plastic wrap, and cover the wrap with a damp kitchen towel.) Brush the sheet of phyllo with butter and dust with crushed hazelnuts and parsley. Repeat twice again with sheets of phyllo, butter, nuts, and parsley for 3 layers. Work quickly so as not to let the phyllo dry out.

Spoon the vegetable mixture along one long end of the pastry and roll the strudel up. Tuck the ends under. Brush the top and outside with melted butter and sprinkle on more hazelnuts, then transfer the strudel to a nonstick baking sheet and bake until golden brown, about 20 to 30 minutes. Cut into serving portions.

BAKED BEETS STUFFED WITH FETA, RED ONIONS, AND ROSEMARY

Serves 4 to 6

Though this dish is weighted with a long moniker, it is in fact simple to prepare. Granted, a hollowed-out root vegetable is a conceit, but how pretentious can a beet be? Besides, it's fun for company, and gives you an opportunity to fuss over guests. Of course, the very same flavor can be achieved less dramatically by combining the ingredients and tossing with sliced or diced beets.

Thin, crisp croutons will bring out the flavor of the cheese best. Use bread that is a day or two old, stale but still soft enough to cut. If you can find it, a creamy, mild feta, one that is not salty, is exceptional with baked beets. A fresh chèvre will be outstanding, too.

- ▶ 6 medium beets, 3 to 3 1/2 inches in diameter, trimmed and washed
- Olive oil
- Kosher salt
- 2 cloves garlic, minced
- 6 to 8 very thin slices of country bread or baguette
- 1 cup cubed feta or chèvre that is slightly aged and firm enough to cut into cubes
- 1/2 cup finely chopped red onion
- 2 tablespoons minced fresh rosemary
- Salt and ground black pepper to taste
- Fresh lime juice
- Pernod

Rub whole beets with a teaspoon of olive oil. Place in a pie plate or baking dish with 1/4 cup of water and sprinkle with kosher salt. Cover tightly with foil and bake in a 325-degree oven for 40 minutes to 1 hour, depending on the size of the beets, or until a beet is tender enough to be pierced with a knife. When the beets are cool enough to handle, carefully scoop out the middles: Use a knife to cut a circle down into the beet and then use a melon baller, an apple corer, or a spoon to remove the inside and form a cup.

Preheat the oven to 375 degrees. Mix the garlic with 2 tablespoons of olive oil and brush the bread slices on both sides with the mixture. Put on a baking sheet and bake for about 5 minutes or until the bread is golden and crisp but not brown. The bread should be crunchy enough to break into bite-size croutons when tossed with the cheese and onion. Season with rosemary, salt, and pepper. Stuff each beet with some of the crouton mixture. Drizzle olive oil, a squeeze of fresh lime juice, and a drop of Pernod over all before serving.

WHOLE STUFFED SAVOY CABBAGE
BRAISED IN RIESLING

▶ 1 large (3-pound) savoy cabbage

STUFFING

1 tablespoon olive oil

1 cup minced onion

1 teaspoon sugar

2 cloves garlic, minced

2 cups cooked millet

1 1/4 cups lightly toasted unsalted cashews, crushed but not ground

1 teaspoon vanilla extract

3 egg whites

2/3 cup cubed tofu

1/2 cup ricotta

2/3 cup grated Parmesan cheese

2 tablespoons chopped fresh rosemary, or 2 teaspoons dried

A head of cabbage presents a lot of potential for a willing and creative cook. Few vegetables offer as many layers to chop, stuff, or wrap. This entire stuffed head of cabbage is an attractive dish for company. It has the kind of drama that inspires oohs and aahs from friends, who will then feel obliged to make something special when it is their turn to have you over for dinner.

If you cannot get Le Puy lentils, which are small and hold their shape, do not replace them with regular lentils, which will only make the sauce seem murky and heavy. Use navy beans or white beans instead. If you can't find savoy cabbage, substitute green cabbage.

LENTILS

1 cup shallots

2 tablespoons olive oil

2 cups Riesling or other fruity white wine

3 cups vegetable broth

1 cup Le Puy lentils or presoaked white beans

3 cloves garlic, minced (1 teaspoon)

2 tablespoons chopped fresh rosemary, or 2 teaspoons dried

1 tablespoon chopped fresh sage, or 1 teaspoon dried

Salt and ground black pepper to taste

For the cabbage, use a small, sharp knife to carve out as much of the cabbage stem and core as you can remove. Blanch the whole cabbage in a large pot of boiling salted water; simmer for about 10 minutes or until the cabbage turns color and softens. Refresh in ice water or under cold tap water. Invert and let the cabbage drain. When it is cool to the touch, shake and squeeze the head so that more excess water drains from the head. Turn the cabbage so that the core is pointing up. Gently remove the rest of the core. Being careful not to tear any leaves, spread the cabbage apart and remove the small inner leaves that are the heart of the cabbage. The cabbage will form a kind of leafy bowl which you can now fill with stuffing.

Make the stuffing: Heat the olive oil in a small skillet and sauté the onion until softened. Add the sugar and stir over high heat to caramelize, but do not burn. Stir in the garlic. Combine in a bowl with the cooked millet, cashews, vanilla, egg whites, tofu, ricotta, Parmesan, and rosemary. Mix well.

Stuff the bowl, or heart, of the cabbage with the filling. Close the leaves around this to re-form the ball shape of the cabbage. You may wrap the entire cabbage in a 2-foot square of cheesecloth, or simply tie the cabbage with string.

Make the lentils: In a casserole large enough to hold a head of cabbage, sauté the shallots in the olive oil. Add the wine and boil to reduce by one-quarter, about 5 minutes. Add the vegetable broth. Stir in the lentils, garlic, rosemary, sage, salt, and pepper. Bring to a simmer.

Nestle the cabbage into the beans. Cover and bake at 325 degrees for 1 1/4 hours or until the beans are tender. Check the liquid and add more broth from time to time if necessary.

Remove the cabbage to a platter and the lentils to a serving bowl. Slice the cabbage and serve with bean sauce. Offer olive oil, Parmesan cheese, or a drizzle of warmed cream and fresh garlic to those who wish it.

ACORN SQUASH
FILLED WITH CORN PUDDING

▶ 1 small acorn squash, cut in half lengthwise and seeded

Canola oil

1 cup milk or rice milk

1 egg plus 2 egg whites

1/2 cup fresh corn kernels

1/2 teaspoon anise seed, chopped fine

1 teaspoon chopped scallions

Freshly grated nutmeg

Salt and ground black pepper to taste

1/4 cup grated white Cheddar cheese (optional)

This is a fine dish to serve with braised greens such as collards, spinach, or chard or with a salad. Cooking time may differ depending on the variety of squash you use. I have based this recipe on a squash cup that is about 3/4 inch to 1 inch in width. Most squash take between 45 minutes and 1 hour to cook through. Bake the squash until it is almost half done, then pour the custard mix into it.

Preheat the oven to 375 degrees.

Brush the interior of the squash with canola oil, place cut side up on a baking sheet, and cover with foil. Bake for 35 minutes or until the squash seems to be getting tender and can almost be pierced by a fork, but not all the way through.

In a bowl mix the milk, eggs, corn, anise seed, and scallion with nutmeg, salt, and pepper to taste. Pour even amounts of the pudding mixture about three-quarters to the top of the squash. Continue baking uncovered for another 20 minutes or longer, until the pudding is firm in the center and the squash is tender. Top with Cheddar cheese, cook until it melts, and serve at once.

LOAVES, CAKES, AND PIES

VEGETABLES: LOAVES, CAKES, AND PIES

CONTENTS

In this chapter, I have tried to include very different types of loaves, cakes, and pies in order to give a broad spectrum of vegetable combinations and baking ideas. Vegetable loaves have a great deal in common with vegetable burgers, but they are baked. They are made up of various combinations of vegetables, grains, and beans. They may be bound with tofu or egg whites, and often puréed beans can do the trick. Though I like including egg whites and cheese in many of these loaves, if you are a vegan, it is not necessary to add these ingredients, as the loaves will bind as they bake, anyway. If you have a favorite pastry crust or tart shell, use it in place of mine in the relevant recipes, which will work just as well.

CABBAGE TART

▸ SPICED PASTRY CRUST

1 1/3 cups all-purpose flour

1/4 teaspoon grated nutmeg

1/8 teaspoon ground ginger

1/8 teaspoon ground cloves

Pinch of salt

6 tablespoons unsalted butter, at room temperature

1 whole egg

CABBAGE FILLING

6 cups shredded green or savoy cabbage

1 cup finely chopped leeks, white and green parts

1 1/2 tablespoons olive oil

2 cloves garlic, minced

1/2 cup white wine

1/2 to 1 teaspoon good curry powder, to taste

1 teaspoon ground cumin (optional)

Salt and ground black pepper to taste

2 whole eggs plus 1 egg white

1 1/2 cups buttermilk

Inspiration for adding quatre épices to a pastry crust belongs to Josephine Araldo, remarkable cook and teacher whose spirit and influence have spread far and wide.

Make the pastry: Whisk together the flour, nutmeg, ginger, cloves, and salt in a mixing bowl. Cut the butter into 6 pieces, add to the flour, and blend with a fork until the texture is grainy. Mix the egg into the dough. Form into a ball, wrap in waxed paper, and refrigerate for at least 30 minutes before rolling out.

Make the filling: Put the cabbage in a steamer basket, in batches if necessary. Cover and steam over boiling water for 12 to 14 minutes, until tender but still crisp. Cool.

In a saucepan, sauté the leeks in the olive oil until softened. Stir in the cabbage and garlic. Add the wine and reduce completely over high heat until the cabbage has absorbed all the liquid. Add curry powder, cumin, salt, and pepper.

Beat the eggs and egg white lightly in a mixing bowl and add the buttermilk. Add to the cabbage and mix well. Preheat the oven to 350 degrees.

Roll out the pastry and fit it into a 10-inch tart pan or a pie pan. Pour in the cabbage mixture and bake for 1 hour or until the custard has set.

Serves 4 to 6

Pale green, pear-shaped chayotes, also known as mirlitons, have a delicate texture and flavor that remind me somewhat of seedless cucumbers. Here they are steamed, then marinated in a vinaigrette, tossed with feta cheese and roasted yellow peppers, and then placed inside a pastry shell and served at room temperature.

Try to avoid peeling chayotes raw, as they give off an enzyme that irritates the skin. Either peel under running water or parboil for 3 minutes before cutting away the bumpy skin.

▶ Spiced pastry crust (see page 294)

1/2 cup olive oil

1/4 cup fresh lemon juice

1/4 cup fresh lime juice

1 tablespoon sugar, or to taste

1 teaspoon fresh ginger cut into thin matchsticks

1 teaspoon fresh ancho purée

2 tablespoons freshly grated Parmesan cheese

2 teaspoons chopped fresh herbs: thyme, rosemary, oregano

Salt and ground black pepper to taste

3 or 4 medium chayotes

1 1/2 cups soft, creamy feta cheese or goat cheese

1 cup roasted yellow bell pepper strips

Preheat the oven to 400 degrees.

Roll out the pastry and fit it into a 9-inch pie pan. Place a sheet of parchment or foil over the pastry; fill with beans or pie weights to hold down the crust as it bakes. Bake for 20 minutes or until the pastry is set. Carefully lift out and remove the parchment holding the beans. Prick the crust all over with a fork and return to the oven. Bake for 10 minutes longer or until the pie shell is golden brown. Set aside to cool.

To make the vinaigrette, combine the olive oil, lemon and lime juice, sugar, fresh ginger, ancho purée, Parmesan cheese, and fresh chopped herbs. Add salt and pepper to taste.

Plunge the chayotes into a large pot of boiling water for 3 minutes. Remove the skin with a vegetable peeler. Depending on the size of the chayotes, the flesh may already be cooked after parboiling. Slice or cube the chayotes and, if necessary, steam for a few seconds, just long enough to finish cooking through so that it is tender enough to pierce with a fork. While still warm, place in a bowl; add the vinaigrette. Marinate for 30 minutes, and toss frequently. Drain off the liquid. If the feta cheese seems salty, rinse it well, squeeze dry, and crumble it coarsely. Combine the feta cheese and roasted yellow peppers with the chayotes. Heap in the pie shell and serve immediately.

MILLET AND CASHEW LOAF

▶ 1 cup diced onion

1 tablespoon canola, fruity olive, or toasted sesame oil

1 1/2 cups millet

1/2 cup soy grits

3 3/4 cups vegetable broth

2 teaspoons fruity olive oil

1 1/4 cups cashews, chopped fine

1 cup grated raw parsnips

1 egg plus 4 egg whites

1 cup ricotta cheese

1 teaspoon minced garlic

1 teaspoon fresh ginger cut into thin matchsticks

1 1/2 teaspoons ground cardamom

1/2 teaspoon ground allspice

Salt and ground black pepper to taste

The delicate flavors of cashew and parsnip are a light and satisfying combination in this colorful yellow loaf. I prefer to toast my cashews, though raw nuts provide a decidedly aromatic, sweet, and subtle quality. Soy grits are toasted soybean bits usually made from ground defatted soybeans. They resemble large-grain yellow polenta and lend a protein boost as well as a nice nutty taste to any dish. Soy grits take 30 to 50 minutes to cook, and can be added to a dish raw or cooked, depending on the length of time it cooks and the texture you want.

In a pot, sauté the onion in the oil until softened. Add the millet, grits, and vegetable broth. Simmer covered for 25 to 30 minutes or until the millet is tender. Let stand for 10 to 15 minutes to steam through and finish cooking.

Preheat the oven to 375 degrees. Brush a 13 × 9 × 2-inch baking dish with 1 teaspoon of olive oil.

Combine the cashews, grated parsnips, egg and egg whites, ricotta cheese, garlic, ginger, cardamom, allspice, and salt and pepper to taste. Add the millet and combine well.

Pour and pat the mixture into the prepared baking dish. Brush the top with the remaining teaspoon of olive oil. Bake uncovered for 45 minutes or until the top is nicely browned.

GREENS BAKED IN PIE CRUST

This pie can be made with any greens you especially like. I have made it with collards and chard, or combinations of mustard greens, watercress, chard, collards, and spinach. If you prefer, the crumbled tofu can be replaced by ricotta or farmer cheese. The pastry dough — an olive oil dough is based on one by Nick Malgieri, master baker and author of How to Bake *— is easy to work with and can be made in a food processor or by hand.*

▶ SAVORY OLIVE OIL PASTRY

1 1/2 cups unbleached flour

3/4 teaspoon garlic salt, or to taste

2 teaspoons sugar

1/2 teaspoon baking powder

2 tablespoons kefir or cream cheese

1/4 cup olive oil

GREENS FILLING

2 tablespoons olive oil

2/3 cup chopped leeks, both white and green parts

1 large bunch greens, or 4 cups chopped, to cook down to 2 1/2 cups

3 cloves garlic, minced

2 tablespoons puréed sun-dried tomatoes (optional)

3 tablespoons chopped kalamata olives, or 7 olives, chopped

2 tablespoons golden raisins (optional)

3/4 cup crumbled tofu

1/4 cup grated Parmesan cheese

3/4 teaspoon grated nutmeg

1 egg plus 1 egg white

1/2 egg yolk mixed with 1 teaspoon olive oil and 1 teaspoon water

Make the pastry: Combine the flour, garlic salt, sugar, and baking powder. If you are using a food processor, pulse a few times. Add the kefir and olive oil. Pulse long enough for the dough to form a ball. Turn out onto a floured surface and lightly roll out or shape into two patties, one slightly larger. Wrap in plastic wrap and chill in the refrigerator for at least half an hour before you roll them out.

Make the filling: Heat the olive oil in a saucepan and sauté the leeks until softened. Add the chopped greens and garlic and cover the pot. Sweat the greens over low heat. Add no liquid, but cook slowly. When the greens have turned color and wilted down, place them in a bowl and add the sun-dried tomatoes if desired, olives, raisins, crumbled tofu, Parmesan, and nutmeg. When the mixture is cool enough, add the whole egg and egg white.

Preheat the oven to 350 degrees.

Roll the larger circle of dough out on a lightly floured surface and drape it over an 8-inch springform pan. Fill it with the greens mixture. Roll out the remaining circle of dough and cover the pie. Make air vents with your fork. Cut away extra dough and crimp the sides along the top. Paint the top of the dough sparingly with a mixture of egg yolk, olive oil, and water.

Bake for 35 to 45 minutes. If the dough browns too quickly, cover with foil to keep it from burning.

VEGETABLE BISTEEYA

Classically, this Moroccan pie contains layers of poultry, almond, and lemon-curdled egg, which serves as a flavored binder. I have kept its traditional almonds and spices and have used instead of poultry a savory tempeh mincemeat mixed with lemon-flavored tofu and egg, chopped chard, and eggplant, all baked in a phyllo crust.

▶ 1 pound Swiss chard, to yield 1 cup chopped steamed leaves

3 Japanese purple or white eggplants, to yield 1 cup steamed

2 tablespoons olive oil

1/2 cup finely chopped onion or shallots

3 cloves garlic, minced

1 tablespoon fresh oregano, or 1 teaspoon dried

1 cup steamed crumbled tempeh

1/3 cup golden raisins

1/2 teaspoon ground cinnamon

1/2 teaspoon grated nutmeg

1/2 teaspoon ground coriander

1/4 teaspoon ground allspice

1 teaspoon lemon zest

3/4 cup blanched, lightly toasted, chopped almonds

2 tablespoons sugar

1 egg plus 1 egg white

1/2 cup finely crumbled tofu

1 teaspoon fresh lemon juice, or to taste

1/2 teaspoon butter

1 teaspoon toasted sesame oil

2 to 3 tablespoons butter, melted

6 phyllo leaves

Put the chard leaves in a steamer basket, cover, and steam over boiling water for 10 to 12 minutes or until softened. Cool, chop fine, and measure out 1 cup.

Cut the eggplants into 1-inch-thick rounds, then into 2-inch pieces. Place in a steamer basket, cover, and steam over boiling water for 3 to 5 minutes or until tender. Cool and measure out 1 cup.

Heat the olive oil in a skillet. Add the onion and sauté until softened, about 5 minutes. Squeeze any liquid out of the greens; combine greens and onion. Gently squeeze the eggplants to remove any liquid; combine the eggplants with the greens and stir in 2/3 of the garlic and the oregano. Set aside.

In a small mixing bowl, combine the tempeh with the raisins, cinnamon, nutmeg, coriander, allspice, lemon zest, almonds, and sugar. Set aside.

In a separate bowl, combine and lightly beat together the egg, egg white, crumbled tofu, remaining garlic, and lemon juice. Heat the 1/2 teaspoon of butter in a small nonstick omelet pan and quickly scramble the mixture. Transfer to a strainer and let excess liquid drain out. When the mixture is cool, press down with a wooden spoon to release any other liquid.

Combine the steamed vegetables with the tempeh and tofu mixtures in a large bowl and stir well.

Preheat the oven to 350 degrees. Have ready two 9- or 10-inch pie pans or similarly sized shallow baking dishes. (One of the pans will serve briefly as a lid.)

Mix the sesame oil and melted butter. Drape one of the baking pans with a phyllo sheet, and brush it with sesame butter. (Cover the remaining phyllo with plastic wrap and cover the wrap with a damp kitchen towel.) Repeat 5 times, using 6 phyllo sheets. Lay the sheets in such a way that the corners overlap each other and fan out into a circle. Work quickly; the phyllo must not dry out.

Mound the eggplant-tempeh-tofu filling on top of the phyllo. Carefully cover with the overlapping leaves and brush again with butter. Place a matching pan or dish that has been oiled or buttered on top of the bisteeya and turn the pan over so that the overlapping leaves become the bottom and the top of the pie is smooth.

Butter the top and bake uncovered for 25 to 35 minutes until the phyllo has turned a golden brown. If the phyllo browns too quickly, lower the heat and cover lightly with foil. Remove foil for the last 5 minutes of cooking.

VARIATION: This dish can also be assembled free-form on a cookie sheet or any baking tray. Any round or square shape will do; just remember to invert before baking for a prettier presentation.

WILD MUSHROOM BREAD PUDDING

Serves 6

Your favorite mushroom, or combination of mushrooms, will be delicious in this earthy yet elegant dish. Dried mushrooms can be used in addition to fresh ones for a more robust flavor. Save the soaking liquid and use it in place of or in addition to the vegetable broth.

▶ 1 pound wild mushrooms: chanterelles, shiitake, porcini, portobello

2 tablespoons fruity olive oil

1 cup chopped shallots

2 cloves garlic, minced

1 1/2 tablespoons chopped fresh thyme, or 2 teaspoons dried

1/3 cup dark rum or cognac

1 cup vegetable broth

Salt and ground black pepper to taste

1 large or 2 medium loaves Italian or French bread

2 whole eggs plus 5 egg whites

2 cups milk or rice milk

2 tablespoons medium sherry

1 teaspoon freshly grated nutmeg

Pinch of ground red pepper (cayenne)

1/2 to 3/4 cup grated Gruyère cheese

1/2 cup grated Romano cheese

Preheat the oven to 375 degrees. Butter a 2-quart baking dish.

Put the mushrooms in a steamer basket, cover, and steam over boiling water until tender when tested with a knife tip. Cool and slice; set aside.

Heat the olive oil in a small skillet, add the shallots, and sauté for 3 to 5 minutes, until softened. Stir in the garlic and thyme. Add the rum and cook down until the rum evaporates. Pour in 1/2 cup of the vegetable broth and boil to reduce completely until the mushrooms have absorbed all the liquid and flavor. Season with salt and pepper. Set aside.

Remove the crusts from the bread and cut the loaves into 1/2-inch-thick slices. You will need about 3 1/2 to 4 cups. Set aside.

Lightly beat the eggs and egg whites. Combine with the milk, vegetable broth, sherry, nutmeg, and cayenne.

Line the prepared baking dish with bread slices. Add a layer of mushrooms and a layer of mixed cheeses. Top with a layer of bread, then with another layer of mushrooms and of cheese. Top with bread. Pour the egg and milk mixture over all.

Bake for 30 minutes or until custard has set. Slice and serve with sautéed broccoli raab.

HOISIN SEITAN KASHA LOAF

▶ 1/2 ounce dried mushrooms

1 teaspoon toasted sesame oil

1 cup kasha

1 tablespoon shoyu

1 to 2 cups vegetable broth

1/4 pound fresh white mushrooms
(2 generous cups whole)

1 tablespoon olive oil

1/2 cup minced onion

1/4 cup chopped celery

1/4 cup chopped carrots

1/3 cup chopped red bell pepper

1 1/4 cups ground seitan
(see page 202)

1/4 cup good-quality hoisin sauce

2 egg whites (optional)

2 teaspoons ground dried sage

1 teaspoon dried savory

1 teaspoon grated nutmeg

1/2 teaspoon ground cinnamon

1/4 teaspoon ground cloves

2 teaspoons fruity olive oil

Soak the dried mushrooms in hot water to cover for 30 minutes or until they are reconstituted. Squeeze them dry and chop fine. Strain the soaking liquid through a double thickness of cheesecloth and reserve. Set aside.

Preheat the oven to 350 degrees.

Heat the sesame oil in a nonstick skillet, add the kasha and shoyu, and stir over medium-high heat until the grains are separate and brown.

Pour the mushroom liquid into a 4-cup measure and add enough vegetable broth to measure 2 cups. Add to the kasha, bring to a boil, and reduce the heat. Cover and simmer for 20 minutes. Remove from the heat and let stand for another 10 minutes to steam through. Let cool.

Put the whole mushrooms in a steamer basket, cover, and steam over boiling water for 3 minutes or until tender. Let cool, then chop fine and add them to the chopped dried mushrooms in a mixing bowl.

In a small skillet, heat the olive oil and add the onion, celery, carrots, and bell pepper. Sauté over medium-high heat until the vegetables soften. Transfer to the mixing bowl with the mushrooms. Add 2 to 2 1/2 cups of the cooked kasha, the ground seitan, and the hoisin sauce. Stir in the egg whites if desired, sage, savory, nutmeg, cinnamon, and cloves. Mix thoroughly and shape into a loaf.

Brush a shallow baking dish with 1 teaspoon of olive oil. Place the loaf in the baking dish. Brush the top with the remaining teaspoon of oil. Bake uncovered for 35 to 45 minutes or until the top is nicely browned.

SWEET POTATO, RICE, AND BARLEY LOAF

Serves 8

If you are looking for supper ideas that your children will actually eat, a loaf as sweet as this one will agree with both them and grownups. My seven- and nine-year-olds like this loaf when it is hot, and they also eat it cold in sandwiches. Granted, they devote long blocks of concentrated time to picking out every visible centimeter of sautéed onion if I am foolish enough to include it in this or any other recipe, so unless you are preparing this for an adult audience or your table is graced with sophisticated eaters, large or small, leave out the onions, or purée and hide them as I so sneakily suggest here.

▶ 1 1/2 cups vegetable broth

1/2 cup brown rice

1/4 cup barley

2 cloves garlic, sliced, plus 3 cloves garlic, minced (1 scant teaspoon)

1 2/3 cups grated yam or sweet potato

1 cup grated carrots

3/4 cup crumbled tofu

1/2 to 2/3 cup grated Parmesan cheese

1/2 cup puréed raw onion

4 egg whites

1 tablespoon chopped fresh rosemary, or 1 teaspoon dried

1 tablespoon chopped fresh savory, or 1 teaspoon dried

Salt and ground black pepper to taste

2 teaspoons olive oil

Bring the vegetable broth to a boil in a saucepan and add the rice, barley, and sliced garlic. Simmer covered for 40 minutes. Remove from the heat and let stand for another 10 minutes to steam. Put the rice and barley in a large mixing bowl and allow to cool.

Preheat the oven to 375 degrees.

Combine the grated yam, carrots, tofu, cheese, raw onion, crushed garlic, and egg whites with the cooled grains. Season with rosemary, savory, salt, and pepper.

Brush a shallow baking dish with 1 teaspoon of olive oil. Pour and pat the mixture into the baking dish. Brush the top with the remaining teaspoon of olive oil. Bake uncovered for 45 minutes or until the top is nicely browned.

NUT AND TEMPEH LOAF

Serves 8

▶ 1 cup (8 ounces) tempeh

1/4 pound fresh mushrooms
(2 generous cups whole)

1 tablespoon plus 2 teaspoons
olive oil

2/3 cup chopped onion

1/3 cup finely diced carrots

1/3 cup finely diced celery

3 cloves garlic, minced

1/4 cup medium sherry

1/2 cup lightly toasted cashews

1/2 cup lightly toasted walnuts or
pecans

1/2 cup lightly toasted sunflower
seeds

1 cup cooked brown rice

This dinner loaf has a different quality from the pâté made with some similar ingredients on page 74. It is baked and it intentionally packs in more nutrition. Though it can be used on sandwiches or served on crackers or with crudités, it is meant for mealtime. Try serving this with mashed or baked sweet potatoes and a light salad for a contrast of tastes and textures.

1 egg plus 3 egg whites

1 1/2 teaspoons fresh sage leaves,
or 1/2 teaspoon ground sage

1 teaspoon fresh thyme, or
1/3 teaspoon dried

1 teaspoon fresh marjoram, or
1/3 teaspoon dried

1/2 teaspoon freshly grated nutmeg

1/4 teaspoon ground allspice

1 teaspoon brown sugar

Put the tempeh in a steamer basket, cover, and steam over boiling water for 20 minutes. Let cool, then crumble.

Steam the mushrooms for 2 minutes or until they are soft and cooked through. Let cool, then chop fine.

Heat 1 tablespoon of olive oil in a skillet and sauté the onion, carrots, and celery until softened. Add the garlic and stir. Add the sherry and boil to reduce until all the liquid is absorbed by the vegetables. Add the tempeh and mushrooms.

Chop or individually grind the cashews, walnuts, and sunflower seeds. In a food processor, pulse the rice just long enough to break the grain.

Combine the chopped nuts and rice with the vegetable and tempeh mixture. Add the egg, egg whites, sage, thyme, marjoram, nutmeg, allspice, and brown sugar. Mix well and shape into a loaf.

Brush a shallow baking dish with 1 teaspoon of olive oil. Place or pat the loaf into the baking dish. Brush the top with the remaining teaspoon of oil. Bake uncovered for 30 to 45 minutes or until the top is nicely browned.

ROASTED OR GRILLED

VEGETABLES: ROASTED OR GRILLED

CONTENTS

BARBECUED RUTABAGA STEAK

Serves 4 to 6

Barbecue sauce is good on anything, but try it on a large, thick, round slice of rutabaga, and I think you'll be very happy. Serve it alongside red onions barbecued in the same sauce, and you will be even happier. Either tomato or mango barbecue sauce will work for this dish.

▶ 2 medium or 1 large rutabaga, peeled and cut into 1/2- to 3/4-inch rounds

1 large red onion, peeled and sliced vertically into thick rounds so that core holds layers together

2 cups barbecue sauce (see pages 365–66)

Lay the rutabaga slices flat in a steamer basket, cover, and steam over boiling water just long enough for them to heat through, so that the surface may be pierced with a fork but the center of a slice offers resistance.

In a shallow bowl or pan, cover the hot rutabaga and the onion slices with barbecue sauce. Marinate for 1 hour.

Prepare a charcoal fire or preheat a gas-fired grill. Place the rutabaga steaks and onion rounds on an oiled rack and grill on both sides just long enough to cook through.

GRILLED LEEKS
STUFFED WITH BLACK OLIVE PASTE

Serves 4 to 6

▶ 1/2 cup pitted black olives

2 cloves garlic, crushed

1/4 cup fine dry bread crumbs

1 tablespoon chopped fresh thyme, or 1 teaspoon dried

4 to 6 medium to large leeks

Olive oil

You can find black olive paste in Italian or specialty food stores. Or you can make your own by puréeing pitted black olives. I prefer kalamata, but any imported black olive will do, as long as it is neither canned nor oil cured.

In a food processor, purée the black olives with the garlic. Remove to a small bowl and add the bread crumbs and thyme.

Trim off the dark green leaves and the root ends of the leeks. Open the leeks by slicing them lengthwise so that the core layer, or heart, is visible, but do not slice them completely through. Rinse under cold running water to remove all sand and dirt; drain well. Place in a steamer basket. Cover and steam over boiling water just long enough for them to turn color and become pliable.

Remove the core or heart of the leeks and reserve for another purpose. Stuff each leek with some of the black olive mixture. Close the leeks and tie with kitchen string. Generously oil a flameproof shallow pan. Arrange the leeks in the pan and turn to coat with oil. Slide the pan under the kitchen broiler and grill the leeks, turning them frequently but carefully with tongs, until lightly browned on all sides.

ROASTED SPAGHETTI SQUASH
WITH EGGPLANT FLAN

An eggplant flan provides a silken contrast to the long strands of sweet roasted spaghetti squash.

▶ 1 medium to large spaghetti squash

1/2 teaspoon canola oil

1/2 teaspoon toasted sesame oil

1 pound eggplant, preferably the long, thin seedless Japanese type

1 tablespoon olive oil

1 1/2 teaspoons sugar

2 cloves garlic, minced

2 slices or 1 1/2 ounces French or Italian bread, crusts removed

1/2 cup vegetable broth or milk

2 eggs, or 1 egg plus 2 egg whites

1 teaspoon fresh marjoram, or 1/2 teaspoon dried

3/4 teaspoon ground cardamom

Salt and ground black pepper to taste

Chèvre (optional)

Preheat the oven to 350. You can bake this more speedily at 375, but I have found that the lower heat, especially in electric ovens, gives you more control over the way this dish bakes.

Cut the squash in half lengthwise and remove the seeds. Combine the canola and sesame oils and rub the squash inside and out. Place cut side up on a baking sheet and bake for about 45 minutes. At this point, the squash should be about half cooked. You should be able to pierce some of its flesh with a fork, but you should meet too much resistance to pierce it fully.

While the squash is baking, peel the eggplant, cut it into 3/4-inch chunks, and put in a steamer basket. Cover and steam over boiling water until cooked through. Cool, then squeeze out any moisture from the eggplant. Heat the olive oil in a skillet and sauté the eggplant. As it cooks, stir in the sugar and garlic. Remove from the heat.

In a small bowl, soak the bread in the broth. Squeeze dry. Discard the liquid.

In a food processor combine the eggplant, bread, and eggs. Pulse until puréed. Season with marjoram, cardamom, salt, and pepper. Pour into the squash. Continue baking another 35 minutes or until flan has set. If the squash appears to be browning too fast, cover it with foil and continue baking, removing the foil covering for the last 5 minutes.

Serve if desired with a dollop of fresh chèvre.

ROASTED CARROTS, PARSNIPS, AND QUINCES

▶ 3 large or 6 medium carrots, peeled and cut into 3-inch pieces

3 large or 6 medium parsnips, peeled and cut into 3-inch pieces

2 quinces, peeled, cored, and quartered

2 large or 4 small crisp, rich apples: Rome, Jonathan, Empire, Cortland, or Macoun type, peeled, cored, and halved or quartered depending on size

Fruity olive oil

1 cup apple cider, or as needed

1 teaspoon toasted sesame oil

1 teaspoon honey (optional)

1 sprig rosemary

What you pick as your favorite vegetable probably says a lot about you. I am a carrot person. (Well, I am very fond of collards, too, but that is another story.) The carrot is an underrated vegetable and much taken for granted because of its basic thereness — reliable, always available in the market, ready to report for cooking action. I am especially moved by the way the carrot's underlying philosophy is brought out through baking, which sweetens it and brings out its deep, rooty complexity. Life reveals the true nature of a person, but only roasting can reveal the true nature of a carrot.

Try using large, deep orange carrots for this recipe. (They are often referred to as soup carrots.) This is essentially a fall dish, when parsnips and quinces are available. If you cannot find quinces, just use apples.

Preheat the oven to 300 degrees. Have ready a shallow baking dish, preferably glass or Pyrex.

Rub the carrots, parsnips, quinces, and apples with olive oil. Place in the baking dish. Combine 1 cup of the apple cider with 1 cup of water, 2 teaspoons of olive oil, the sesame oil, and the honey. Pour into the bottom of the baking dish with the rosemary sprig. Roast slowly, uncovered, for 1 1/4 to 2 hours, or until the vegetables and fruits are tender. It is important to baste the vegetables often while they are roasting. Do not let the liquid totally evaporate; add more as necessary. Since the baking time of these fruits and vegetables may vary, you may wish to remove pieces when they are done and add them back to the pan for the last few minutes to heat through.

Serve hot or warm, with the basting juices.

ROASTED VEGETABLES
OVER COUSCOUS AND BARLEY

Serves 6

The slow roasting of the vegetables at low heat makes a big difference; they are richer and more succulent than they would be if cooked at moderate or high heat.

▶ VEGETABLES

1/2 head cauliflower cut into florets

3 Japanese-style eggplants, white or purple, cut into 2-inch chunks

4 large sweet carrots, preferably organic, peeled and cut into 3-inch chunks

3 large parsnips, preferably organic, peeled and cut into 3-inch chunks

6 Yukon gold or yellow Finn potatoes, skins on, kept whole if small or quartered if large

8 baby beets, skins on, or 4 large beets, peeled and quartered

2 ears fresh corn, cut into thirds

MARINADE

2 cups fruity olive oil

1/2 cup soy sauce

6 garlic cloves, minced

2 to 3 tablespoons honey or sugar, to taste

1 tablespoon grated fresh ginger

GRAINS MIXTURE

2 cups whole wheat couscous

1 1/2 cups chopped onion

2 tablespoons olive oil

3/4 cup barley

1 1/2 cups vegetable broth, heated

2 1/2 cups uncooked fresh corn kernels

1/2 cup chopped chives

Salt and ground black pepper to taste

Assemble and prepare the vegetables.

For the marinade, combine the 2 cups of olive oil, soy sauce, garlic, honey, and ginger. Coat the vegetables one variety at a time in the marinade; place in a large roasting pan, grouped by variety. This makes turning the vegetables easier and gives you a choice in presentation.

Put the vegetables in the oven at a very low heat of 300 degrees, or 275 in an electric oven. Roast uncovered for at least 2 hours. Keep turning the vegetables while they are roasting.

For the grains, wet the couscous with 1 1/4 cups of water and let stand for 10 minutes. Break up any clumps. Line a steamer basket with a double thickness of cheesecloth and transfer the dampened couscous to the steamer. Cover and steam over boiling water until tender. Do not overcook the couscous and stir only with a fork to keep it fluffy and light.

Sauté the onions in 2 tablespoons of olive oil until golden and add the barley. Stir in the hot vegetable broth, cover, and simmer for about 35 minutes or until tender. Let stand for another 10 minutes to steam through.

Combine the hot couscous, barley, and corn kernels and mix with a long serving fork or with chopsticks. Add chives, salt, and pepper.

Serve the roasted vegetables with the barley and couscous. If you have leftovers, serve them as a salad the next day, tossing with fresh lemon and lime juice to taste.

ROASTED YELLOW FINN POTATOES
OVER ONION MIREPOIX

Serves 4

Yellow Finns embody what I would call the unique essence of potato, as they possess the very sweetness of the flavor of the earth. I prefer using yellows whenever possible, but in this recipe any good roasting potatoes will do. Here they are roasted over a mirepoix of onion. Keep your bed of onion moist, check on it from time to time, stir it to keep the onion from sticking to the pan, and add liquid only if necessary.

▶ 1/2 cup olive oil, or as needed

4 cups chopped onion (6 to 8 medium onions)

1 tablespoon sugar (optional)

1/2 cup cider vinegar or balsamic vinegar

1/2 cup whole large garlic cloves

1 1/2 pounds yellow Finn potatoes, unpeeled and cut into 2-inch chunks or cubes

Kosher salt and ground black pepper to taste

3 sprigs thyme

Preheat the oven to 300 degrees. Have ready a shallow baking dish, preferably glass or enameled cast iron.

Heat 1/2 cup of olive oil in a saucepan, add the onion, and sauté over moderate heat for 5 minutes. Stir in the sugar if desired. When the onion has just begun to soften, add the vinegar and garlic cloves. Remove from the heat. Add 1/4 cup of water. Transfer to the baking dish.

Rub the potatoes with olive oil and sprinkle with kosher salt and pepper. Place potatoes on the onion and tuck in the thyme sprigs. Roast uncovered for 1 hour or until golden-crusted and tender. Serve hot.

BEETS ROASTED OVER RADICCHIO, RADISHES, AND CHERRY BEER

Serves 4

▶ 1 1/2 bunches of radishes, leaves and root ends removed (about 1/2 pound)

1/4 cup olive oil, or as needed

1 cup chopped red onion

6 cups shredded radicchio, or radicchio and savoy cabbage

3/4 cup cherry beer such as Grolsch

1 teaspoon molasses (honey or sugar may be used as a substitute)

3/4 cup vegetable broth, or as needed

Salt and ground black pepper to taste

1 to 1 1/4 pounds beets, trimmed and peeled

The concept of roasting over a mirepoix or bed of vegetables is again interpreted in this dish where beets are roasted over a leafy bed of shredded radicchio and sliced peppery red radishes. If you are not a fan of cherry beer, substitute a fruity white wine instead for the braising liquid. If you don't favor using any alcohol, stick with broth or try a rich but slightly watered-down apple cider. If radicchio seems too expensive, try using savoy cabbage with the radicchio or in place of it. The point is, never let an ingredient keep you from trying out a recipe.

Preheat the oven to 300 degrees. Have ready a shallow baking dish or pan.

Cut any especially large radishes into halves or quarters, leaving the rest whole. Set aside.

Heat 1/4 cup of olive oil in a large skillet, add the onion, and sauté over moderate heat until softened. Add the radicchio and stir until coated with oil. Add the cherry beer and simmer long enough for the radicchio to wilt slightly. Stir in the molasses, vegetable broth, and salt and pepper; bring to a simmer. Remove from the heat and transfer to the baking dish.

If the beets are very large, halve or quarter them. Rub the peeled beets with olive oil. Place the beets and radishes on top of the radicchio, and roast uncovered for 1 to 1 1/2 hours or until the beets are tender, depending on their size. If the liquid cooks out, add broth, not beer.

FRIES AND FRITTERS

VEGETABLES: FRIES AND FRITTERS

CONTENTS

If our palates were fixed at basic childhood taste, most of what we ate would be fried. We love foods that are crisp, moist, crunchy, rich, salty. It hurts my arteries to say this, but if most of us could fry with impunity, we would. Our current collective food conscience is made of sterner stuff, that of eating healthier foods in the service of living those longer lives we lust after but don't necessarily know what to do with. At any rate, when following our personal food compass, we need to leave room for the occasional fry or fritter. Fried food is not only the contemporary elixir of the gods, it is celebration food, lazy food, and plain old kick-back-and-throw-caution-to-the-wind food. Here are some recipes to ease your conscience as you journey to the altered spheres of fried food paradise and back.

BEET AND CHÈVRE SANDWICH FRITTERS

Makes 6 to 8 sandwich fritters

▶ 2 medium raw beets, peeled and sliced into thin rounds

4 ounces goat cheese, preferably fresh chèvre, in small log form, not aged or crumbly

1 egg plus 2 egg whites

1 1/2 cups panaka or fresh unflavored bread crumbs

Oil for deep frying

It never ceases to amaze me what a sucker I am for beets and goat cheese; the earthy, metallic beet is so sweetly transformed by the simple yet elegant chèvre. If possible, use panaka for this, the crunchiest bread crumb known to the civilized world, available in Japanese specialty stores or in the Asian section of large supermarkets. Wipe the beet slices dry before filling them with cold goat cheese, and chill these little sandwiches before frying, if you have the time.

Pat each slice of beet dry with a paper towel. Place a pat or thin slice of goat cheese on half the slices and cover with the other slices to form sandwiches.

Beat the egg and egg whites together.

Carefully dip the beet sandwiches into the beaten egg, then dredge in the bread crumbs. Press the crumbs onto the beets, making sure the surface is completely covered. Refrigerate for an hour if possible.

Pour 1 inch of oil into a heavy saucepan or skillet and heat to about 350 degrees. Place a few of the beet and chèvre fritters into the hot oil and fry on one side until golden brown. Turn and fry the second side. Drain excess oil on paper towels and serve hot or warm.

RUTABAGA AND BEETS
FRIED IN CHERRY BEER BATTER

Serves 2 to 4

Either rutabaga or beets go nicely with this batter. If you plan to serve them together, cut the beets in wedges and the rutabaga in contrasting sticks.

- 1 medium rutabaga, peeled and cut into 3/4-inch-thick sticks
- 2 medium beets, peeled and each cut into eighths
- 3/4 cup all-purpose flour
- 1 tablespoon baking powder
- 1/2 teaspoon sugar
- 6 ounces cherry beer or other sweet beer
- 1 egg white
- Salt and ground black pepper to taste
- Vegetable oil for deep frying

Put the vegetables in a steamer basket, cover, and steam over boiling water until hot though not quite pierceable with a knife. The vegetable should remain hard in the center, just beginning to soften at the outside. Cool and pat dry on paper toweling.

Combine the flour, baking powder, and sugar in a bowl. Add the beer, egg white, and salt and pepper to taste.

Pour 1 inch of oil into a heavy saucepan or skillet and heat to about 350 degrees.

Dip the root vegetables into the batter and deep fry until golden. Serve hot.

BRUSSELS SPROUTS
FRIED IN CHICK-PEA BATTER

- ▶ 1/2 cup chick-pea flour
- 1/2 cup whole wheat flour
- 1/2 teaspoon baking powder
- 1/2 teaspoon ground cumin
- 1/2 teaspoon ground cardamom
- 1/2 teaspoon ground cinnamon
- Salt and ground black pepper to taste
- 1 pint brussels sprouts, trimmed
- Vegetable oil for deep frying

Here is a delicious batter with a rich, cakey texture. Chick-pea flour can be found at Indian specialty stores or natural food stores.

In a mixing bowl, combine the flours, baking powder, cumin, cardamom, cinnamon, salt, and pepper to taste. Mix with 3/4 cup of water into a smooth batter.

Cut the sprouts in half lengthwise through the root. Place in a steamer basket, cover, and steam over boiling water long enough for the vegetables to turn color and soften somewhat. Remove from the steamer, cool, and pat dry.

Pour 1 inch of oil into a heavy saucepan or skillet and heat to about 350 degrees.

Dip the sprouts into the batter and deep fry until golden brown.

EGGPLANT AND ONIONS
DEEP-FRIED IN HERB BATTER

Serves 2 to 4

An herbaceous fragrance and taste set these apart from other fritters. Use any herbs and vegetables you like; I have found the following to be an especially good combination. This recipe works best if you remember to mince the herbs very fine.

▶ 2 purple or white Japanese-style eggplants, long, seedless variety

1 large sweet onion, such as Vidalia or Maui

1 cup all-purpose flour

1 teaspoon dried chervil

1 teaspoon dried thyme

1 teaspoon dried oregano

2 egg whites

2/3 cup milk

1/2 teaspoon garlic salt, or to taste

Ground black pepper to taste

Vegetable oil for deep frying

Cut the eggplants crosswise on the diagonal into 1/2-inch slices. Place in a steamer basket, cover, and steam over boiling water just long enough to heat the eggplants and to begin to soften them. A fork should not be able to pierce them through. Remove from the steamer, cool, and pat dry.

Cut the onion lengthwise so that the root holds the leaves of each piece together. Cut into slices about 1/2 inch thick.

In a mixing bowl, combine the flour with the herbs. In a separate bowl, beat the egg whites and stir in the milk, garlic salt, and pepper. Add to the flour and mix the batter well.

Pour about 1 inch of oil in a heavy saucepan or skillet and heat to about 350 degrees.

Dip the vegetables into the batter and fry a few at a time until golden. Drain on paper towels and serve hot.

JESSICA BARD'S
MACADAMIA NUT BEIGNETS

▶ 8 ounces toasted chick-pea flour

8 ounces macadamia nuts, toasted and coarsely chopped

2 to 4 tablespoons vegetable oil

1 tablespoon baking powder

2 tablespoons sugar

1 cup soy milk

Oil for deep frying

Powdered sugar for dusting

I loved teaching writing at the Culinary Institute of America, where I met students who worked, cooked, and ate harder than many professional chefs I have known. This recipe belongs to Jessica Bard, student extraordinaire.

If the chick-pea flour you buy is not already toasted, dry-toast it in a hot sauté pan until it releases its fragrance and turns a shade darker. Be careful not to overcook or burn.

Process the chopped nuts with the oil to make a nut butter. Transfer to a bowl and add the chick-pea flour, baking powder, and sugar. Stir in the soy milk.

Heat about 1 inch of oil in a heavy saucepan or skillet until hot, 365 degrees.

Drop dough by the scant tablespoonful into the oil and fry a few beignets at a time until puffed and golden on both sides. Blot with paper towels and sprinkle with powdered sugar to serve.

HUBERTS PUMPKIN FRITTERS

Makes about 24 fritters

We served these at Huberts Restaurant.

▶ 1 tablespoon olive oil

1/2 cup minced onion

1 1/4 cups pumpkin purée

1 egg plus 1 egg white

6 ounces milk or rice milk

1/2 cup grated Cheddar cheese

1 3/4 cups all-purpose flour

1/2 teaspoon ground cloves

1 tablespoon baking powder

1/2 teaspoon salt

Vegetable oil for deep frying

Heat the olive oil in a saucepan, add the onion, and sauté over moderate heat until golden. Remove from the heat and cool slightly. Add the pumpkin purée, egg and egg white, milk, and grated cheese.

Whisk together the flour, cloves, baking powder, and salt. Sift this mixture over the pumpkin mixture. The batter should not be runny but should be thick enough to drop from a tablespoon. Add a little more flour if needed.

Heat at least 1 inch of oil in a heavy saucepan or skillet to 360 degrees. Drop batter by the tablespoonful into the hot oil. Fry a few at a time. Cook on both sides until golden brown. Drain on paper towels.

MILLET AND BASIL CHILES RELLENOS

1/2 cup plus 1 tablespoon olive oil

1/2 cup minced onion

1 1/2 cups millet

3 cups vegetable broth

2 teaspoons vegetable bouillon powder

1/2 to 1 teaspoon Thai green curry paste, or to taste (optional)

1 cup finely chopped fresh basil, divided

6 to 8 ounces crumbled goat cheese: Montrachet, Bucheron

8 long mild chile peppers, Anaheim type

Salt and ground black pepper to taste

1 egg plus 2 egg whites

1 tablespoon milk

1 cup fine cornmeal

1 teaspoon garlic salt

If possible, try to use the millet while it is still hot or warm. The texture of the stuffing will be much fluffier and lighter.

Heat 1 tablespoon of olive oil in a heavy saucepan. Add the onion and sauté until golden. Add the millet and stir for a few minutes. Add the broth, bouillon powder, and green curry paste. Cover and simmer for 45 minutes or until tender and let stand for 10 minutes to steam. Transfer to a bowl. Add 1/2 cup of the fresh basil, goat cheese, and salt and pepper to taste.

Slice off the top of each pepper and remove the seeds and veins. Stuff with the millet and goat cheese mixture.

In a shallow bowl, beat the egg and egg whites with milk. In another bowl, combine the cornmeal, the remaining basil, and garlic salt. Dip the peppers in egg, then dredge in cornmeal.

Heat 1/2 cup olive oil in a small skillet. Fry 2 chilies at a time, carefully turning them over until they are golden brown all over. Keep them warm in a 200-degree oven until you are ready to serve the chilies all at once.

Serves 4

These are so unctuous it's hard to believe they are basically just rice. I have added cabbage, leeks, and garlic, but you might wish to add instead a little chopped apricot, or coriander, or even chopped umeboshi or pickled plum. An entertaining approach to this dish is to make different-flavored balls and offer them all at once. You can use fresh or leftover rice — just make sure it is cool enough to handle.

▶ 3 cups cooked brown rice

1 tablespoon olive oil

1 cup finely shredded cabbage

1/4 cup minced onion

2 cloves garlic, crushed

1 teaspoon dried savory

Pinch of ground red pepper (cayenne)

Salt to taste

Vegetable oil for deep frying

Put the rice in a food processor and briefly pulse just long enough to break or split the grain. Set aside in a bowl.

Heat the olive oil in a skillet and sauté the cabbage, onion, and garlic until the cabbage wilts, about 10 minutes. Add to the rice. Stir in the savory, cayenne, and salt to taste. The mixture should hold together.

Heat 2 inches of oil in a heavy pan to about 360 degrees. Form rice balls by molding the rice into rounded ovals using two teaspoons, one to shape, one to scrape. Drop the rice balls into the oil and deep fry until golden. Do not fry too many at once. I use a small, deep pot and make no more than 3 at a time. Drain on paper towels.

ROOT VEGETABLE FRITTERS
WITH SCALLIONS

▶ 1/2 cup finely grated parsnips

1/2 cup finely grated carrots

1/2 cup finely grated turnips

1/2 cup chopped scallions, green
part only

1 egg plus 2 egg whites

2 tablespoons grated onion and its
liquid

1/4 cup whole wheat flour

1 teaspoon baking powder

1 teaspoon sugar

Salt and ground black pepper
to taste

Vegetable oil for deep frying

Grated onion and scallions add a hearty, down-home flavor to these delicious fritters.

In a bowl, mix the grated parsnips, carrots, and turnips with the scallions. Add the egg and egg whites beaten with the grated onion. Whisk together the whole wheat flour, baking powder, sugar, salt, and pepper. Stir into the vegetable mixture.

Heat about 1 1/2 inches of oil in a heavy pot to 375 degrees. Drop batter in the hot oil by the tablespoonful. Turn over when golden brown and fry the other side. Don't cook too many at the same time or you will risk lowering the temperature of the oil. These cook best when they are small and not too thick. Drain on paper towels.

DEEP-FRIED TEMPEH FINGERS

Serves 2 to 4

Tempeh fingers are simple but delicious, especially when dipped into mango barbecue sauce. Although you really need not presteam the tempeh before you deep fry it, steaming will mellow its flavor.

▶ 8 ounces tempeh

Whole wheat flour for dredging

Vegetable oil for deep frying

Cut the block of tempeh in half. Place in a steamer basket, cover, and steam over boiling water for about 10 minutes. The tempeh will still be firm. When cool, cut into fingers about 3/4 inch thick. Dredge in flour. Heat 1 to 2 inches of oil to about 360 degrees in a heavy pot. Add the tempeh fingers, a half dozen at a time, and deep fry until golden brown. Drain on paper towels.

ZUCCHINI RICOTTA FRITTERS

▶ 1 1/4 cups grated zucchini (about 2 medium zucchini)

3/4 cup grated raw potatoes

1 cup ricotta cheese

1/4 cup grated onion

1 garlic clove, crushed (optional)

1 egg, or 2 egg whites

1/2 to 3/4 cup flour, to taste

1 teaspoon dried marjoram

Salt and ground black pepper to taste

1/2 cup combined olive and canola oils

Squeeze the zucchini dry. Squeeze the potatoes dry. Combine the zucchini and potatoes in a mixing bowl. Add the ricotta, grated onion, garlic if desired, egg, flour, and marjoram. Use more flour if the batter seems too thin. Season with salt and pepper.

Heat the oil in a skillet and drop in batter by the spoonful, as for pancakes. Fry the zucchini fritters until golden brown on both sides. Drain on paper towels and serve hot with applesauce on the side.

SAUSAGES

VEGETABLES: SAUSAGES

CONTENTS

The concept of a vegetable sausage requires a certain leap of faith, a willing suspension of your preconception as to what a sausage *is*. By definition, a sausage is composed of a mixture of chopped or ground ingredients, of the sort that might be used for pâtés or farces, that are shaped by being poured or pushed into a casing, or rolled in plastic, then poached, baked, or sautéed. In general, sausages have a bold savor achieved through the use of seasonings and herbs, and sometimes through smoking or the incorporation of smoked ingredients. Sausages are synonymous with great bursts of big flavor, come by honestly. They enliven whatever dish in which they are used and bring it down to earth.

How can that skinny little brother, the vegetable sausage, compete with its fat-filled older sibling? Since a vegetarian sausage uses no animal product casing, consideration must be given to its ability to hold together, and its shape becomes as important as its contents. The recipes in this section suggest not only ingredients but shaping techniques, and are meant to be used as guidelines for your own sausage creations. Some may consider the vegetable sausage a culinary oxymoron, but I prefer to think of it as an idea whose time has come. I have tried to suggest a few different approaches to widen the concept of *sausage* in a Brave New World cuisine. It should be remembered that some of us like Italian sausages full of oregano and red pepper flakes, others prefer their sausages oozing with garlic, while still others must have Parmesan and parsley — proving that sausages, like everything else, are a matter of personal taste.

SOURDOUGH BULGUR SAUSAGE

1 tablespoon olive oil

3/4 cup chopped onion

1 teaspoon sugar

2/3 cup white wine

1/3 cup dark rum

1 tablespoon minced garlic

3 cups stale sourdough bread torn into pieces, any favorite variety

1 1/2 cups bulgur wheat, soaked but not cooked

1 1/2 cups fresh buttermilk

1 tablespoon vegetable bouillon powder

3/4 to 1 cup sunflower seeds

1/2 cup chopped prunes or apricots (optional)

2 tablespoons fresh thyme, or 1 tablespoon dried

2 tablespoons fresh rosemary, or 1 tablespoon dried

Salt and ground black pepper to taste

Olive oil

If you like stuffing, you will love this scrumptious sausage. I prefer the basic mixture moistened with buttermilk, but milk, rice milk, or vegetable broth will work equally well. Also, I like what sunflower seeds and a few chopped prunes do here, but walnuts or cashews and apricots will also be delicious.

Preheat the oven to 350 degrees.

Heat the oil in a heavy saucepan. Add the onion and sauté until softened. Add the sugar and cook until lightly caramelized. Add the white wine and boil until reduced. Add the dark rum and reduce again by at least half, or until the alcohol has cooked out. Stir in the garlic and remove from the heat.

In a mixing bowl, combine the torn bread, bulgur wheat, and buttermilk. Mix and squeeze with your hands as you would a meatloaf. Add the bouillon powder, sunflower seeds, prunes, thyme, rosemary, salt, and pepper. Correct the seasoning according to your own taste. The mixture should be moist but firm, not unlike a meatloaf. Shape into 2 × 5-inch sausages. Set on a baking sheet and brush with olive oil. Bake, turning occasionally, until golden brown.

SPICY POTATO AND SPINACH CHIPOTLE SAUSAGES

Call these what you will — vegetable sausages, glorified gnocchi, bastard croquettes. Whatever you decide they are, you'll find them to be tasty and satisfying. The millet and goat cheese have a lightening effect. For a different version, try using a sweet potato. The chipotle adds a spicy, smoky flavor.

▶ 1 large potato (3/4 pound)

1/3 pound loose spinach leaves

1/4 cup cooked millet

1/4 cup grated Parmesan cheese

1/4 to 1/3 cup crumbled goat cheese

1 whole egg plus 1 egg white

2 or 3 cloves garlic, minced

1/2 to 1 teaspoon chipotle powder or cayenne to taste

1 teaspoon freshly grated nutmeg

1 teaspoon salt, or to taste

1/2 cup semolina flour, or more to taste

1/2 cup all-purpose flour

Fine, dry unflavored bread crumbs or flour for dredging

Equal parts melted butter and olive oil

Peel and cube the potato, place in a steamer basket, cover, and steam over boiling water until tender. Allow to cool and dry out. Measure 1 cup and set aside.

Clean the spinach leaves, place in the steamer basket, and steam until tender. Cool and squeeze dry. Measure out 1/4 cup.

In a food processor, combine the potato and spinach. Pulse until the two are homogeneous; leave in the processor. Add the millet, Parmesan cheese, goat cheese, egg and egg white, garlic, chipotle powder, nutmeg, and salt to taste. Add the semolina and all-purpose flours. The mixture should be sticky, but with the addition of the flour, it should be firm enough to ball up in the processor when pulsed. Add a little more semolina flour if you need a firmer mix and pulse again. Turn out into a bowl or onto a lightly floured surface. Form into sausage shapes. Experiment with the size you prefer, but these should be no bigger than 1 inch wide and 4 inches long.

Poach the sausages in boiling water or stock until firm and cooked through. Cool and pat dry.

Roll the sausages in bread crumbs or flour and sauté in equal amounts of butter and oil, turning frequently, until sausages are golden brown. Serve while hot and crispy.

SEITAN BULGUR SAUSAGES

Makes about 16 to 20 sausages

▶ 1/2 cup bulgur wheat

1 1/3 cups ground seitan
(see page 204)

1 1/2 teaspoons ground sage

1 1/2 teaspoons poultry seasoning

1 teaspoon grated nutmeg

1/2 teaspoon ground ginger

1/2 teaspoon ground cardamom

1/2 to 1 teaspoon ground red
pepper (cayenne) or chipotle
powder to taste

1 cup vegetable broth

2 teaspoons vegetable bouillon
powder

2 teaspoons minced garlic

Though seitan bulgur sausages take time to cook, they are quick and easy to prepare. They are very sausagelike in that they hold together well, sauté easily with other vegetables, and are great with onions and sautéed greens such as broccoli raab.

1/2 cup shoyu

1 onion, sliced

6 cloves garlic

1 knob ginger, sliced

1 cup white wine

Flour or fine, dry unflavored bread
crumbs for dredging

Olive oil, canola oil, or clarified
butter

Soak the bulgur in 1 1/2 cups of water for several hours, but do not cook.

Combine the seitan and 1 1/2 cups of the bulgur wheat in a bowl. Add the sage, poultry seasoning, nutmeg, ginger, cardamom, and cayenne and mix all the ingredients well.

Heat the vegetable broth in a small saucepan and add the bouillon powder and garlic. Pour into the dry ingredients and mix with a wooden spoon for about 1 minute or until the mixture feels cool enough to knead by hand. Knead for 3 to 4 minutes, until the bulgur wheat is well incorporated into the seitan. Try placing a little mix on your tongue to help you adjust seasoning.

Fashion the mixture into sausage shapes about 1 inch thick and 4 inches long.

Bring 7 cups of water to a boil in a kettle. Add the shoyu, onion, garlic cloves, ginger, and white wine. Adjust the heat to a simmer and add the sausages. Simmer covered for 2 to 2 1/2 hours. If liquid evaporates, add more water.

Remove the sausages and let cool, or refrigerate until ready to use. Pat dry, lightly dredge in flour or bread crumbs if desired, and sauté in olive oil, or canola oil and clarified butter. Serve hot.

TEMPEH SAUSAGE

This meaty, savory sausage can be rolled into small sausage links, but I like it best as thin, crisply fried sausage patties, sautéed in a nonstick pan with canola oil and a little butter. The smoked flavor of soy bacon bits adds an interesting touch, but it is not necessary.

▶ 1 (8-ounce) package tempeh

2 tablespoons flour

1 egg white

4 cloves garlic, minced
(2 teaspoons)

1 1/2 teaspoons packed brown
sugar

1 1/2 teaspoons ground sage

1 teaspoon freshly grated nutmeg

1 teaspoon chopped dried rosemary

1 teaspoon ground cardamom

1/2 teaspoon ground allspice

1/4 cup soy bacon bits (optional)

1/2 teaspoon Chipotle Purée (see
page 370), or 1/4 teaspoon ground
chili powder

Salt and ground black pepper
to taste

Slice the tempeh into 3/4-inch-thick slices. Place in the basket of a bamboo steamer, cover, and steam for 20 minutes. Transfer to a bowl and mash.

Add the flour and mix well. Add the egg white, minced garlic, brown sugar, sage, nutmeg, rosemary, cardamom, and allspice. If you wish to add soy bacon bits, you may want to soak them in a few tablespoons of water for about 30 seconds. Added dry, they give a slight crunch to your sausage, something you may actually enjoy. Add the chipotle purée, salt, and pepper to taste.

The mixture should look crumbly but hold together very well when pressed or rolled into a shape. Fashion into sausage patties and sauté in a skillet until brown and crisp.

The mixture can also be rolled into a log, wrapped in plastic, and refrigerated. Slices can be cut and sautéed as desired. This freezes very well.

These sausages are good with applesauce, apples sautéed with onions, or apples and sauerkraut.

VEGETABLE BOUDINS

For those readers who want to experiment using animal casing to make vegetable sausages, the following recipes are ideal. In fact, any vegetable custard or pudding can be the basis of a vegetable boudin, or sausage. The secret to stuffing a vegetable mixture into a casing is to remember to leave plenty of room for the mixture to expand, with about one-quarter to one-third the casing left empty. If you overfill the casings they will only break, and your poaching liquid will swim with its contents.

I prefer making a batter that is thick enough to sit on a piece of plastic film that can then be rolled up, twisted closed on either side, rolled again, and poached. I have also placed the wrapped rolls in zipper-locked plastic bags and poached them that way. I relied on this method when I cooked beet boudin, because I was trying out several different types of vegetable sausages at once, and did not want the poaching water to turn red.

Boudins are generally larger than sausages and are served in slices that are browned in a little olive oil or butter, but if you make your sausages small enough, just sauté them whole and serve them as is.

336

CAULIFLOWER BOUDIN

Makes about 8 to 10 sausages

I use a silken tofu in this recipe because of the smooth texture it gives the sausage. Silken tofu is creamier because it is made with more whey, and it is available in soft, medium, and firm textures. It comes sealed in an aseptic cardboard package and can be found in any natural food store. Steam your cauliflower rather than boiling it in water. You want as little additional liquid in the boudin mixture as possible. You can substitute broccoli for cauliflower, and you can certainly use regular-textured tofu if you prefer.

▶ 1 cup cooked cauliflower purée

1/2 cup firm silken tofu cubes

1/2 cup coarsely ground raw rice, grain split or broken in food processor

1 egg plus 2 egg whites

1 teaspoon minced garlic

2 to 4 tablespoons Parmesan cheese (optional)

1/2 teaspoon freshly grated nutmeg

1 teaspoon fresh thyme, or 1/3 teaspoon dried

1 teaspoon fresh marjoram, or 1/3 teaspoon dried

Salt and ground black pepper to taste

Olive oil or clarified butter

Combine all the ingredients in a bowl and stir together until well blended. Season to taste with more herbs, salt, and pepper.

Place a square of plastic wrap on a work surface. Brush lightly with oil, if desired. Place about 2 generous tablespoons of the mixture in the middle of the plastic wrap. Fold the wrap over so that the sausage mixture is at the bottom, closed part of the fold. Now roll the sausage along the wrap until it has been completely enveloped. Twist the ends until they twist and curl around themselves. Repeat, rewrapping the sausage in a second piece of plastic wrap. Continue making boudins until the sausage is used up.

If you are using a casing, fill it by hand or according to manufacturer's directions on whatever heavy-duty mixing machine you are using.

Bring a kettle of water to a boil. Add the wrapped sausages and poach in boiling water for 35 minutes or longer until the sausages seem firm to the touch. Carefully remove from the water, cool, and remove the plastic wrapper by cutting both twisted ends off, then cutting across the length of the plastic and peeling it away from the sausage.

Serve the boudins hot as is or sauté in olive oil or clarified butter until golden brown if desired. They are delicious served with a slice of goat cheese and an arugula salad.

BEET BOUDIN

▶ 1 cup beet purée

1 cup coarsely ground raw rice, grain broken in a food processor

1/2 cup firm silken tofu

1 egg plus 2 egg whites

1 teaspoon sugar

1 teaspoon grated fresh ginger

1/2 teaspoon orange zest (optional)

1/4 cup crumbled goat cheese (optional)

1/4 teaspoon ground allspice

Salt and ground black pepper to taste

1/4 to 1/2 cup short matchsticks of mozzarella or gjetost cheese (optional)

Olive oil or clarified butter

You have to be charmed by the idea of a red sausage for a beet boudin to appeal to you. I like this best with a dollop of cheese hidden in its center — a little mozzarella, goat, or gjetost. It's best served alongside like-minded or similarly colored vegetables: a sauté of radicchio, a medley of root vegetables, or a rich eggplant dish.

Steam your beets until very soft, rather than boiling them, before you purée them.

In a mixing bowl, combine the purée, rice, tofu, egg and whites, sugar, ginger, orange zest and goat cheese if desired, and allspice. Mix well and correct the seasoning with spices, salt, and pepper.

Place a square of plastic wrap on a work surface. Brush lightly with oil, if desired. Place 2 generous tablespoons of the mixture in the center of the plastic wrap.

Tuck a few matchsticks of mozzarella or gjetost inside the mixture if desired so that it is stuffed in the center of the sausage and doesn't sit next to the plastic wrap.

Fold the wrap over so that the sausage mixture is at the bottom, closed part of the fold. Now roll the sausage along the wrap until it has been completely encased. Twist the ends until they twist and curl around themselves. Repeat, rewrapping the sausage in a second piece of plastic wrap. Continue making boudins until the sausage is used up.

If you are using an animal casing, fold the mozzarella or gjetost into the mixture and fill by hand or according to manufacturer's directions on whatever mixing machine you are using.

Poach the boudins in boiling water for 35 minutes or longer. Carefully remove from the water, cool, and remove plastic wrappers. Serve hot as is or sauté in olive oil or clarified butter until golden brown if desired.

CARROT TOFU SAUSAGE

These mild, sweet sausages are very good served with garlicky lentils and roasted red peppers.

▶ 1/2 cup carrot purée

1/4 cup squash purée

1/4 cup sweet potato purée

2 teaspoons sugar

3/4 cup raw rice

3/4 cup crumbled tofu

3 medium egg whites

1/2 teaspoon ground cardamom

1/2 teaspoon ground allspice

Salt and ground black pepper to taste

In a mixing bowl, combine the carrot, squash, and sweet potato purées and stir in the sugar.

Using a food processor, pulse the rice until the grains break or split. Add to the puréed vegetables. Now add the tofu, egg whites, cardamom, and allspice.

Correct the seasoning with salt and pepper.

Place a square of plastic wrap on a work surface. Put about 2 generous tablespoons of the mixture in the center of the plastic wrap. Fold the wrap over so that the sausage mixture is at the bottom, closed part of the fold. Now roll the sausage along the wrap until it is completely enveloped. Twist the ends until they twist and curl around themselves. Repeat, rewrapping the sausage in a second piece of plastic wrap. Continue making sausages until the filling is used up.

If you are using an animal casing, fill by hand or according to manufacturer's directions on whatever mixing machine you are using.

Poach the sausages in boiling water for 35 minutes or longer, until they seem firm to the touch. Carefully remove from the water, cool, and remove the plastic wrapper by cutting both twisted ends off, then cutting across the length of the plastic and peeling it away from the sausage.

Serve hot as is or sauté in olive oil or clarified butter until golden brown if desired.

EGGPLANT, CHARD, AND
SUNFLOWER SEED SAUSAGE

Makes 18 to 24 sausages

▶ 1 medium eggplant, about
3/4 pound (1/2 cup purée)

4 medium large leaves Swiss
chard (1/4 cup purée)

3/4 cup sunflower seeds, lightly
toasted

1 teaspoon vegetable bouillon
powder

3 egg whites

3/4 cup cooked buckwheat groats,
or kasha

3/4 cup cubed firm tofu

2 teaspoons minced garlic, or
more to taste

2 tablespoons fresh thyme, or
2 teaspoons dried

Salt and ground black pepper
to taste

Try to find the long and thin Japanese "pickling" eggplant for this delicious recipe. They are less bitter than larger eggplant and have almost no seeds. Add a green Thai curry powder or mix a curry to your own taste if you prefer it spicy, and substitute finely chopped basil leaves for the thyme. This mixture freezes well either as a mix or prewrapped in plastic in sausage shape.

Preheat the oven to 375 degrees.

Cut the eggplant in half, place on a baking sheet, and roast for 40 minutes or until soft and cooked through. Let cool.

Put the chard leaves in a steamer basket, cover, and steam over boiling water until tender. Let cool. Squeeze dry.

In a food processor, pulse the sunflower seeds until they are ground but still textured — a little pasty but not yet a butter. Remove and set aside.

Put the eggplant and chard in the workbowl and add the bouillon powder, egg whites, buckwheat groats, tofu, garlic, and thyme. Pulse until combined. Add the sunflower seeds and pulse again to mix. Taste and correct seasoning with salt and pepper.

Put a square of plastic wrap on a work surface. Place 2 generous tablespoons of the sausage mixture in the center of the plastic wrap. Fold the wrap over so that the sausage mixture is at the bottom, closed part of the fold. Now roll the sausage along the wrap until it has been completely wrapped up. Twist the ends until they twist and curl around themselves. Repeat, rewrapping the sausage in a second sheet of plastic. Continue making sausages until the filling is used up.

If you are using an animal casing, fill by hand or according to manufacturer's directions on whatever mixing machine you are using.

Poach the sausages in boiling water for 35 minutes or longer, until the sausage seems firm to the touch. Carefully remove from water, cool, and remove the plastic wrap by cutting both twisted ends off, then cutting across the length of the plastic and peeling it away from the sausage.

Serve hot as is or sauté in olive oil or clarified butter until golden brown if desired.

11

DESSERTS

DESSERTS

CONTENTS

Makes one 8-inch cake to serve 6 to 8

Imagine a rich chocolate cake made without eggs or butter. Instead, a purée of unsulfured prunes is added to the batter. Prunes, rich in sorbitol and pectin, hold moisture like butter, and the moisture does not evaporate during the baking process. I like to add ground pistachios to this cake, but hazelnuts or almonds will work just as well.

- ▶ 1/4 cup rum
- 2 tablespoons sugar
- 1/2 cup (4 ounces) dried prunes
- 8 ounces semisweet chocolate
- 1/2 cup ground shelled and lightly toasted pistachios
- 1/2 cup all-purpose flour
- 8 egg whites (1 cup)
- 3/4 cup sugar
- Chocolate frosting (see page 346)

Bring rum, 2 tablespoons of water, and sugar to a simmer in a small pan and remove from the heat. Soak the prunes, covered, in this mixture for about 15 minutes or until they are plump. Add more boiling water only if necessary. Drain and purée.

Preheat the oven to 350 degrees. Line the bottom of an 8-inch springform pan with a circle of waxed paper or baking parchment. Oil or butter the paper, then dust with flour.

Melt the chocolate in the top part of a double boiler over boiling water. When it is melted, slowly add the warm prune purée. Mix the ground pistachios with the flour. Combine the chocolate-prune and flour-nut mixtures.

With an electric beater, whip the egg whites until stiff but not dry. Slowly add the sugar, beating all the while. Continue beating at high speed until a soft meringue is formed. Fold the meringue into the chocolate mixture.

Pour the batter into the prepared cake pan. Bake for 30 minutes or until the top is firm and not jiggly. The center of the cake will remain moist but not runny.

Let cool before removing from pan. Frost with chocolate frosting.

CHOCOLATE FROSTING

▶ 8 ounces semisweet chocolate

2/3 cup cold kefir or low-fat sour cream

1 tablespoon rum

Melt the chocolate in the top part of a double boiler over hot water. Add the kefir and beat over ice until the frosting firms. Add rum and beat until light and fluffy.

PARSNIP CARAMEL CAKE

Here is my version of a spiced parsnip cake I first saw published in Sally and Martin Stone's excellent The Essential Root Vegetable Cookbook.

▶ 1/4 cup dark rum

1/2 cup yellow raisins

1 3/4 cups all-purpose flour

2 teaspoons baking soda

1 teaspoon ground cinnamon

2 teaspoons freshly grated nutmeg

1 1/4 cups packed brown sugar

6 egg whites

1/2 cup applesauce

1/4 cup canola oil

1/2 cup chopped walnuts, lightly toasted, loose skins rubbed off

1/2 cup butterscotch chips (optional)

1 3/4 cups finely grated peeled parsnips

Caramel Meringue Frosting (see page 348) (optional)

1/2 teaspoon cinnamon mixed with 1 1/2 tablespoons sugar (optional)

Preheat the oven to 350 degrees. Line the bottom of a 10-inch square cake pan with waxed paper or baking parchment to fit. Oil or butter the paper, then dust with flour.

In a small saucepan, bring the rum to a simmer; remove from the heat and steep the raisins, covered, until they are plump.

Combine the flour, baking soda, cinnamon, and nutmeg on a sheet of waxed paper or in a bowl.

Put the brown sugar in the bowl of an electric mixer. Beat the egg whites, one at a time, into the sugar. Beat the applesauce and oil into the egg mixture. Fold in the dry ingredients. Fold in the walnuts, chips, raisins, and grated parsnips.

Pour the batter into the prepared pan. Bake for 1 hour and 10 minutes or until the center is firm but moist.

Either frost this with caramel meringue frosting, or, more than halfway through the baking time, sprinkle the top with the cinnamon sugar. This will help make the top of the cake sweet and crunchy.

CARAMEL MERINGUE FROSTING

▶ 1 1/2 cups packed brown sugar

1/4 teaspoon cream of tartar

Pinch of salt

2 egg whites

This wonderful frosting has a rich caramel flavor but none of the fat of a buttercream.

In a large heavy saucepan, mix the brown sugar with 1/3 cup plus 1 tablespoon of water, cream of tartar, and salt. Bring to a boil, then lower the heat to medium or medium-low and boil gently until the sugar syrup reaches 234 to 240 degrees on a candy thermometer or forms a soft ball that flattens when dropped into cold water. You will notice the sugar syrup darkening and making harder, glassier bubbles as it caramelizes. Don't let the syrup get too dark too quickly. Remove it from the heat and use it right away.

With an electric beater, whip the egg whites until stiff, then slowly pour the syrup teaspoon by teaspoon in a thin, slow stream into the whites, continuing to beat until the frosting is cool, thick, and spreadable, about 3 minutes. Try to keep the hot syrup from landing on the beaters, which will splatter the caramel instead of incorporating it into the meringue. Cover with plastic wrap and refrigerate until you are ready to use it.

Serves 8 to 10

This roulade was a longtime favorite at Huberts. Save it for a celebration and serve with peppered pears or figs.

- ▶ 1/4 cup all-purpose flour
- 2 teaspoons ground ginger
- 1 teaspoon ground cinnamon
- 1 teaspoon freshly grated nutmeg
- 1 teaspoon ground cardamom
- 5 egg yolks
- 1 1/2 teaspoons grated orange zest
- 1 tablespoon molasses

- 3/4 cup plus 1/4 cup confectioners' sugar, sifted twice
- 10 egg whites
- 1/4 cup unsweetened cocoa powder
- 4 ounces semisweet chocolate
- 6 tablespoons unsalted butter
- 1 tablespoon brandy
- 1 1/2 cups plus 1 tablespoon heavy cream
- 2 tablespoons Grand Marnier

Preheat the oven to 350 degrees. Butter the bottom of a 17 × 11-inch jelly-roll pan; line the bottom with baking parchment or waxed paper. Butter and flour the paper and the sides of the pan. Tap out any excess flour.

Into a small bowl, sift together the flour, ginger, cinnamon, nutmeg, and cardamom. In a large bowl, combine the egg yolks, grated orange zest, molasses, and 3/4 cup of sifted confectioners' sugar. Beat until thickened and slightly yellow, about 3 minutes. Fold in the sifted flour and spice.

In another large bowl, beat the egg whites until they stand in soft peaks. Fold into the egg yolk mixture until no streaks remain. Pour the batter into the prepared pan and spread evenly. Bake until the top springs back when lightly pressed, 15 to 20 minutes.

Meanwhile, sift the cocoa powder evenly onto a clean kitchen towel. Run a knife along the edges of the pan to release the cake while it is still hot. Invert the cake onto the kitchen towel and remove the pan. Carefully peel off the parchment; let the cake cool to room temperature.

In a double boiler, melt the chocolate with the butter. Stir in the brandy and 1 tablespoon of the heavy cream. Remove from the heat and let cool to room temperature. With a flexible spatula, spread the chocolate glaze evenly over the cake.

Combine the remaining 1 1/2 cups of heavy cream and 1/4 cup of confectioners' sugar with the Grand Marnier. Beat until stiff. Spread the whipped cream evenly over the chocolate-glazed cake. Beginning with a long side and using the towel to guide you, roll up the cake, jelly-roll fashion. Transfer to a platter, cover with plastic wrap, and refrigerate for up to 6 hours.

Slice and serve. Delicious with poached pears or figs.

LINGONBERRY UPSIDE-DOWN CAKE

Fresh lingonberries are sweet, but refreshing. A good substitute would be fresh cranberries or reconstituted dried sour cherries.

▶ 3 tablespoons unsalted butter, softened

1/2 cup packed brown sugar

1/2 cup granulated sugar

2 cups fresh lingonberries

CAKE

4 tablespoons (1/2 stick) butter

1/2 cup granulated sugar

1 egg yolk plus 3 egg whites

1 teaspoon lemon zest

1 teaspoon orange zest

1 1/2 cups all-purpose flour

1 tablespoon baking powder

1/2 teaspoon salt

1/2 cup milk

2 teaspoons vanilla extract

Preheat the oven to 375 degrees. Line the bottom of an 8-inch springform pan with a circle of waxed paper or baking parchment cut to fit. Spread the 3 tablespoons of soft butter evenly over the bottom of the pan. Combine the 1/2 cup each of brown and granulated sugar. Spread over the butter. Top with the berries, and press them firmly into the sugar.

Make the cake: Cream the 4 tablespoons of butter in an electric mixer, using the whisk attachment, until pale yellow, about 3 minutes. With the mixer running, add the sugar in a steady stream; continue beating for 3 or 4 minutes. Scrape down the sides of the bowl when necessary. Beat in the egg yolk first, then the whites one by one. Add the zests. Set aside.

Sift together the flour, baking powder, and salt onto a sheet of waxed paper. Combine the milk and vanilla in a cup.

With a large rubber spatula, fold half the flour into the butter-sugar mixture. Fold in half the milk; scrape down the pan and fold in the remaining flour and milk alternately. Spread this batter smoothly over the berries. Place in the oven and bake for 45 minutes. A toothpick inserted into the center of this cake should come out dry.

Run a knife along the edge of the pan to release the cake. Let cool for a few minutes, then invert the cake onto a platter and release and remove the springform. Carefully peel off the parchment. Serve the cake warm or cool.

LEMON SOUFFLÉ TART

▶ 8 egg yolks

2/3 cup sugar

Zest of 1 lemon

1 tablespoon flour

Juice of 4 lemons (3/4 cup)

1 tablespoon butter

8 egg whites

Pinch of salt

Pinch of cream of tartar

1 (10-inch) prebaked tart shell

This superb tart had its origins at Sally Darr's restaurant, La Tulipe, in New York.

Preheat the oven to 400 degrees.

In an electric mixer, beat the yolks with 1/3 cup of the sugar, the zest, and the flour until thick and pale yellow. Add the lemon juice. Pour into the top part of a double boiler and whisk over boiling water until the mixture sets. Remove from the heat and whisk in the butter. Cover with a sheet of waxed paper placed directly on the hot mixture and set aside.

With an electric mixer, beat the whites with salt and cream of tartar until they form soft peaks. Add the remaining 1/3 cup of sugar and continue beating until the peaks are stiff but not dry. Gently stir one-third of the whites into the yolk mixture. Using a rubber spatula, fold in remaining whites.

Transfer the mixture to the tart shell. Level the top. Place in the oven and bake for 18 minutes, rotating the tart after 9 minutes. Remove and cool.

RASPBERRY-RHUBARB TART

A very simple tart to prepare.

▶ 1/2 cup seedless raspberry preserves

1 (10-inch) unbaked tart shell

1 cup plus 1/3 cup granulated sugar

Zest of 1/2 orange (about 1 teaspoon)

2 tablespoons flour

1 pound rhubarb stalks, cut into 1-inch slices

1 pint raspberries

Confectioners' sugar

Preheat the oven to 400 degrees.

Put the preserves in a small pan over medium heat and stir until softened and hot. Using a pastry brush, apply a thin layer, about half, of the hot raspberry glaze over the bottom of the tart shell. Set aside to cool.

In a bowl or food processor, combine 1/3 cup of granulated sugar with the orange zest and flour. In a separate bowl, toss the rhubarb with 1 cup of granulated sugar.

Sprinkle the orange sugar evenly on the bottom of the glazed tart shell. Cover with the rhubarb and tent the tart with aluminum foil. Bake for 35 to 40 minutes. Cool on a rack.

Arrange the raspberries on top of the cooled rhubarb.

Heat the preserves again and, using the pastry brush, glaze the berries. Place the tart in the refrigerator to set. Dust with confectioners' sugar. Serve with cinnamon ice cream if desired.

FIGS IN PEPPERED WINE

▶ 3 cups fruity red wine

3/4 cup sugar, or more to taste

Whole (not chopped) orange zest cut from 1 orange

24 peppercorns

4 cloves

8 allspice berries

1 pound figs, Black Mission or green

I love figs, but just in case you don't, this poaching liquid will do for any fruit you would like to serve in a sweet red wine sauce. Some suggestions would include apples, pears, quinces, plums, or any combination of dried fruits, especially apricots. Poaching is a good way to use firmer figs that are not yet ripe.

Bring wine, 1 cup of water, and sugar to a boil in a stainless-steel saucepan. Make a spice bag by wrapping the whole orange zest, peppercorns, cloves, and allspice in a length of cheesecloth. Tie with string and submerge in the poaching liquid. Simmer for 10 to 15 minutes or until the flavors emerge.

Cut off any hard stems from the figs. I prefer whole figs, but for more infused flavor, cut the figs in half. Place the figs into poaching liquid and simmer no more than a minute, until the figs are tender. Do not let the figs fall apart or melt. If you are using a harder fruit, such as an apple or a pear, let it poach longer until it is tender but still holds its shape. If the figs are ripe, omit poaching and go on to the next step.

Remove the figs from the poaching liquid. Boil the liquid until it is reduced to the consistency of heavy cream. Pour over the fruit and chill. If the poaching liquid is spicy enough for you, remove the cheesecloth full of spices before you reduce the sauce.

Serve warm or chilled with the poaching liquid, with or without whipped cream.

QUINCE AND APPLE STRUDEL

Serves 6

Quince is fragrant and mixes well with apples in this light and easy to pre-pare strudel. The softer apple provides a sauce for the chunkier bites of quince.

▶ 2 quinces

1 cup plus 3 or 4 tablespoons sugar, divided

1 vanilla bean, split

4 apples: Cortland, Empire, Winesap

1/4 cup golden raisins

1/2 teaspoon ground cinnamon

1 teaspoon lemon zest

1 to 2 tablespoons fresh lemon juice, to taste

5 sheets phyllo pastry

2 tablespoons clarified butter

1/2 cup hazelnuts, toasted and ground

Peel, halve, core, and chop the quinces. In a saucepan, combine 1 cup of sugar with the vanilla bean and enough water to cover the quinces and bring to simmer. Poach the quinces uncovered until tender. The pieces will maintain their shape and will not melt to produce a sauce like apples. Strain the quinces, save some liquid, and set aside.

Peel, halve, core, and chop the apples. Place in a saucepan with 3 tablespoons of the quince poaching liquid and 2 tablespoons of sugar. Cook covered over a medium-low heat, stirring occasionally and adding water if necessary, until the apples are tender and a little sauce has been made.

Preheat the oven to 375 degrees. Butter a baking sheet.

Combine the apples, quinces, golden raisins, cinnamon, zest, and lemon juice. Add 1 or 2 tablespoons of sugar, to taste. You should have about 3 to 3 1/2 cups.

Lay out a single sheet of phyllo on a work surface (keep the remaining phyllo covered with plastic wrap and a damp towel). Brush lightly with clarified butter, dust with sugar, and sprinkle with ground hazelnuts. Cover with another single sheet of phyllo, brush with butter, top with sugar and nuts, and repeat for 5 layers.

Spoon the filling in a strip along one of the long ends of the pastry, leaving a 1-inch margin from the edge. Roll up as you would a traditional strudel, sealing the ends by tucking them under as you roll. Place on the prepared baking sheet. Brush the outside with a light coating of butter and dust with nuts. Bake for 15 to 20 minutes or until brown and crisp.

MACADAMIA TART

▶ 1/4 cup sugar

4 tablespoons (1/2 stick) butter, softened

1/2 teaspoon orange zest

3 egg yolks

3 tablespoons honey

3 tablespoons half-and-half

1 teaspoon vanilla extract

2 teaspoons Kirsch

1/4 teaspoon ground cinnamon

1/2 cup toasted shredded dried coconut

1 cup macadamia nuts

1 (10-inch) prebaked and egg-wash-glazed tart shell

Rich, but a knockout.

Preheat the oven to 350 degrees.

Using an electric mixer, cream the sugar and butter together for 3 minutes or until very fluffy. Beat in the zest, egg yolks, honey, half-and-half, vanilla, Kirsch, and cinnamon.

Spread coconut and macadamia nuts into the prebaked and egg-glazed tart shell. Pour the batter over the nuts until the shell is two-thirds full. Bake until just set, about 20 to 25 minutes.

MEXICAN CHOCOLATE ICE CREAM

This ice cream was created by Susan Rosenberg, a very talented baker who met her husband, chef Peter Hoffman, while they were both working at Huberts. They fell in love while eating this ice cream and now they own the restaurant Savoy in New York City.

▶ 2 ounces Mexican chocolate (see Note)

2 ounces semisweet chocolate

2 cups milk

1 vanilla bean, split

3 egg yolks

3/4 cup sugar

1/2 teaspoon ground cloves

1/2 teaspoon ground cinnamon

1/4 cup Grand Marnier

1/2 cup heavy cream

Melt the chocolates together in the top part of a double boiler over hot water.

In a stainless-steel saucepan over low heat, steep the milk together with the split vanilla bean. Do not let it boil. In a stainless-steel bowl whisk the egg yolks together with the sugar, cloves, and cinnamon. Slowly stir in a little of the warm vanilla milk and mix. Return to the saucepan and cook over medium-low heat, stirring, until thickened. Remove from the heat.

Stir one-third of the custard into the melted chocolate until dissolved. Then stir in the remaining custard. Add the Grand Marnier, then stir in the cold heavy cream.

Freeze in an ice cream freezer according to manufacturer's directions.

NOTE: A grainy, sweet, cinnamon-flavored chocolate that comes in bar form, Mexican chocolate can be purchased in Mexican markets and some supermarkets.

GRAPEFRUIT AND TEQUILA SORBET

Serves 4

▶ 3/4 to 1 cup sugar, or to taste

2 cups pink grapefruit juice

Juice of 1 lemon, or 3 tablespoons lemon juice

1/4 to 1/3 cup tequila, to taste

Combine sugar and 1/4 cup of water in a saucepan and make a simple syrup by cooking over low heat until clear, then boiling for a minute or two. Add to the rest of the ingredients and freeze in an ice cream maker according to manufacturer's directions.

CINNAMON-CLOVE ICE CREAM

Serves 4

▶ 2 cups milk

3 cinnamon sticks

6 whole cloves

1 vanilla bean, split

3 egg yolks

3/4 cup sugar

1/2 cup cold heavy cream

In a stainless-steel saucepan over medium heat, bring the milk to a simmer. Turn off the heat and steep the cinnamon sticks, cloves, and split vanilla bean in the hot milk, covered, for at least 30 minutes.

In a stainless-steel bowl whisk the egg yolks together with the sugar. Slowly pour in the warm spiced milk through a strainer and mix. Return to the saucepan and cook over medium-low heat until the custard has thickened. Remove from the heat. Chill over ice and keep whisking until cool. Add the cold heavy cream. Freeze in an ice cream freezer according to manufacturer's directions.

RUM RAISIN TAPIOCA

I grew up eating my aunt Ethel's tapioca, which was light and frothy and never too sweet.

▶ 1/2 cup rum

6 tablespoons sugar

1/2 cup raisins

1 3/4 cups milk

1 vanilla bean, split

1/4 cup quick-cooking tapioca

3 egg whites

Pinch of cream of tartar

Bring the rum and 1 tablespoon of sugar to a simmer in a small saucepan. Remove from the heat and steep the raisins, covered, in the liquid until they are plump.

In a medium saucepan, heat the milk, stir in 5 tablespoons of sugar, add the vanilla bean, and let steep, off the heat, for 10 minutes. Bring the milk back to a simmer, add the tapioca, and stir. Cover, remove from the heat, and let stand for 5 minutes. Then cook over a low heat, constantly stirring, for about 5 minutes. The tapioca should be fully cooked and transparent. Remove the vanilla bean, scraping out the seeds. Add the raisins and rum. Mix and cool to room temperature.

Whip the egg whites with the cream of tartar until they stand in soft peaks. Fold the whites into the tapioca. Serve at once or chill in the refrigerator for up to 3 hours before serving.

CONDIMENTS

CONDIMENTS

CONTENTS

MANGO CHUTNEY

I don't bother canning this delicious chutney, because it gets eaten immediately. If you can't find a hard mango, substitute barely ripe apricots and unripe peaches or nectarines, without skins.

▶ 3/4 cup peeled and sliced green or unripe mango

1/4 cup dried apricots, chopped

1/4 cup raisins

1/2 cup finely chopped onion

2 or 3 cloves garlic, sliced

1 inch knob of ginger cut into small matchsticks

1 teaspoon orange zest

1/4 cup cider vinegar

1/2 cup packed dark brown sugar, or to taste

Pinch of salt

1/4 teaspoon chopped jalapeño or ancho purée, to taste

Combine all ingredients in a stainless-steel saucepan with 1/2 to 1 cup of water. There should be enough liquid to just cover the ingredients. Adjust flavor with sugar, vinegar, garlic, and jalapeño. Simmer covered for at least 30 minutes, then cook uncovered until the liquid reduces to a sauce. Use immediately.

PAPAYA KETCHUP

2 cups puréed papaya pulp

1/4 teaspoon ground allspice

1/4 teaspoon ground cloves

1/4 teaspoon ground cinnamon

1/2 teaspoon minced fresh ginger

1/4 cup minced onions

1/8 teaspoon Chipotle Purée (see page 370), or pinch of chili powder

1 tablespoon brown sugar

Pinch of salt

1 1/4 tablespoons cider vinegar

Combine all the ingredients with 1/4 cup of water in a stainless-steel saucepan and simmer slowly, adding more water if necessary. Cook over low heat, uncovered, until the sauce darkens and thickens. Adjust seasonings to taste.

VEGETARIAN COMPASS BARBECUE SAUCE

This has an excellent smoky flavor, and the puréed onions thicken the sauce substantially.

- 1/4 cup olive oil
- 1 cup raw onion puréed in a food processor
- 1 cup marsala wine
- 1 cup puréed peeled, seeded tomatoes
- 1 teaspoon tomato paste
- 2 cups ketchup
- 1/4 cup honey
- 2 to 4 tablespoons cider or balsamic vinegar, to taste
- 2 or 3 cloves garlic, minced
- 1 teaspoon minced or grated fresh ginger
- 1 tablespoon miso paste
- 1 tablespoon Chipotle Purée (see page 370)

In a stainless-steel saucepan, heat the oil and add the onion purée. Cover tightly and sweat the onions over low heat until golden. Uncover, add the marsala, and boil for 1 minute or until the alcohol has cooked out. Add the puréed tomatoes and tomato paste, and simmer until reduced and slightly thickened. Add all the other ingredients and simmer uncovered for 15 to 30 minutes or until the sauce reduces, darkens, and thickens.

MANGO BARBECUE SAUCE

- 2 cups mango purée
- 1/4 cup rum
- 1/4 cup honey
- 3 tablespoons olive oil
- 3 tablespoons cider vinegar
- 2 tablespoons fresh lemon juice
- 2 cloves garlic, crushed
- 1/2 teaspoon dry mustard (optional)
- 1/4 teaspoon chili powder, or to taste

Here is a great little barbecue sauce that is good on anything, including the rutabaga steak on page 307. It can be refrigerated for up to 2 weeks, and frozen or canned for months longer. It offers a lovely, fruity alternative to tomato-based barbecue sauces, though I have also extended this sauce by adding 1 cup of ketchup and simmering a minute or two longer.

Combine all the ingredients in a stainless-steel saucepan and simmer for 3 to 5 minutes, or just long enough to reduce and darken the sauce slightly, and to cook out the alcohol. Use immediately or refrigerate up to 2 weeks.

ROASTED RED PEPPER AND CASHEW SAUCE

Serve this with vegetable mousses or timbales, or use as a spread to flavor sandwiches.

- 3/4 cup unsalted cashews, toasted
- 1/3 cup roasted red bell pepper strips
- 1 to 3 tablespoons fresh lemon juice, to taste
- 1 or 2 cloves garlic, crushed, to taste
- Salt and ground black pepper to taste
- 2 tablespoons olive oil or toasted sesame oil, or 1 tablespoon tahini (optional)

Combine the cashews, roasted pepper, 1 tablespoon of lemon juice, and 1 clove of garlic in a food processor. Process until creamy. Season with salt, pepper, more garlic, and lemon juice to taste. Stir in the oil or tahini if desired.

MALAY SLAAI

- 1/2 cup chopped pineapple
- 1/2 cup chopped green papaya
- 1/2 cup chopped mango
- 1/2 cup minced onion
- 1/2 cup toasted crushed peanuts or macadamia nuts
- 1/4 teaspoon minced jalapeño
- 1 teaspoon sugar
- 1/4 cup cider or raspberry vinegar, or 1/4 cup fresh lime juice
- 1 teaspoon ground cardamom

Traditional South African dishes were influenced by the Malaysian Muslim community, who were originally brought over to the Cape from Java Sumatra and the East Indies to work, and cook, for the Dutch in the seventeenth century. The Cape Malay, as they came to be called, brought to the table many dishes, including a variety of shredded and sliced salads called slaai. Slaai goes very well with Yassa au Tempeh (see page 187), or any other spicy dish you want to dress up with this African Malay version of salsa. Traditionally, a Malay slaai is never dressed with oil.

Combine the pineapple, papaya, mango, and onion in a bowl. Sprinkle on the nuts. Toss with the minced jalapeño, sugar, vinegar, and cardamom. Adjust seasoning.

For a very interesting, though seasonal, variation, substitute 1 cup of chopped ripe nectarines in place of the red tomato.

▶ 1 cup tomatillos, husked, rinsed, and chopped

1 cup ripe red tomatoes, peeled, seeded, and chopped

1 cup chopped jicama

1/4 cup chopped scallions, green part only

1/4 cup olive oil

1/4 cup fresh lime juice

1 garlic clove, minced

1/2 cup chopped fresh cilantro

1/2 teaspoon Chipotle Purée (see page 370)

1 teaspoon sugar

Toss the tomatillos, tomato, jicama, and scallions in a bowl.

Combine the olive oil, lime juice, garlic, cilantro, chipotle purée, and sugar. Mix well and pour over the tomatillos. Stir to combine.

TOMATILLO SALSA II

- ▶ 1 cup tomatillos, husked, rinsed, and chopped
- 1/4 to 1/2 jalapeño, minced
- 1 cup seedless green grapes, sliced thin
- 1/2 cup chopped jicama or green mango
- 2/3 cup cilantro leaves, chopped
- 1 to 2 teaspoons sugar
- 1 tablespoon fresh lime juice
- 2 tablespoons olive oil
- Salt and ground black pepper to taste

Sliced grapes underscore the fruitiness of the tomatillos. Use cold, firm grapes and keep this sauce chilled before you set it out to serve. Jicama or green mango adds another dimension to this piquant salsa.

Combine all the ingredients in a serving bowl and toss until mixed well.

CHIPOTLE PURÉE

- ▶ 4 chipotle chilies, stems removed
- 1 clove garlic, peeled
- 1 tablespoon fresh lime juice
- 1 teaspoon ground cinnamon

Soak the chipotle in boiling water for about 30 minutes to reconstitute. Don't try to remove the seeds. Place the whole chilies in a blender with the garlic, lime juice, and cinnamon. Purée until smooth. This holds well in the refrigerator. Use for chili, mole, in sauces, dressings, or spreads.

CHIPOTLE SAUCE

Fold the chipotle purée into the kefir a drop or two at a time. When it seems hot enough to suit your taste, add the garlic and lime juice. Save whatever chipotle purée you do not use to flavor such things as sweet potatoes, mashed potatoes, stews, soups, and salad dressings.

▶ 1/2 teaspoon Chipotle Purée, or more to taste (see page 370)

1 cup kefir, Yogurt Cheese (see page 375), or low-fat sour cream

1 clove garlic, minced

1 teaspoon fresh lime juice, or more to taste

PICKLED FIGS

Wash the figs. Put the sugar, vinegar, 1 cup of water, cinnamon, and cloves together in a stainless-steel saucepan and boil gently for about 10 minutes. Add the figs and return to a boil. Remove from the heat. Spoon the figs into a clean jar, cover with the boiling syrup, and let stand, covered, for one day before serving.

▶ 12 to 16 figs

1/2 cup sugar

1/2 cup cider vinegar

1 cinnamon stick

3 whole cloves

PICKLED RED CABBAGE

1/2 head red cabbage, shredded
(about 4 cups)

1 cup white wine

1 cup white wine vinegar

1/2 cup sugar

1/4 teaspoon ground allspice

2 or 3 juniper berries

1 bay leaf

1/2 teaspoon minced fresh ginger

This makes a nice accompaniment for a blue cheese soufflé.

Dunk the cabbage into a large kettle of boiling water for about 30 seconds, or just long enough for it to deepen in color. Drain.

Place the cabbage in a glass or stainless-steel bowl.

Bring to boil in a nonreactive saucepan 1 cup of water, the white wine, vinegar, sugar, allspice, juniper berries, bay leaf, and ginger. Pour the hot dressing over the cabbage and stir to combine. This is best if it stands and marinates for 1 to 2 days. It can be served hot or cold.

Preheat the oven to 350 degrees. Remove the outer layers of papery skin from whole heads of garlic. With a sharp knife, slice off and discard the top third of each head to expose the cloves. Rub the garlic heads with olive oil and place in a baking dish or on a sheet of aluminum foil. Cover tightly and bake for 35 to 40 minutes or until the skin is brown and papery and the cloves soft to the touch. Remove and cool until easy to handle. Unpeel the cloves and squeeze out the pulp.

For a faster, though somewhat more wasteful, approach bake an extra head or two of garlic, cut the entire bulb in half and squeeze the soft cloves right out. One head of garlic yields about 1 tablespoon of roasted garlic purée.

GOMASHIO

2 tablespoons sea salt

3/4 cup black sesame seeds

3/4 cup white sesame seeds

The seasoned salt called gomashio can be found in any natural food store. It can also be made with toasted sea salt and sesame seeds. This unusual and pretty version uses both black and white sesame, though the white seed is more commonly used. Toasting the sea salt adds to the flavor. Traditionally gomashio is ground using a mortar and pestle, or a ceramic suribachi, but you can easily use a food processor. This is a good seasoning for rice, grains, pasta, and fish.

Heat a cast-iron skillet over medium heat. Place the sea salt in the skillet and toast for about 1 minute or until the salt gives off a slight briny aroma. Put the salt in a food processor.

With the skillet still hot, and over medium-low heat, combine the black and white sesame seeds in the skillet. Move the seeds constantly, either with a wooden spoon or by shaking the skillet back and forth as you would when making popcorn. In about 1 minute, the seeds will turn golden and give off a nutty aroma. The seeds will also crack easily between your nails. Immediately remove the seeds from the skillet, as they will continue to cook in their own heat for a few seconds. Add to the salt in the processor and process for a few seconds until the mixture is coarse, sandy, and dry, not fine or pastelike. You want to be able to shake this out of a container, or sprinkle it onto food, so you don't want a nut butter.

Yogurt cheese makes a fine dip for corn chips and is a satisfying substitute for sour cream. It can be mixed with chives or scallions and garlic and other herbs for a savory flavor, or with dried fruit and walnuts for a sweet one. Regular yogurt is the most flavorful, but the technique works just as well with the low-fat variety. (It cannot be used, however, with nonfat yogurt that contains gelatin.)

▶ 1 quart (4 cups) plain yogurt

Cut a large enough piece of cheesecloth to hold the quart of yogurt and allow for the ends to be tied hobo style. Attach the package to a chopstick. Balance the chopstick over the rim of a container that is deep enough to catch the drippings of the yogurt whey, or water. The yogurt package will hang down into the container, but should remain far enough above the bottom so that it does not touch the water collecting there.

Refrigerate this way for at least 6 hours — the longer the time, the richer the cheese will be. I like to let the yogurt cheese sit for a day, even two. Transfer the cheese to a bowl and discard the liquid. Pour off any liquid that accumulates.

Savory or sweet flavors may be added before making the cheese or after. If you add the scallions before, however, they will lose their color. Nuts will turn soft unless added later.

THICK COCONUT MILK

Add 1 cup of boiling water to 3 cups of freshly grated coconut meat. Let stand at least 15 minutes. Strain through a double thickness of cheesecloth, squeezing out as much milk as possible. Thick coconut milk is used for sauces and desserts.

THIN COCONUT MILK

Add 2 to 3 cups of boiling water to 3 cups of freshly grated coconut meat. Let stand at least 15 minutes. Strain through a double thickness of cheesecloth, squeezing out as much milk as possible. Thin coconut milk is used to prepare rice and add to stews.

carrots *(continued)*
    in mousse, 77–78
    in salad, 16
cashews, 296, 367
cauliflower, 20, 66, 240, 337–38
    with grains, 94, 98
caviar, amaranth, 87
celeriac, 18, 219
celery root, 239
champagne, 135, 219
chanterelles (mushrooms), 135
chard
    red, 232
    Swiss, 227, 269, 277, 340–41
chayote (squash), 32, 152, 295
cheese
    blue, 89–90, 244
    on burgers, 62
    Cheddar, 54
    chèvre, 268, 318
    feta, 221, 287
    fromage blanc, 99
    gjetost, 258, 266
    goat, 56, 126
    Gorgonzola, 153
    Parmesan, 252
    Quark, 147
    ricotta, 52, 131, 259–60, 271, 328
    Roquefort, 117, 261
    yogurt, 375
cherries, dried, 114, 154
chèvre (cheese), 268, 318
chick-peas, 53, 69, 320
chicory, 137
Child, Julia, 44, 107
chiles rellenos, 324
chili, 150
chilies, 257, 280, 324
    puréed, 120, 194, 370, 371
    in sausage, 194, 333
Chinese vegetarian cuisine, 62,
    176
chipotle chilies, 333
    purée of, 120, 194, 370, 371
chives, 12

chlodnik (sour cream), 38
chocolate, 345–46, 357
cholesterol, 251
chutney, mango, 363
cinnamon, 358
cloves, 358
cobbler, vegetable, 272–73
coconut
    milk of, 94, 184, 282, 376
    young Thai, 33–34
coleslaw, 15
collards, 11, 114, 229, 270
    kitfo, 221
condiments, 363–76
coriander, 32, 57
corn, 12, 290
coulis, tomato, 242
couscous, 12–13, 311–12
*Couscous and Other Good Foods from
    Morocco* (Wolfert), 107
cream, 14, 188, 267
    sour, 38
crêpes, 192–93, 278–79
cucumbers, 70
Culinary Institute of America,
    322
cumin, 32
currants, 218
curry powder, 33
custard, ricotta, 271

daikon (Japanese turnip), 17
Darr, Sally, 352
dashi (seaweed), 17
dates, 113
dau gok (Chinese long beans),
    233
dengaku (roasting style), 35
desserts, 345–59
dosas (crêpes), 192–93
doughs, 141, 272–73
    pastry, 294, 297
dressings. *See* salad dressings
dumplings, tofu, 37

eggplant, 35, 67–68, 321
    Asian pickling, 281, 309, 340–41
eggs, 61, 251
    substitute for, 244
enchiladas, tofu, 169–70
escarole, 156
The Essential Root Vegetable Cookbook
    (Stone & Stone), 347

fennel (bulb), 36, 239, 248
    beans with, 14, 91, 158
    in salads, 14, 20
feta cheese, 221, 287
figs, 66, 354
    with fennel, 14, 248
    pickled, 371
    in salads, 14, 15
    in stuffing, 207–08
fillings, 277–90, 308
    for bean curd, 176–77
    cabbage, 288, 294
    of greens, 270, 297–98
    lentil, 147–48
    for seitan, 207–08
    tempeh, 192–93
flan, 179, 309
Flour, Vital Wheat, 202
fritters, 318, 323, 326, 328
fromage blanc (cheese), 99
frostings, 348
fruit
    apples, 33–34, 117, 230, 355
    apricots, 111
    cherries, 114, 154
    currants, 218
    dates, 113
    figs, 14, 15, 66, 207–08, 248, 354,
        371
    grapefruit, 358
    grapes, 56, 220
    mangoes, 15, 19, 57, 184, 363
    papaya, 15, 96, 364
    prunes, 345
    quince, 99, 310, 355

raspberries, 10, 101, 353
ratatouille, 242
ravioli, tofu, 174
rémoulades, 18, 244
Reynolds, Robert, 218
rhubarb, 102, 191, 269, 353
rice, 105–20
  arborio, 107
  basmati, 110, 184
  in burgers, 61
  Japanese sweet (mochi), 113, 116
  noodles made from, 37, 128, 129, 185
  paper made from (banh trang), 281
  risottos of, 107–09, 190
  in salad, 120
  sticks made from (mai fun), 37
  with tempeh, 184, 190
  wild, 114
rice, brown, 113, 118, 120, 303
  with cheese, 115, 117
  deep-fried, 325
  dirty, 106
  with lentils, 110, 192–93
  with nuts, 111, 114
  with other grains, 88, 102
  with pasta, 112
  tempeh in, 184, 190
The Rice Book (Owen), 105
Rice Dream, 157, 172, 265, 332
ricotta cheese, 52, 131, 259–60, 271, 328
rigatoni, 124, 155
risottos, 107–09, 190
Roquefort cheese, 117, 261
rosemary, 239, 287
Rosenberg, Susan, 357
roulades, 207–08, 280, 349–50
roux (bouilli), 251, 261
rum, 359
rutabagas
  batter-fried, 319
  gratin of, 266
  grilled, 307

mousse of, 77–78
in salad, 18
and squash, 246
See also turnips

sage, 44–45, 137
salad dressings
  chipotle, 120
  citronette, 144
  lemon cream, 14
  ponzu, 17
  sesame-ginger, 11
  tofu rémoulade, 18
  vinaigrettes, 10, 13, 19, 82–83, 95, 135
  white miso, 243
salads, 7–21
  bean, 14, 137, 144
  beet, 10, 16
  coleslaw, 15
  collard, 11
  daikon, 17
  grain, 12, 120
  vegetable satay, 20–21
salsas, 280, 368–70
salt, 26, 192, 252, 374
sandwiches, 51–58
  beet, 52, 318
  brushchetta, 8, 19
  chick-pea, 53
  fava crostini, 143
  garlic and tofu, 55
  grape, 56
  kimchi, 54
  seitan steak, 58
  tempeh BLT, 57
sauces
  apple bourbon, 117
  barbecue, 365, 366
  bean pesto, 155
  chipotle, 370, 371
  hoisin, 255, 302
  lime dipping, 282–83
  mole, 138–39, 159

peanut, 20, 21, 185
ponzu, 17
red pepper and cashew, 367
rémoulade, 244
rhubarb, 102, 191
sorrel cream, 188
tahini, 119
Thai, 125
tomato, 127, 145–46, 167–70, 242
wild mushroom, 97
sauerbraten, seitan, 209
sauerkraut, 136, 195, 230
sausages, 222, 331–41
  with grain, 332, 334, 339, 340–41
  potato, 333
  seitan, 334
  sourdough, 332
  tempeh, 335
  with tofu, 339, 340–41
Savorex, 62
Savoy restaurant (New York City), 357
scallions, 326
scalloppine, seitan, 210
seasonings, 26, 61, 62, 137, 321
  basil, 324
  bumbu, 43
  cardamom, 57, 245
  chilies, dry, 194, 280, 370
  cinnamon, 358
  cloves, 358
  coriander, 32, 57
  cumin, 32
  curry powder, 33
  ginger, 15
  gomashio, 192, 374
  lemongrass, 152
  nutmeg, 246
  oregano, 153
  rosemary, 239, 287
  sage, 44–45, 137
  salt, 26, 192, 252, 374
  Savorex, 62
  sorrel, 188
  Spike, 175, 252